The Business
of Commerce

T0124857

The Business of Commerce

Examining an Honorable Profession

James Chesher
and
Tibor R. Machan

HOOVER INSTITUTION PRESS

Stanford University   Stanford, California

URL: http://www-hoover.stanford.edu

Hoover Institution Press Publication No. 454
Copyright © 1999 by the Board of Trustees of the
Leland Stanford Junior University

Photo credits:
Background photo: © Boden/Ledingham/Masterfile
Stack of coins: by Stephen Gladfelter, Stanford Visual Arts, 1999

First printing, 1999

05   04   03   02   01   00   99   9   8   7   6   5   4   3   2   1

Manufactured in the United States of America

The paper used in this publication meets the minimum requirements
of American National Standard for Information Sciences—Permanence
of Paper for Printed Library Materials, ANSI Z39.48–1984. ♾

Library of Congress Cataloging-in-Publication Data
Machan, Tibor R.
   The business of commerce : examining an honorable profession /
Tibor R. Machan, James Chesher.
      p.   cm.
   Includes bibliographical references and index.
   ISBN 0-8179-9622-2
   1. Commerce—Moral and ethical aspects.   2. Social responsibility
of business.   3. Business ethics.   4. Businessmen—Conduct of life.
I. Chesher, James, 1941–   .   II. Title.
HF1008.M33   1999
174'.4—dc21   98-47216
                                                              CIP

CONTENTS

PREFACE

Honor sinks where commerce long prevails.
—Oliver Goldsmith,
"The Traveler" (1764)

Some years ago, when business ethics courses began to appear in university catalogs, the punsters quipped, "Business ethics—isn't that an oxymoron?" The joke would not have flown with, say, biomedical ethics. This tells us a great deal about the reputation of business.[1] It's curious, to say the least, that our culture has a disdainful attitude toward commerce generally and the profession of business in particular. This moral distrust, at times bordering on contempt, is evident throughout much of Western culture, especially in philosophy, theology, the arts, and the press.

The great irony here is that so much of what makes our lives comfortable, safe, enjoyable, and at times uplifting would not exist but for the flourishing of business, which provides employment, productivity, research and development, and an abundance of goods, services, and opportunities. We are in debt to business for the necessities as well as the amenities of life. And yet, though it's easy enough to see the great value of business, our culture has

---

1. By commerce we mean all trade, including that carried out by ordinary shoppers, whereas by business we mean professional commerce carried out mainly by those whose formal occupation is to make a profit or help in that endeavor at some firm.

not granted this profession the moral respect that it may be due. Instead, business bashing has become a cultural phenomenon, a favorite pastime.

Why is business so widely maligned, especially by intellectuals, those who reflect on and write about matters of morality, values, politics, and culture? Is the inclination to denigrate commerce beneficial to us, or might this attitude actually be "hazardous to our health"?[2] Given that the activity of business is so life affirming, and so conducive to our well-being, it seems ungrateful, if not unjust, to condemn this profession.

The purpose of this book, the deep concern that propels it, is to call attention to the phenomenon of business bashing, to show not only that it is unjust but that business bashing is harmful to us all. Those who embark on the profession of business, as well as the rest of us who engage in commerce, are victims of a deeply rooted cultural prejudice, all the more vicious for its unchallenged acceptance. In the end, this book will show, the profession of business is honorable and no less worthy of respect than the professions of medicine, science, art, or education.

If anyone doubts that there is a widespread disdain of business in our culture, he or she need only consider that business is the only profession that is asked repeatedly to redeem itself, to prove itself worthy, by means of philanthropy and other noncommercial good deeds. Firms, executives, and business managers are continually being reminded of their "social responsibility," independent of their performing their jobs well and conscientiously. For example, during his successful career as CEO of General Motors, Lloyd Royce received no moral praise from the prominent pundits who guard the moral conscience of the nation.

---

2. This phrase is to be taken suggestively. Business bashing, it will be argued here, is hazardous to our overall well-being, not just our health, although, to be sure, it is that as well.

But when it was learned that in his retirement Lloyd was contributing generously to his Michigan hometown and its vicinity, accolades abounded, even from such politically correct sources as National Public Radio.

Thus, to merit respect, people in business are more forcefully and insistently called on to perform extraprofessional good deeds than are their counterparts in education, science, medicine, the arts, the media, and farming. These latter professions are seen as inherently worthy and their practitioners as praiseworthy simply for doing their work conscientiously. Teachers are admired for teaching well, artists for their creative productions, journalists for their proficient delivery of the news, doctors for healing, scientists for making discoveries, and so on, for nearly all of the professions but business. Einstein is morally praiseworthy as the great physicist, Edison as the inventor, Socrates, the teacher, Dostoyevsky, the novelist, and Lincoln, the president.

One does not become a cultural hero, however, by succeeding as an entrepreneur; such a person must go on to become a philanthropist, must "earn" respect by doing more than performing excellently in business. Why must people in business do double duty? It is this issue and its permutations that the present work addresses.

First, a word of caution. A thorough exploration of our topic requires frequent reference to the writing of prominent thinkers throughout history, but this immediately poses a problem, for written evidence can introduce a bias in estimating general trends and opinions. In other words, the negative attitude toward business by those who *wrote* may not be indicative of how people in general may have regarded business. After all, most writers have chosen for themselves goals other than economic or commercial success. As thinkers, they often explicitly differentiate themselves from other professionals by what they deem to be a "higher skill" or a "higher calling." And so they may exhibit a tendency, in comparing their craft with those of others, to assign their own a unique and higher significance.

Philosophers are no exception: Starting with Plato, they have tended to see their own line of work as the noblest. This has contributed to the denigration of trade as "merely mechanical," one of the lower professions.[3] As we'll soon see, it is rare for a philosopher or literary figure to sing the praises of those who enable us to have houses, food on our tables, transportation, health insurance, opportunities to finance a college education, and the myriad amenities that make life enjoyable.

Similarly, and equally unfortunately, when people in business compare their profession to others, they tend to belittle artists and intellectuals as "unrealistic" and inept in practical affairs. One often hears this theme when "practical" men and women describe academics and theoreticians, those generally involved with ideas. Such people, it is thought among the practical minded, lack common sense and are wasting their efforts on "useless," "abstract," or "inconsequential" matters.[4]

---

3. As Peter Green notes, "The indifference to the lower orders and the contempt for them [in Hellenic Greece] is all pervasive. Intellectual activity was hierarchical to such a degree that Archimedes found even applied science beneath his dignity. . . . The ideal of this elite was an inherited, or otherwise unearned, fortune. Work, especially work for others, was a social disgrace. The economic ideal was stability rather than growth." From "The Care of the Soul," *New Republic*, September 5, 1994, p. 38.

4. Examples abound, but one very interesting case is the late George Stigler, who has argued that ideas are inconsequential when it comes to world affairs. What matters most are the concrete interests that drive people to do what they do. See George Stigler, *The Economist as Preacher and Other Essays* (Chicago: University of Chicago Press, 1982). It is interesting that in this respect Stigler is closer to Karl Marx than to most champions of capitalism. (Marx, too, believed that it was mainly economic forces, not ideas, that made things happen. He regarded it as idealism, which he took to be standing things upside down, to believe that ideas per se made any difference to human affairs. How curious that captains of industry agree with the scourge master of capitalism!)

Although each side tends to diminish the value of the other, writers, theoreticians, academics, and intellectuals generally broadcast their opinions as a matter of course, sometimes to a relatively wide audience, and so their opinions take deeper root. Thus Plato, Aristotle, Augustine, Locke, Hume, and Marx, to name but a few, as well as media scriptwriters and newspaper editorial writers, may not be impartial sources for determining the importance of professions far removed from their own.[5] Historians of ideas may be equally unreliable concerning whether a given opinion was prominent, since they rely so heavily on what the literati of an age thought about some activity, practice, or profession. How would one learn what the ordinary citizen believed about producing wealth? What did the slaves think? What did the merchants themselves believe? It is difficult for us to tell, except from the writings of an era.

Still, though the written record of human opinion may lean in one direction, widespread conduct may indicate an opposite, albeit unwritten, opinion. For example, we cannot ignore the fact that commerce, trade in goods and services, has become increasingly prominent in Western civilization. Nevertheless, writers reporting on prevailing opinion have registered public condemnation or have themselves held commerce in contempt. Most renowned writers of our own day have low regard for commerce, despite the fact that many who write depend on the success of commerce for their own livelihood.[6]

---

5. Of course, this is not unavoidable, only somewhat probable. Certainly one ought to consider the arguments of such theorists and only after finding these wanting should one explore their possible motivation. From afar it is difficult to tell why particular persons may have become biased in favor of certain values.

6. The numerous slights of big business in the movies is nearly incredible, considering that all these are made possible by the successful management of the companies for which the moviemakers work.

The best method of determining whether a culture or era or even civilization is dominated by a certain viewpoint is, no doubt, a complete enumeration. Short of this nearly impossible task is the method of sampling, such as a sampling of prominent views. This method, inductive generalization, always faces the challenge of being fair, accurate, and representative. It is hoped that the following work meets those requirements.

This book hopes to demonstrate that Western culture, as represented by the bulk of stellar figures throughout its history, has unjustly held commerce and business in low esteem. In contrast, the practices of millions of people attest to a good measure of respect for the profession. What has emerged is a kind of cultural schizophrenia in regard to commerce and business.

Many people in business are admired for their savvy, cleverness, industry, perseverance, and even public-spiritedness. Consider, for example, Lee Iacocca, Ross Perot, Donald Trump, or earlier figures such as Andrew Carnegie and J. Paul Getty, all of whom have been praised for their achievements. That praise, however, is empty of moral significance and at times even smacks of cynicism. The admiration is not moral respect, any more than champion athletes and celebrities in general are admired for exhibiting outstanding moral virtues.

There are some exceptions to this dominant view that business is at best a nonmoral profession. Ayn Rand has made her name in literature in part because of her masterful, if not persuasive, depiction of commerce and business as noble and morally virtuous pursuits. Michael Novak, Robert Sirico, and others have produced works showing the compatibility of commerce and Roman Catholicism. Calvinists and other Protestants have also had kind words for the mundane endeavors of business.

In addition to some filmmakers, essayists, and playwrights, a few of the popular writers of our time have painted business and commerce in a reasonably favorable light. For example, Cameron

Hawley, in novels such as *Cash McCall* and *Executive Suite*, treats business so as to distinguish between those who are decent, upstanding professionals and those of questionable character, without requiring the former to prove their virtue beyond simply doing their job well. Even more notable is the mystery writer Dick Francis, whose thirty-odd novels involving the horse-racing profession have included an adjacent story of some kind of entrepreneurship such as banking, brewing, veterinary medicine, toy making, and the like. All the professionals in these fields are depicted by Francis as doing business and seeking profits without compromising their respectability.

Evidently, then, in its attitude toward commerce, our culture tends to vacillate between intense interest and occasional admiration, on the one hand, and suspicion, even outright scorn, on the other. This may be due largely to the mundane role of commerce in human life, despite the often considerable influence that commerce exerts on our lives and actions. Even among the friends of commerce a distinction is often drawn that devalues our economic and prudential concerns. Consider, for example, Senator Barry Goldwater, who, in his *The Conscience of a Conservative*, observes that "the economic and spiritual aspects of man's nature are inextricably intertwined." But, just prior to this, Goldwater betrays the dichotomous view of human nature that so many champions of commerce embrace and that contributes to our cultural ambivalence regarding commerce:

> The Conservative believes that man is, in part, an economic, an animal creature, but that he is also a spiritual creature with spiritual needs and spiritual desires. What is more, these needs and desires reflect the superior side of man's nature, and thus take precedence over his economic wants.[7]

7. Barry Goldwater, *The Conscience of a Conservative* (Chicago: Regnery, 1962), pp. 12, 10–11. Conservatism's major champion, the late Russell Kirk,

In other words, the concerns of the mind are of greater value than those of the body, and the faculty of the mind, which is one part of our nature, is somehow ontologically and morally superior to the rest. In this traditional view of the dualistic nature of human beings, we are a composite of two basic parts, which often conflict and one of which is subordinate to the other. Both the Greek philosophical and the Christian theological traditions have conspired to make this view a deeply ingrained feature of Western thinking. But, in fact, we are whole beings, with minds, bodies, and whatever else indispensable to our being human.

This belief in a kind of ultimate paradox or conflict inherent in our nature may well be the most lamentable aspect of the situation: society's admitting to, and, indeed, wanting, both aspects of our humanity and their practical impact and rewards, while denying their equal worthiness in the kind of lives we want to live. Such disunity not only deprives us of the ability to benefit fully from the practice itself but leaves us fundamentally unsettled, mentally and emotionally ambivalent, and at odds with ourselves. We are suffering a kind of metaphysical schizophrenia.

If this dualistic view of human nature is correct, and if this earthly life is inherently base and depraved, why should we take seriously any striving for earthly improvement? Why honor in the slightest any effort to that end? Why lament poverty, disease, or misfortune? A logical consequence of the dualistic view should

---

produced his *The Conservative Mind* (Chicago: Regnery, 1953) in part to stress the fundamental tendency of human beings toward evil. This modern-day Manichaeanism (the doctrine important to many ascetic notions from Hindu ethics, including the fundamental obstacle of our body to reaching full human excellence) is influential within American conservative circles. Arguably the reason conservatives do not support government intervention in the economy is not so much because of their principled belief in the free market system but because economic concerns, pertaining as they do to earthly well-being, are of no ultimate importance within their thinking.

be a form of nihilism, asceticism, or stoicism regarding things of this world, not the attitude and practice of business bashing that has in fact resulted.

If we hold commerce—perhaps the most forthright way that people embrace this world—in contempt, then our sexuality, our endeavors in science, art, medicine, education, politics and the rest, which also embrace and flourish within this world, ought also to be held in contempt. Indeed, many religious leaders, such as Ignatius of Loyola, the sixteenth-century founder of the Roman Catholic Jesuit order, have held precisely this view.

Following the chronicling of business bashing and a demonstration of the serious error in deriding this profession, the aim of this book is to convince readers, by means of analysis and explanation,[8] that it is a mistake to continue with the dichotomization of human life, at least as far as the relationship between commerce and the true enrichment of our existence is concerned. As will be shown, such a dichotomy is a fabrication, an illusion, not an inherent feature of the human condition.

The intended audience of this book is the educated layperson who reads such publications as *Time, Newsweek,* the *Wall Street Journal,* the *New York Times,* who reads novels by such authors as John Grisham, Laurie Colwin, Scott Thurow, Phillip Roth,

---

8. We should clarify that by explanation we do not mean a mechanistic or efficient-causal story about something, akin to explaining why a car broke down or a geological formation appeared in Colorado. Those types of explanations certainly have their place. What is sought here, however, is an account, a rendering intelligible by whatever means are suited to the task, of certain ways of thinking and acting in human affairs. Such an explanation could well make use of purposes, failures to pay heed, misconceptions, confusions, and so on, along lines Ludwig Wittgenstein would seek in the process of reaching an understanding about thought that has gone astray. Nor do they exclude explanations of the other sort, as when some event in history (e.g., the collapse of some banking system or even some disastrous harvest) is invoked to help show the reason some folks developed a distrust of commerce.

and who keeps abreast of current affairs. There is good reason to believe that the reader, while at college, experienced a rather negative view of commerce and business. This book is offered as an antidote to that miseducation and as a response to such damaging works as *A Nation of Salesmen* and *The Illusions of Choice*, both unabashed and unjustified assaults on commerce.

It would be arrogance of the highest order to think that this book alone will overturn centuries of prejudice and misunderstanding. A more modest and realistic hope is that the reader will finish this book with a greater respect for the profession of business than with which she or he no doubt began.

ACKNOWLEDGMENTS

We wish to thank *Public Affairs Quarterly, Jobs & Capital, Mid-Atlantic Review of Business, Critical Review*, and *Business and Professional Ethics Journal* for permitting us to make use of previously published materials.

We also wish to thank the Earhart Foundation and the Hoover Institution on War, Revolution and Peace for the support we have received in the preparation of this work. Thanks also to our friends Laurie and Alex Alexiev, Michael and Sharon Blasgen, Douglas J. Den Uyl, Randall R. Dipert, Robert Hessen, Jan Narveson, Tom Palmer, Douglas B. Rasmussen, Aeon Skoble, Mark Turiano, and Jack Wheeler for their continued support and critical comments on portions of the manuscript. Barbara Dodsworth helped with the copyediting, and we are grateful to her. We wish to thank John Raisian for his support in bringing this work to completion.

Is Commerce Really Maligned?

Free trade abjures patriotism and boasts cosmopolitanism. It regards the labor of our own people with no more favor than that of the barbarian on the Danube or the coolie on the Ganges.
—Justin Morril, Republican senator from Vermont (1855)

BAD PRESS FOR COMMERCE: THE EVIDENCE

A moment's reflection reveals a serious negative attitude toward commerce. Consider the attitudes toward the role of the "middleman," or retailer, she who buys from the producers and in turn sells, at a higher price, to consumers. This, the entrepreneur, often called the profiteer, has been held in moral contempt by many important thinkers and creeds throughout human history. In "Middleman Minorities, Why the Resentment?" Thomas Sowell underscores this point in concluding his essay:

> Even beyond a racial or ethnic context, there are grim implications to the widespread tendency to resent productivity, and to attack those who create it, even as the benefits of that productivity are welcomed and more of those benefits are sought.[1]

Ample evidence exists of a prevalent anticommerce attitude. John McVeagh, in his book *Tradeful Merchants: The Portrayal*

---

1. Thomas Sowell, "Middleman Minorities, Why the Resentment?" *American Enterprise*, May/June 1993, p. 41.

of the Capitalist in Literature,[2] points out that, beginning in the sixteenth century, one finds antagonism toward business throughout important English literature. For instance, in Marlowe's *The Jew of Malta* (ca. 1589) we read: "Avarice is the medieval representation still in use . . . but also . . . is a more up-to-date concept reflecting the new money spirit, and methods, of contemporary society. The spirit was felt as usually, but not always, malign."[3] So, even before the modern era, commerce and business were treated with contempt, along with the socioeconomic system most hospitable to them, capitalism. In some works, such as the drama *New Custom* (1571), the degree of contempt motivates the transformation of the vices of cruelty and avarice into the allegedly phony virtues of (severe) justice and cruelty. As McVeagh observes, "It can hardly be reading too much into this exchange . . . to see in it the accommodation of worldly acquisition of an otherworldly tradition of thought, its motion to assimilate a new robust economic energy."[4] Consistent with this is the observation of Francis Bacon, one of the recognized founders of the modern view. In 1605 Bacon noted that "the wisdom touching negotiations or business hath not been hitherto collected into writing, to the great derogation of learning. . . . It is by learned men for the most part despised, as inferior to virtue, and an enemy to meditation."[5] We will explore these observations throughout this work.

What follows is not a defense of any given commercial endeavor or, certainly, of any commercial agent, either individual or corporate. Nor is it argued that commercial societies, now

---

2. John McVeagh, *Tradeful Merchants: The Portrayal of the Capitalist in Literature* (London: Routledge & Kegan Paul, 1981).

3. Ibid., p. 6.

4. Ibid., p. 9.

5. Francis Bacon, *The Advancement of Learning* (Oxford, England: W. A. Wright, 1868), p. 181.

manifested in Western "democracies," always function in an exemplary way. The authors do believe, however, that on the whole such societies are more just and supportive of a quality human life than most, perhaps all, known alternatives, as the historical evidence suggests.

We also acknowledge that some values are simply not as likely to be evident in societies hospitable to commerce as they might be in others. For example, valor, honor, or chivalry are not likely to play as prominent a role in classical liberal societies given to economic capitalism as they would in feudal systems. Conversely, prudence, industry, and thrift are widely exhibited in commercial societies. Some of this may only be a matter of public appearances rather than substance, for appearances can be mistaken. In certain societies some virtues may be less publicly exhibited in contrast with others.

We argue that the institution of commerce and its professionals, the men and women who engage in business, are demeaned in much of Western culture, often to the extent of being thought morally pernicious, and that much of what is morally decent about human life is enhanced in societies where commerce is free to flourish, even if one allows for some measure of abuse. (What matters in comparative socioeconomic analysis is not whether certain modes of life are subject to abuse but whether the abuse from one basically decent form of life will be more destructive and rampant than that from another. Thus Aristotle compared different forms of government to see which constitution would be most suitable for human community life.)[6]

In any case, our culture is ambivalent about the moral merits of commerce and its professional expression, business. On the

---

6. Aristotle, *Politics*. See also the book attributed to one of Aristotle's students but listed under Aristotle's authorship, *The Athenian Constitution*, trans. P. J. Rhodes (Middlesex, England: Penguin Books, 1984).

one hand, we prize commerce and depend on it for the well-being of our society as well as for the private and government support that we give to other societies. On the other hand, our society ranks business low on the ladder of moral standing among professions. From the podiums of politicians and the pulpits of ministers to the works of dramatists and novelists, as well as in the messages and tone of ordinary works of entertainment, we find commerce, business, and capitalism held to be morally deficient. As one of the Founders of this country put it: "There seem to be but three ways for a nation to acquire wealth. The first is by war, as the Romans did, in plundering their conquered neighbors. This is robbery. The second is by commerce, which is generally cheating."[7] This characterization of the moral status of commerce remains part of many college texts in business ethics courses. It also permeates much of popular culture.

The main support for business comes from a morally neutral source, scientific neoclassical economics. This discipline precludes what people ought or ought not do, makes no pronouncements on whether institutions are ethically praiseworthy, and avoids inquiring into what is more or less worthy in human life. The closest this discipline comes to a normative judgment is in its message that capitalism is an instrument for advancing prosperity. In other words, if prosperity is to be desired, then capitalism is the most efficient system for achieving it. What we ought and ought not value or seek is beyond the scope of the science of economics. As the financial writer Garret Garrett wrote in 1922, business "is neither moral nor immoral. It represents man's acquisitive instinct acting outside of humanistic motives."[8] This

7. Ralph L. Ketcham, ed., *The Political Thought of Benjamin Franklin* (Indianapolis, Ind.: Bobbs-Merrill, 1965), p. 229.

8. Garret Garrett, "Business," in Harold E. Stearns, ed., *Civilization in the United States: An Inquiry by Thirty Americans* (New York: Harcourt, Brace, 1922), p. 410. This view is what most neoclassical economists seem to embrace

limited perspective allows capitalism its qualified respectability in the academic world, and capitalism's unchallenged efficiency is its redeeming feature, as evidenced by the words of praise for capitalism from political and diplomatic podiums. In 1992, former U.S. secretary of state James Baker announced to a crowd of Albanians that "I came to say to you that freedom works."

Is this the best that can be said for freedom? And for what does freedom work? Surely this is the crucial question. After all, sufficiently powerful totalitarianism also "works" if, for instance, one wishes to control the behavior of citizens despite their preferences! In short, what we need to know is whether our political system, which protects and maintains the right of individuals to freedom, is noble and just. Does it have moral significance? How does the free society, with its strict protection of the rights to life, liberty, and property, compare with socialism, unchecked democracy, communism, and even certain kinds of (theocratic) dictatorships, all of which have enjoyed moral praise from a variety of prestigious sources, intellectual and otherwise?

Socialism, capitalism's main alternative in the twentieth century, is a political economic system embodying certain features of the other systems just mentioned, including collective and central economic planning as well as social planning. But, even as recent events in Eastern Europe have demonstrated the bankruptcy of socialism, skepticism concerning the moral status of capitalism continues, so deeply rooted is the anticommerce prejudice.

In this book we explore the intellectual origins and develop-

---

with their subjectivist theories of ethical value. The view derives from the standard understanding of Thomas Hobbes's philosophy of human life. Hobbes is most frequently credited with having laid out the case for the amoral conception of human life, meaning the absence of moral agency with its underlying acceptance of free will and objective moral standards.

ment of this prejudice to shed some light on the ambivalence that our culture exhibits regarding the merits of commerce. Various traditions of thought converge to produce the prevailing attitude; many are disdainful, some, neutral, and a few are somewhat complimentary toward commerce and business. The practical result of this hybrid genealogy is confusion in the free marketplace, leading occasionally to professional misconduct. Some of this misconduct, it can reasonably be argued, is the result of the common belief that business is inherently immoral at worst and nonmoral at best. After all, ideas do have consequences, and one's beliefs about one's profession and its host system can influence one's professional conduct. We explore which of the three attitudes toward business is most credible and sensible: moral contempt, indifference, or respect? The hostile tradition certainly has been dominant throughout the humanities and liberal arts of academe, as well as in the literary arts and in entertainment, all of which are vital influences on the popular culture generally.

This book also cautions those who are jubilant about global developments in the direction of privatization, including Eastern European, Russian, African, and Asian trends toward democratization and liberalism. Many who prize the free society and its free marketplace believe that we are witnessing a powerful world transformation in the direction of freedom and human dignity; but this belief may be premature, and the temptation to relax vigilance, dangerous. We have not reached the "end of history" with the triumph of democratic capitalism and liberalism. No such end is forthcoming, and there is little basis for believing that current developments amount to even a significant temporary trend.[9]

The embrace of privatization during the early 1990s, including

---

9. The reversals in the 1993 Russian parliamentary elections support this cautious view.

the softening of the Soviet and Eastern European attitudes toward some elements of private enterprise, was not motivated by the view that commerce is honorable. Rather, it rested largely on the pragmatic perspective that commerce, however distasteful, is a useful way to achieve some measure of economic prosperity. The admittedly dramatic initial move toward privatization will likely be short lived unless it is grounded in the valuing of liberty and freedom of commerce, including the right to liberty for the profession of business. Without this normative basis, as soon as government believes that the economy is sufficiently vital, or decides that it may get work from its citizens by means other than free individual motivation, it will revive the old agenda of sacrificing everything in the name of securing universal and equal welfare through government regimentation. Lacking support for the moral principle that men and women not only have the right to seek prosperity but have in fact for the greatest part acted properly, virtuously (i.e., prudently) when they do so, the privatization and liberalization movement will fail to steer most cultures away from their fundamental and tragic ambivalence about commerce. An honorable institution and its practitioners will be condemned to a morally inferior status.

The intellectual community of America gives business and commerce a mixed review, at best. For the most part, opinion among the educated in the liberal arts and social sciences follows Charles Baudelaire's view that "commerce is satanic, because it is the basest and vilest form of egoism."[10] Along with many Hollywood television and movie writers, many intellectuals would prefer to eliminate or subdue commerce.

Ambivalence toward business goes back to ancient times. Plato, for example, consigned the trader to the lowest rung of the

---

10. Charles Baudelaire. The source of this quotation has been lost.

ideal community.[11] In reviewing Charles Taylor's book *Sources of the Self,* Joseph Baldacchino observes that, in Plato's hierarchy of social reality, the philosopher, who devotes his life to contemplation of the unchanging Good, is placed at the top.

> The citizen, who contributes to the political life of the state, is less exalted than the philosopher, yet nonetheless participates in the order of the Good and shares in the good life. By contrast, those who provide the material without which life would be impossible, the household workers and those in commerce, are excluded from participation in the good life.[12]

Plato regarded the values of profiteers as plebeian and unworthy of respect.[13] Although less of an intellectual elitist than Plato, Aristotle is just as severe against trade in his ethics and politics. Despite their brilliance in so many spheres of human concern, the classical philosophers were unable to resist the temptation to elevate to the status of most favored their own mode of pursuing the good.

Medieval Europe unequivocally embraced disdain for commerce. The biblical proverb that the rich will struggle in vain to

11. In "The Laws" Plato's central character tells us, "For there are in all three things which every man has an interest; and the interest about money, when rightly regarded, is the third and lowest of them; midway comes the interest of the body; and, first of all, the soul."

12. Joseph Baldacchino, "The New Public Order: Within and Above," review of Charles Taylor's *Sources of the Self, Humanitas,* fall 1992/winter 1993, p. 50.

13. Allan Bloom tells us that "the companion, hence, belongs to, and represents, that lowest class of the Republic which Socrates calls the money-loving or profiteering class, even though the companion professes to berate profiteers." Bloom, *Giants and Dwarfs* (New York: Simon and Schuster, 1990), p. 109. Bloom was one of the most astute translators and interpreters of Plato. See his Plato's *Republic* (New York: Basic Books, 1972).

enter heaven clearly disapproves of the pursuit of wealth.[14] And Jesus' only act of violence is when he "cast out all those who were selling and buying in the temple, and he overturned the tables of the money-changers."[15] In short, Jesus attacked merchants, moneylenders, who were conducting business in a temple. But what of the others, at least some of whom may have been less than reverent as well, only in other ways? Why did Jesus cast the stone, so to speak, at the merchants, when no doubt many others were there who were not without sin?

In modern European thought perhaps the most sustained critique of commercial life may have been advanced, albeit mostly implicitly, by Immanuel Kant.[16] For Kant, the pursuit of any material (empirical) object is, at least, irrelevant to the moral quality of one's actions and, at most, pernicious. Moral worth issues precisely and only from intending to do what the moral law commands and only because it commands it. The moral law is totally independent of any goal or end that we might choose to pursue; it is a force all its own, based on pure reason. This, the heart of Kant's immensely influential moral view, though fraught

14. For a good discussion, see J. D. M. Derrett, "A Camel through the Eye of a Needle," *New Testament Studies* 32 (July 1986): 465–70. Derrett argues that the rich must at least unload their wealth before they can gain God's favor.

15. New Testament, Matthew, 21:12–13. Jesus is quoted as saying "My house shall be called a house of prayer; but you have made it a den of thieves." Are we not to infer from this that Jesus regarded selling and buying and money changing as no better than theft?

16. A start on developing this line of analysis is made in Leonard Peikoff, *The Ominous Parallels* (New York: New American Library, 1982). The central idea is that Kant's influence strengthened the belief that any practical, productive undertaking lacks moral significance unless it was done without any desire to benefit anyone but only to realize some formal moral law. If one acts so as to reap benefits, the act has no moral value whatsoever. And since commercial activities and business primarily aim at profiting the agent or someone the agent wishes to benefit, such conduct and business cannot possess moral value.

with philosophical difficulties, has commanded considerable respect in subsequent moral philosophy.[17]

In modern Europe, Jews were both envied and later systematically liquidated for flourishing in the world of commerce. Marxism, supposedly a radical departure from Western culture, joined the chorus, using Jews as the typical bourgeois citizens, the models of callous capitalists whose pursuit of prosperity was dismissed as crude commodity fetishism.[18] "Blessed are the poor," Jesus proclaimed, from which much of Christianity inferred that the pursuit of wealth is itself sinful. Less harsh is the prescription guiding the Jews: As Curator Magen Broshi of the Shrine of the Book Israel Museum put it, "Normative Judaism claimed . . . that it isn't a shame to be poor, but it is neither something to be proud of."[19] Contrast this with the view advanced by a Christian clergyman, but shared by many, that, "strictly speaking, a rich Christian is a contradiction in terms."[20]

17. Consider Amitai Etzioni's highly critical book about economics, *The Moral Dimension* (New York: Free Press, 1988), in which he embraces a moderate yet pointed deontological or Kantian view of morality from which commerce and business are evaluated. Etzioni is an influential sociologist and business ethics teacher who edits the journal *Responsive Community*, a publication dedicated to promoting communitarianism and criticizing the kind of individualism associated with economics and commerce.

We share Etzioni's dismay with the imperialistic tendencies of economic science, its professed value-free stance, and many of its practitioners' disdain of ethics. But Etzioni's insistence on a purely deontological approach to ethics throws the baby out with the bathwater.

18. See Karl Marx, "On the Jewish Question," in Robert C. Trucker, ed., *The Marx-Engels Reader* (New York: W. W. Norton, 1978), pp. 26–52. Consider the passage in the concluding section of this essay: "As soon as society succeeds in abolishing the empirical essence of Judaism, huckstering and its conditions, the Jew becomes impossible, because his consciousness no longer has an object."

19. Magen Borshi, "Children of Light," correspondence in the *New Republic*, May 2, 1994, p. 5.

20. George D. Herron, 1890 sermon, "The Message of Jesus to Men of

Despite this unenviable reputation, business as a profession and commerce in general have seen their highest development in the West. This is due in large part to another element of Western civilization, and one closely related to Christianity, the flourishing of the individual, resulting from the ideal of individual rights, particularly the right to private property. It is no coincidence that the recent "communitarian" movement, suspicious of "unchecked market forces," which are seen as a corrupting influence on society, places a great deal of the blame on individualism, which is characterized as greedy, aggressive, and antisocial.

An irony in this is that the very mistrust of commerce is itself partly responsible for much of the misconduct in business that goes unidentified and remains unchecked. Since the profession of

---

Wealth," cited in *Reason*, December 1986, p. 34. Consider also Paul Tillich, "Any Serious Christian Must Be a Socialist," cited in Michael Novak, *The Spirit of Democratic Capitalism* (New York: Simon & Schuster, 1982), p. 242. "I believe that here is one system which, thanks to the grace of God, we have not dared to label Christian explicitly and directly even when Christian ideology had reached its most abject levels, namely, Capitalism. Today it seems that we are all agreed that it must be rejected." Archbishop Mendez of Cuernavaca, cited in John Eagleson, ed., *Christians and Socialism* (Maryknoll, N.Y.: Orbis Books, 1975), p. 153.

There is, of course, much dispute about how to understand the Christian faith vis-à-vis the topic of wealth. Michael Novak, in his aforementioned work, argues persuasively that Christianity is compatible with capitalism and the business society, although even he does not defend the morality of profit seeking per se. Nonetheless, consider the way England's King Edward dealt with Jews when, as David Hume wrote, "he let loose the whole rigour of his justice against that unhappy people [Jews]. Two hundred and eighty of them were hanged at once for this crime [adulteration of the coin] in London alone, besides those who suffered in other parts of the kingdom. No less than fifteen thousand were at this time robbed of their effects and banished from the kingdom." David Hume, *The History of England*, vol. 2 (Indianapolis, Ind.: Liberty Fund, 1983), p. 83. The reason this is not a widely discussed fact is probably that relatively speaking it isn't something remarkable in the context of the history of most European countries.

business is nearly synonymous with huckstering, genuine criticism gets overshadowed by the pervasive cynicism. In addition, the proper standards of the profession remain largely unacknowledged and untapped, obscured by the attitude that the field is inherently ignoble and thus certainly absent of standards.[21]

Evidence of this prejudice can be found throughout contemporary culture. Consider the entertainment field alone: The movies regularly depict people in business as shady characters; sitcoms play into the stereotype; dramas, from the highbrow, such as *Death of a Salesman*, to the ordinary, such as *Wall Street*, often characterize people in business as morally deficient, on a continuum from insensitive and greedy to viciously evil.[22]

---

21. In a mid-1980s broadcast on the CBS television news program *60 Minutes*, Diane Sawyer labeled the loot trained young Italian pickpockets garner as "profit" in one of her reports.

22. An intense effort to demean business may be encountered in Earl Shorris, *A Nation of Salesmen: The Tyranny of the Market and the Subversion of Culture* (New York: W. W. Norton, 1994). This work, while prominently featured (e.g., in an extract in *Harper's*, October 1994), is filled with anecdotal support for claims about the underhanded nature of selling, repeating nearly all the well-known claims of Karl Marx about the supposedly corrosive impact of commerce on the rest of culture. No less vehement is the energetically distributed populist tirade by Ralph Estes, *Tyranny of the Bottom Line* (San Francisco, Calif.: Berrett-Koehler, 1996). Here the usual story about the heartlessness of corporate business is recounted, with no concern at all for the rights of stockholders to have their investment protected and vigilantly increased by management. This fallacy of what is seen versus what is not seen was identified by the nineteenth-century French political economist Frederick Bastiat, in his book *The Law*. Never mind how much downsizing and salary competition at the executive level improves the earnings of stockholders (the millions of pensioners, insurance clients, mutual funds owners) so they can take good care of their families, reinvest in new enterprises, and thus create jobs where they are actually wanted. The Shorrises and Esteses of the world can only lament the lot of the old guard. They would be the ones opposed to the vacuum cleaner or can opener because these take jobs away from workers who did those jobs by hand. See Tyler Cowen, *In Praise of Commercial Culture* (Cambridge, Mass.: Harvard University Press, 1998).

The other professions are largely exempt from this indictment, except insofar as they are closely associated with making money. Medicine is generally respected, as is law (when divorced from money), education (all the more so because teachers are not highly paid), science, and art. Politics has come under heavy fire mostly because of its close ties to "big business," fund-raising, and various scandals invariably related to money. Yet even in politics there are some honored figures, those characterized as "statesmen," such as George Washington, Abraham Lincoln, Adlai Stevenson, J. William Fulbright, Helmut Schmidt, Winston Churchill, and Mikhail Gorbachev. When the practitioners of these respected professions do well in their craft or art, they are praised and admired for that alone; when professionals in business excel at their craft, their very success is reason for suspicion, as though one cannot make a profit except by some form of trickery, fraud, or underhanded dealing. Those few in business who are admired, such as Lee Iacocca, Henry Ford, Bernard Baruch, and Andrew Carnegie, tend to be so despite their profession. They have had to prove their worthiness, so to speak, by giving back some of their money in contributions to the arts, sciences, or education. They then merit the accolade of "philanthropist."

And so it is business itself, the profession and its underlying activity and purpose, that is the object of contempt. Commerce is so widely maligned that the word "commercial" has become a pejorative term, as seen in expressions such as "Christmas has become commercial" or "dentistry is so commercialized these days." Is it that the various professions have leaned toward corruption as they eye the bottom line? Is it indeed morally odious to seek prosperity, especially by making money? Certainly innumerable influential thinkers, from Plato to Marx and Sartre, as well as countless contemporary followers, have held this view. Plato's main character in the dialogue "Laws" puts it succinctly:

To be at once exceedingly wealthy and good is impossible, if we mean by wealthy those who are accounted so by the vulgar, that is, the exceptional few who own property of great pecuniary value—the very thing a bad man would be likely to own. [So] that one who is exceptionally good should be exceptionally wealthy too is a mere impossibility. (Book five, 742e–743)

Thus it began with Western civilization's most influential philosopher and continues to this day among most of the intellectual elite. In the words of John Kenneth Galbraith, spoken in his famous PBS television program *The Age of Uncertainty* (1977), "Wealth is the relentless enemy of understanding."

In ironic harmony with this chorus of disapproval is the wide acceptance of business, large and small, as extremely useful, by making possible the host society that we enjoy. Repair shops, stores, retail merchants of all varieties, dams, factories, massive shopping centers, huge aircraft, saving and loan services, franchising establishments, hotels and motels, credit cards, newspapers, television, recreation facilities, amusement parks, communication technology, and thousands of other products and services could not function as efficiently as they do in society without the institution of the freely flowing business corporation.

Big business seems especially indispensable in assuming considerable responsibility for industrial mishaps and their attendant lawsuits.[23] How accommodating would governments be as entrepreneurs, given their near immunity from lawsuits? When governments do assume such tasks, they tend to transform their societies into a kind of forced labor camp, evidenced by what we now know about the grossly irresponsible and inhumane indus-

---

23. For example, the well-publicized figure of the first lawsuit filed against Union Carbide, namely, $15 million, in response to the company's conduct at its Bhopal plant in India, where more than two thousand persons were killed or injured as a result of the company's operations.

trial processes of the Soviet Union. Absent the profit motive, government must resort to fear to induce people to work hard. Even Galbraith, a most reluctant champion of anything resembling capitalism, admits to this. After the collapse of the USSR, the idea that a centrally planned economic system is a desirable alternative to capitalism has few supporters, to put it generously.

And yet, despite the obvious utilitarian[24] benefits of commerce

---

24. By "utilitarian" we mean here the view that an institution or policy supports the goals people actually have, excluding only goals that obstruct others' pursuit of theirs. Utilitarianism is widely championed, notably by some supporters of the free market. (A prominent and very prolific contemporary representative is Richard A. Posner, federal judge and law professor at the University of Chicago, as well as author of numerous books advancing the utilitarian defense of largely free institutions.) Yet, in its normative framework, prosperity, for example, retains the status of only a subjective value; there is nothing objectively right about trying to enrich oneself, about striving to prosper in life.

Utilitarianism is vague about what counts as a good or useful consequence, apart from rendering the idea purely subjective and then devising some measure of summing the attainment of subjective values within some community. Common sense, of course, comes to the aid of the utilitarian when it is noted that most of us know well enough that some things are valuable (education, money, health, recreation, employment) while others are not (disease, destruction of property, ignorance, etc.). Yet, values are commonly more particular than this suggests, so there is a good deal of indeterminacy left about what counts as a utilitarian advance versus a utilitarian retreat. Sophisticated utilitarians will nearly always promote nearly the same public policies as their nonutilitarian critics, mainly because they will argue that once we factor in all relevant value considerations, the utilitarian will have adequately taken care of the critics' values. This, as argued in Tibor R. Machan's "Reason in Economics versus Ethics," *International Journal of Social Economics* 22 (1995): 19–37, comes close to making utilitarianism right by virtue of its stating a tautology. The alternative view relied on herein (that there are objective goods people ought to achieve and a free society makes this more likely than others) denies the subjectivity of the value of human goals but recognizes something that has similar economic consequences, the agent-relativity of values, something that makes what we ought to do and not do frequently dependent on our individual or special situation. Accordingly, in public policy and political-economic matters, the positions reach similar results.

and the flourishing of the profession of business, despite capitalism's undeniably superior capacity to provide what people want, commerce enjoys little moral respect from most of our prominent commentators. It is tempting to trace the anticommercial sentiment to the creation of big businesses by the feudal governments of the tenth through eighteenth centuries, when the great joint stock companies were established by governments to gain wealth and power, especially abroad. This was accomplished by permitting the select establishment of heavily taxed business ventures, by means of public investments in enterprises that were granted monopoly status and limited liability privileges.

Curiously, many noncommercial organizations are large and powerful, especially governments, but there is no comparably generalized disdain toward them. Indeed, despite the widespread misbehavior of politicians, government service is still treated as an honorable calling, at least by those who set the moral tone of a community.

Some argue that commerce is indiscriminate with respect to who receives its particular service or product and thus incapable of upholding any values, of supporting good against evil. Sellers will sell nearly anything to anyone who is willing to pay, making the enterprise appear indifferent to the distinction between right and wrong, good and bad. But this is not unique to business; every craft has this built-in indifference about it: Medicine aids good and bad people with equal skill and attention; lawyers defend both the guilty and the innocent; tailors make clothes for both the bad and the good among us; even preachers serve both those who do good and those who do evil. Once one places one's work, goods, and services at the disposal of others, there is little control over who will obtain them. One can hardly be expected to investigate all those who may make use of one's offerings. Even charities serve their clients indiscriminately, and surely not all who take from charities are in genuine need. So the notion that selling is uniquely indiscriminate is simply false. All those who would share, sell, or give away what others may value necessarily risk giving to the undeserving. And since there is nothing we can do about this, it ought not be lamented. We can guard against evil only by being prepared and by avoiding intentional complicity. Beyond that, we can only hope.

The anticommerce attitude is not based on anything objectively flawed with commerce or business. The underlying reason for this prejudice is that business focuses on profit, on striving for prosperity, and that this motive is widely denounced and renounced as immoral. Happiness, joys, and pleasures, the promise of commerce, are earthly objectives.

Businesses engage in great efforts to satisfy and please people. When entrepreneurs read the market correctly, they often get rich, for the market is simply people spending money for various goods and services that will satisfy or please them. People want to live well, to have as good quality a life as they can afford, and business is complicit in this goal, encouraging and enabling people to live a good life as efficiently as possible. Even the critics of commerce acknowledge this, though many of them go on to observe that the desire to live well is superficial, perhaps even dishonorable and "selfish." But this criticism betrays an antihumanist attitude, a bias against taking care of ourselves in a comprehensive way, as part of a life plan. Such a plan includes minor as well as major personal concerns and desires. Consider, for example, how business thrives from satisfying customers who wish to relieve themselves of minor annoyances such as dandruff, itches, body odors, and so on. These objectives, admittedly insignificant in the larger picture of one's life, are nonetheless a contribution to a comfortable life. Yet these objectives are often demeaned by the critics and condemned as unworthy of pursuit.

It is not always the case that those who seek joy and happiness feel morally confident in doing so. Many tend to be divided: They want to live well, to seek joys and delights, but they also claim to honor and respect those who care little for such "trivial" things. They often express disdain for people and institutions that explicitly pursue such satisfactions or who make a living serving such pursuits. In contrast is the contradictory sentiment, also widely felt, that one ought to pursue professions, crafts, and vocations that give one fulfillment, satisfaction, and prevent alienation from oneself. Commerce assists in this endeavor by allowing one to perform a specialized task at which one excels, while reaping the benefits of innumerable other tasks at which others excel. Thus artists, scientists, educators, athletes, the clergy, business executives, and others can expand their horizons of personal fulfillment. But of all the professions, only business stands foursquare in supporting such an objective. Other callings can, and often do, feign varieties of public-spiritedness; scientists, politicians, lawyers, doctors, professors, novelists, and the rest proclaim the pursuit of goals other than self-satisfaction, even while choosing the field that seems to offer the best chance for their own personal fulfillment.

Anticommercialism amounts to holding as the devil's work, or as submission to our lower instincts, the satisfaction of earthly desires by means of the exchange of goods and services. It sees commerce as unabashedly respectful of our mundane, terrestrial desires, and it deplores our sometimes exclusively economic relationships with other people. Business, which specializes in commerce, makes it possible for everyone to pursue the satisfaction of these desires and the attainment of prosperity by means of trade. Without apologies, business focuses on the fulfillment of earthly desires and seizes the opportunity to do so through trade with others.

This makes the profit motive, disparagingly called "greed," a tolerable but far from respectable trait. It's as though a form of sin had been legitimized. This is illustrated in the highly touted movie *Wall Street*, where the villain, an amoral financial genius, makes a speech spelling out the "virtue" of greed. In harmony, some academic economists (recall the late Proctor Thompson) tell us that "greed is good." This identification of profit with greed perpetuates the myth that commerce is at bottom an ignoble, but necessary, enterprise, and it betrays a misunderstanding of the nature of profit, the seeking of which has a tendency to benefit everyone.

The antimaterialist, antiprosperity viewpoint has a number of major sources: Western philosophy and theology, Eastern philosophy and theology, classical and contemporary literature, history, sociology, and psychology. We will explore many of these sources, as well as explain why contemporary, neoclassical economic science is no antidote to these influences since it ascribes the pursuit of earthly joy and happiness to unconscious motives, the so-called selfish gene.

In contrast with the prevailing cultural view, we will argue that the institution of commerce is noble. Our view is that human beings are doing the right thing when they concern themselves primarily with their own and their loved ones' well-being or with that of their own communities before the welfare of the society at large.[25] This view will be developed more fully in due course.

25. If one equivocates on "loved ones" and insists, unreasonably, that this includes the human race and, for animal rights advocates, many higher animals, then the point does not hold. Yet it would be corrupting the concept of love to include other than those with whom one is reasonably intimate, those one values especially, such as family and friends. One needs also to keep in mind the idea that no one can be responsible toward others if that responsibility cannot be fulfilled; nor can anyone truly love those whom one does not know well enough as individuals. The contrary point rests on a misunderstanding and confusion, mistaking acknowledging the dignity of others with loving them.

Classical liberalism has had some success in battling the prejudice against commerce and capitalism by more or less securing the legality of commerce in Western society. But much more is needed: Commerce must also attain respectable moral standing.

We argue that, once the virtue of prudence is sufficiently understood and appreciated as the prescription that every human being ought naturally to look out for his own well-being and the well-being of loved ones, commerce should no longer suffer a bad reputation. Once commerce is recognized as an honorable endeavor and business takes its place among the respected professions, it will be possible to evaluate the genuine problems that commerce faces and to propose remedies for them. In our present atmosphere of ambivalence, with commerce under a moral cloud, it is difficult to identify the moral principles that should guide the profession. An activity that is thought to be inherently immoral, such as child molestation or rape, has no moral dimension. There can be no ethics of theft or murder, any more than there can be an ethics of breathing or blood circulation—one cannot choose to do them well or badly. If business is thought to be inherently evil, like theft, or beyond choice, like breathing, there can be no question about how one ought to engage in it. As things now stand, with business held under moral suspicion, the very idea of making improvements in how to conduct business loses its meaning. Yet, trying to help, as economists are wont to do, by making business a kind of unconscious human drive, can hardly improve its reputation.[26]

26. One reason the field of business ethics is treated so confusingly within departments of philosophy, where it is usually taught, is this ambivalence about the merits of the profession. We discuss this further in chapter 8.

Succeeding in business means making a profit. This requires producing something or offering a service for which people are willing to pay. In short, business is the profession in which production for profit occurs by addressing the economic needs and desires of people. Thus, the people in business who produce a profit are competent professionals.

Certainly, there is more to living a life than being competent in one's profession. Artists, entertainers, doctors, teachers, politicians, and so on may be competent, even outstanding, in their work and yet fail in other respects as human beings. Professional competence itself is partly guided by the common virtues, and in all the professions excellence involves adherence to ordinary moral principles recognized by everyone. For example, a great writer is not a plagiarist, nor is a great athlete a cheat on the playing field. By the same reasoning, a great business professional or doctor or lawyer does not proceed by immoral means. A professional would hardly be considered competent if success came by way of fraud, deception, force, exploitation, or some other immoral conduct. Such a person would be no more than a clever charlatan.

These and related issues will be explored in this work. We shall advance the thesis that business is the black sheep of the professions precisely because it is forthrightly concerned with pleasing people and satisfying their wishes for a pleasant life here on earth, for taking this life seriously in and of itself. Clearly, this objective detracts from preparing oneself for everlasting spiritual salvation. We will also consider the influence of another prominent view, that all people have an innate drive to seek material riches. We propose in the end that the desire for prosperity in life is morally commendable. Prosperity is a feature of the eudaimonistic life, even if it may not be the highest good for which all human beings should aim.

A QUESTION OF CRITICAL STANDARDS

The moral status of an institution or its members requires that there be fairly stable standards by which to evaluate what human beings do in their lives. Killing, lying, cheating, or stealing as part of one's "profession," as with a career criminal, are almost universally considered unjustifiable and rightly so.

In contrast, most of us are reasonably certain that physicians, scientists, educators, and many other professionals are not inherently under moral suspicion. What they do is regarded as worthwhile, even noble. Their objectives are approved by most (though a Christian Scientist may dispute the merits of medicine and a pacifist the worth of the military). In all these cases it is clear that we depend on standards of value or worthiness in evaluating a vocation and its professionals. Those who admire the spiritual life will regard the ministry as a worthy vocation, whereas those who do not will likely think otherwise. For believers in the paranormal, palmists may be practicing a noble calling, whereas skeptics view them as charlatans or as self-deluded. Some practical-minded people find the activities of poets and philosophers useless, whereas those who prize knowledge for its own sake tend to see the applied fields, such as engineering or business, as less than noble.[27]

But are any of these standards sound? Not only in our own time but throughout history, ingenious thinkers have argued against the very possibility of sound standards. From Heraclitus in ancient times to influential philosophers such as Richard Rorty

---

27. In Plato's ideal state, as presented in *The Republic*, some artists were deemed so destructive that they had to be banished. Of course, Plato also thought that the class of traders is the lowest in the ideal society, concerned with but the most mundane matters. (It needs noting here that Plato likely did not expect the ideal society to be put into practice. It was meant to function as a model, the way a mannequin functions to guide us in selecting clothing.)

and Paul Feyerabend in ours,[28] there have always been those who have argued persuasively that standards have no solid and stable foundation. Today antifoundationalism is in favor among philosophers in various areas, from the philosophy of literary interpretation to the philosophy of science.[29]

The central thrust of these views can be appreciated more fully when one considers developments in Eastern Europe, namely, the demise of communist tyranny and the emergence of democratic politics and free market economic institutions. In a review of the works of Polish philosopher Jan Patock, Richard Rorty claimed that "non-metaphysicians [of whom Rorty and, by his account, all other sensible persons are members] cannot say that democratic institutions reflect a moral reality and that tyrannical regimes do not reflect one, that tyrannies get something wrong that democratic societies get right."[30] In other words, there is no sound, objective moral case to be made in favor of one moral stance and against its opposite, in favor of one political ideal and against its opposite.

Moral and political skeptics have always had champions, but contemporary skepticism is remarkably complex. For the most part, skeptics have aimed their doubts at moral and political standards, following the example of David Hume's famous argument, which holds that no knowledge about the world can lead to conclusions about what we ought to do. In other words, if Hume is correct, we cannot derive an "ought" from an "is." A

28. Charles M. Bakewell, *Source Book in Ancient Philosophy* (New York: Gordian Press, 1873); Richard Rorty, *Objectivity, Relativism, and Truth* (Cambridge, England: Cambridge University Press, 1991); and Paul Feyerabend, *Against Method* (London: Verso Press).

29. See "Rethinking Foundationalism: Metaphilosophical Essays," *Reason Papers*, no. 16 (fall 1991) (special editors, Gregory R. Johnson and Glenn A. Magee).

30. Richard Rorty, "The Seer of Prague," *New Republic*, July 1, 1991.

significant effect of skepticism as it bears on our concerns in this inquiry is that it undermines confidence in our ability to identify standards by which to judge which institutions we ought to support and which to oppose and what professions we ought to honor and which to condemn.

Since our concern here is to explore why our culture maligns commerce and business, and whether this attitude is justified, we will have to establish some standards of evaluation and consider whether those that have been invoked against commerce are sound. When a playwright names one of his characters Avarice in contrast with another named Justice, it is assumed that making such significant distinctions has validity, philosophical merit, or some other important value. Similarly, when Plato regards the professional trader as lowly, or when Christians hold that the poor live more worthwhile lives than the rich, or when Marx sees the capitalist class as in need of abolition or even liquidation, these judgments imply that standards of right conduct are being invoked with confidence.

Granted, some interpreters have observed that Socrates never did find the true standards that he professed to seek and that Socrates himself was aware of this. Nevertheless, it is important to note that those who followed Socrates' thought made at least provisional judgments about those standards and strove for better and better ones. More fundamentally, the very manner of Socrates' examination, including the nature of his questions, demonstrates a profound respect for the standards of correct reasoning, such as clarity, precision, relevance, accuracy, coherence, consistency with known facts, attention to conceptual implications and assumptions, and so on. In another context, organized religions have traditionally been seen as sources for some measure of moral awareness and guidance concerning proper conduct, which is not possible without invoking standards. Skepticism challenges the appeal to standards that human beings make in nearly every area of life, including morality. So, we must ask, is there something inherently flawed in the search for standards, such that persisting in that search is evidence of hubris rather than wisdom?[31]

First, whatever the merits of the skeptical stance, the historical record remains unchanged: Philosophers, theologians, artists, and others have tended to regard commerce as morally base. This fact remains, independent of the problem posed by skepticism.

Second, we have two options available to us regarding the validity of such a widely held view. We can ask whether the prevailing view critical of commerce has validity. More ambitiously, we can go further and attempt to argue for some alternative viewpoint, demonstrating that it has better credentials, everything considered, than either skepticism or the doctrine that holds commerce and business largely in contempt.

Our intention is the more far-reaching one. We wish to argue here that the prominent viewpoint is false and that a better view exists, wherein commerce and business can be seen as worthwhile practices and professions deserving of our long overdue respect.

31. David W. Ehrenfeld, *The Arrogance of Humanism* (London: Oxford University Press, 1978).

CHAPTER ONE

Historical Views
of Commerce

*In the case of dyes and perfumes, for instance, we enjoy them but
think of dyers and perfumers as servile and vulgar people.*
—Plutarch

ANCIENT VIEWS OF COMMERCE

As a matter of anthropological fact, the various cultures of the
world have and do exhibit particular attitudes regarding, among
other things, the different institutions that are part of the culture.
In particular, in Western culture the institution of commerce has
had a dominant reputation or image, partly because of the artic-
ulated opinions of those who have influence over the shaping of
institutions. Just as the institution of the family or the church has
had a reputation, just as science has had a reputation, so too has
commerce been accorded a certain reputation in Europe and
elsewhere. What prominent and influential people have thought
of commerce throughout history can be discerned, including certain shifts in the image of commerce.

The term *image* suggests that something may have been amiss
with how commerce has been perceived. To understand what
exactly, it is necessary to first identify and examine the image. In
this and the following sections we explore how commerce has
been viewed by prominent thinkers and writers, based on contemporary documents. Although other opinions were no doubt

held, what is of interest here is how the main current of thought has evaluated commerce and business as a part of human life.

We can set the stage for our exploration with a particularly illustrative observation from Bertrand de Jouvenel, who noted that "an enormous majority of Western intellectuals display and affirm hostility to the economic and social institutions of their society, institutions to which they give the blanket name of capitalism."[1]

SETTING SOME LIMITS

The origins of this intellectual hostility can be traced as far back as the ancient Greeks, who have had an enormous and sustained influence on Western thought for more than two thousand years. Among them are the familiar names of Homer, Hesiod, Thucydides, Aristophanes, Aeschylus, Sophocles, Pythagoras, Democritus, Socrates, Plato, Aristotle, and others. Following the Greeks, we turn to the Romans and then to the Jews and the Christians, the last exerting the most important influence, which crystallized the dominant perspective on human life in the West. As Victor Hugo so eloquently observed,

> On the day when Christianity said to man: You are a duality, you are composed of two beings, one perishable, the other immortal, one carnal, the other ethereal, one enchained by appetites, needs, and passions, the other lofted on wings of enthusiasm and reverie, the former bending forever to earth, its mother, the latter soaring always toward heaven, its fatherland—on that day, the drama was created. Is it anything other, in fact, than this contrast on every day, this battle at every moment, between two opposing

1. Quoted in Bernard Murchland, *Humanism and Capitalism: A Survey of Thought and Morality* (Washington, D.C.: American Enterprise Institute for Public Policy Research, 1984).

principles that are ever-present in life and that contend over man
from the cradle to the grave?[2]

The dualistic view that Hugo describes gives prominence to a
timeless, unchanging, spiritual dimension of being and applauds
only those human actions that point beyond this world, while it
demeans nature and actions befitting nature. This view has held
sway throughout most of Western civilization.

Ironically, commerce and religion were intimately linked at
one time, and we have reason to believe that the origins of commerce go back to the church. "The religious practice of the period
[of the Old Testament], which made cattle the most important
offering to the gods, also weighed heavily in favor of making
animals the most common currency of barter. The great herds
which thus accumulated at the holy places could not be consumed
but were traded for other goods. Thus the temples became the
oldest places of commerce, the celebration of offerings [became]
the first fairs."[3]

Despite these early ties of commerce and religion, the bulk of
received Christian viewpoint engendered a constant inner division, as Hugo observes. There were a few exceptions, notable for
their rarity, such as Saint Bernardino of Siena (1380–1444) who,
in his book *On Contracts and Usury*,[4] defended trade and private
property and argued that all vocations provide occasions for sin,
not only business.

The ancient Greek view was less radical in its division of body
and soul, although clearly some of the prominent Greek philos-

2. Victor Hugo, *La preface de Cromwell*, Maurice A. Souriau, ed. (Geneve:
Slatkine Reprints, 1973).

3. H. Hamburger, *Money, Coins, Interpreters Dictionary of the Bible*, vol.
3 (Nashville, Tenn.: Abingdon, 1962), p. 423.

4. Saint Bernardino of Siena, *Decontractibus et usuris* (New Haven,
Conn.: Research Publications, 1974), microfilm.

ophers fueled the disdain toward commerce. Socrates, for example, saw the highest goal of human life as the proper ordering of the human soul within its three parts. The highest place belongs to reason because of its unique ability to comprehend the ultimate nature of things; the passions or emotions followed, with the animal appetites at the lowest rung.

This hierarchy suggested not a literal supernatural or spiritual realm of reality but rather a higher, intellectual realm. The two realms were clearly thought to be dependent on one another—no realm of intelligible things makes sense without the realm of the visible things that need to be made intelligible. In other words, these forms served as the standards or criteria by which to know and evaluate the many kinds of things that we encounter in daily life. In short, it is arguable that the realm of ideas is abstracted from the realm of those things, events, actions, institutions, and so on that are necessary to make the latter realm understandable. This is one reason it may be wise not to take strictly literally the standard interpretation of Plato's (Socrates') metaphysical position.

What exactly is the Socratic view of wealth? His stance may be reconstructed from considering some of his discussions about the subject. In a conversation with Adeimantus in book four of *The Republic*, Socrates observes that wealth and poverty are corrupters. Here are some clues:

> SOCRATES: Take the other craftsmen again and consider whether these things corrupt them so as to make them bad.
>
> ADEIMANTUS: What are they?
>
> SOCRATES: Wealth and poverty.
>
> ADEIMANTUS: How?
>
> SOCRATES: Like this: in your opinion, will a potter who's gotten rich still be willing to attend to his art?

ADEIMANTUS: Not at all.

SOCRATES: And will he become idler and more careless than he was?

ADEIMANTUS: By far.

SOCRATES: Doesn't he become a worse potter then?

ADEIMANTUS: That, too, by far.

Furthermore, in the *Republic*, Plato recalls Socrates discussing the vulnerable city, explaining it in part by reference to the soul of the impoverished but money-loving man. As Socrates puts it,

> Humbled by poverty, he turns greedily to money-making; and bit by bit saving and working, he collects money. Don't you suppose that such a man now puts the desiring and money-making part on the throne, and makes it the great king within himself, girding it with tiaras, collars, and Persian swords? (Book eight, 553c)

Socrates seems to be stressing that, once the soul of a person is infected by these desires, he/she will likely lose sight of the higher, noble things. For example, Socrates notes that "unless a man has a transcendent nature he would never become good if from earliest childhood his play isn't noble and all his practices aren't such." Socrates also makes reference to "the stingy element in [a person's] soul," to "bad desires," and to "unnecessary and useless pleasures." These observations arise in the context of an effort to identify the essence of an exemplary human being by exploring the nature of a good and just community. Socrates argues that the city makes itself vulnerable to tyranny if its goal is a comfortable life aimed at the satisfaction of natural or bodily desires. Thus, vesting power in the wealthy, who seek merely to satisfy the lower needs and wants of the people, will incline the city toward tyranny by making it a weak and easy target of conquest.[5]

Thus (Plato) Socrates regards as unworthy humans' attempts to satisfy their desires for an exciting, pleasant, comfortable, and joyful life on earth. Now, we are not to understand Plato as suggesting that it is always wrong to seek to satisfy these desires but that it is wrong to make them our primary goal since human beings ought to transcend these desires and pursue more noble ones. What are these "nobler" desires? They are the philosophical objective of true understanding, namely, knowledge of the forms of things. However, since this objective is not realizable by most people, Socrates can only conclude that few persons can live a truly noble life. We will return to these passages shortly, but let us now consider Aristotle's position, which is more directly stated.

Aristotle shares at least some degree of Socrates' disdain for those engaged in trade or money making. In book one of the *Nicomachean Ethics*, he tells us that the "life of money-making is one undertaken under compulsion, and wealth is evidently not the good we are seeking; for it is merely useful and for the sake of something else." Elsewhere (book three, chapter 12) he praises the liberal or generous person, claiming that

> It is not easy for the liberal man to be rich, since he is not apt either at taking or at keeping, but at giving away, and does not value wealth for its own sake but as a means to giving. Hence comes the charge that is brought against fortune, that those who

5. This suggests that Socrates extrapolates the need for some specific virtues, such as courage, valor, and fortitude, in great demand in communities that are in a state of constant siege, to understanding those virtues as universally primary. Yet would a community not under constant threat from hostile neighbors not require the more peaceable, gentle virtues, including industry, frugality, and liberality?

deserve riches most get it least. But it is not unreasonable that it should turn out so, for he cannot have wealth, any more than anything else, if he does not take pains to have it.

In addition, Aristotle also holds (book one, chapters 8–9 of the *Politics*) that there is something inherently wrong with commerce:

> Hence we may infer that retail trade is not a natural part of the art of getting wealth; had it been so, men would have ceased to exchange when they had enough. In the first community, which is the family, this art is obviously of no use, but it begins to be useful when the society increases. . . . For natural riches and the natural art of wealth-getting are different whereas retail trade is the art of producing wealth, not in every way, but by exchange. And it is thought to be concerned with coin; for coin is the unit of exchange and the measure or limit of it. And there is no bound to the riches which spring from this art of wealth-getting. . . . [Furthermore] in this art of wealth-getting there is no limit of the end, which is riches of the spurious kind, and the acquisition of wealth.

Aristotle reinforces his suspicions about profit making when elsewhere in the *Politics* he claims that

> Some persons are led to believe that getting wealth is the object of household management, and the whole idea of their lives is that they ought either to increase their money without limit, or at any rate not lose it. The origin of this disposition in men is that they are intent upon living only, and not upon living well; and as their desires are unlimited, they also desire that the means of gratifying them should be without limit.

He maintains that of the two kinds of wealth getting, household management and retail trade,

> The former [is] necessary and honorable, while that which consists

in exchange is justly censured; for it is unnatural and a mode by which men gain from one another. The most hated sort, and with the greatest reason, is usury, which makes a gain out of money itself, and not from the natural object of it. For money was intended to be used in exchange, but not to increase interest. And this term interest, which means the birth of money from money, is applied to the breeding of money because the offspring resembles the parent. Wherefore of all modes of getting wealth this is the most unnatural.

By "unnatural" Aristotle does not mean simply "out of the ordinary"—as it would be, say, unnatural for a cat to go swimming. Rather, by "unnatural" here is meant a violation of the most basic moral standards, those objectively identifiable ethics by which we should be guided in living the good life, based on a correct understanding of human nature. Acting against human nature is involving oneself in conduct that thwarts the development or enhancement of oneself as a human being. Going against nature means failing to flourish or, worse, bringing about the diminishing of one's natural capacities. This includes not only acting but also thinking in a way that is inconsistent with human nature.

Aristotle can be shown to be wrong about why people engage in retail trade. He states that they do so because "they are intent upon living only, and not upon living well; and that as their desires are unlimited, they also desire that the means of gratifying them should be without limit." Yet there is no evidence that people do not seek to live well but only on living by means of wealth accumulation through retail trade. In fact, the evidence seems to support quite the opposite observation: Aristotle should have concluded that retail trade ought to contribute to living well, not just to living. Even if it were the case that retail trade contributes to living well per se, it would then perforce contribute to living well since no one can live well without living! Even the most noble life, with or without the elements of trade, will benefit considerably (if only indirectly) from commerce. Thus, those who wish to experience the arts must find the resources to do so. Travel, acculturation, and sometimes even philosophical inquiry require resources, not to mention the pursuit and maintenance of friendships. Commerce is perhaps the only means of earning resources in the modern age, and it is certainly the most efficient, economical, and productive means available to us.

In his conception of human nature, Aristotle elevates the rational element, endowing it with greater significance or nobility than other features of our nature, such as the human capacity for experiencing complex emotions and the satisfaction of physical, chemical, biological, and psychological needs related to a happy life. In short, Aristotle and many other thinkers who came after him, including the very influential Thomas Aquinas, regarded the human capacity to think conceptually and theoretically—our rational faculty—as our most important attribute. For Aristotle, our animal or biological nature was less impressive than our faculty of reason. This may have been part of the legacy of Plato, Aristotle's teacher. Or, quite understandably, it may have been due to Aristotle's observation that rationality is the distinctive feature of human beings, without which we would not be human but just another animal.

Now, in one sense this is quite right: For purposes of understanding human life within the context of nature, that our rationality makes us distinctive is most important, in the way that being winged or having gills or being herbivorous separates one kind of living thing from another. But it doesn't follow from this that for the life of the human individual his or her rationality is more important than, say, nourishment, even if nourishment for us depends on the use of our intelligent minds. We live our lives as one whole, organic being, and it makes sense to care for and nurture all aspects of our being—our health, our emotions, our minds—exactly as the virtue of prudence demands.

Of course, one may perhaps treat what is unique or special about oneself with more care and diligence than those aspects one shares with many others. People typically and not surprisingly tend to themselves and their own more readily than they tend to the concerns of others, and they often enjoy special association with those who share their particular interests. Our distinctions contribute to our individuality, set us apart, and in this sense have greater significance for us than what we have in common with others.

But this should not be confused with attributing greater importance to the distinct element in human nature than to what humans share with other living beings, as Plato and Aristotle seem to have done. Their error was to treat members of their own professional class as deserving of special status, while attributes that they shared with humanity at large were demeaned.[6]

In Plato's and Aristotle's view, that which is special about human beings should be honored more, and, since philosophical and theoretical inquiry are essentially rational activities, philosophy was regarded as the most noble of enterprises. This may explain the tremendous influence that both philosophers have had on the Western tradition of intellectualism and, in time, of spiritualism (though less so with Aristotle, given his metaphysical

6. This may not appear to be a major piece of evidence, yet it is worth noting how often we accept it of intellectuals, that they are absent-minded, meaning that their attention is focused almost exclusively on abstractions and not on concrete reality. Yet why should anyone be excused for failing to have practical intelligence? As we discuss throughout this work, the answer would have to depend on some prior belittling of the significance of practical, earthbound action.

Concerning the impact of such special-interest organization on democratic polities, see Mancur Olson, *The Logic of Collective Action, Public Goods and the Theory of Groups* (New York: Schocken Books, 1971).

monism and his inclusion of the natural sciences as subjects worthy of study).

Admittedly we are speculating here, and it is not a philosophical task to discover why certain mistakes have been made. Psychologists, sociologists, even economists are more suited to this task and may have more illuminating things to say on that question. Still, it is important to consider that the kind of error Aristotle appears to have made—of elevating what is distinctive to the status of most important—may be relatively minor and common. We all do this on occasion, when we take our own individual preoccupations as paramount and universally significant, or when we take our likes and dislikes to be more than what they actually are, namely, choices that may be fitting for us but not necessarily for others. That to which we are accustomed acquires the feel of what is "natural." This tendency is evident as members of one culture learn of the different practices and preferences of other cultures. In any case, it is a common failing of human beings to elevate their own preferences and tastes to the position of general standards. This may derive, in part, from a fear that unless this is done, what we desire, prefer, want will fail to be important. Here we have a clear intimation of the importance of the later emergence of individualism taken to extremes by its initial champions, in particular, Thomas Hobbes.[7]

Of course, distinctiveness does not by itself imply importance. One may be distinctive in being evil or criminal or in having a contagious disease, which would diminish, rather than enhance, one's value. In contrast, what is important for a human being, and vital as the being he or she is, is to think and act consistently

---

7. For more on this see Tibor R. Machan, *The Virtue of Liberty* (Irvington-on-Hudson, N.Y.: Foundation for Economic Education, 1994), as well as *Capitalism and Individualism* (New York: St. Martin's Press, 1990).

with his or her nature.[8] This is how to make oneself an excellent example of one's kind, how to be the best that one can be. By Aristotle's own description, human nature consists of being a rational animal. Clearly, being such an animal is as much a matter of being biological, chemical, physical, and emotional as of being intellectual, social, and political.

Aristotle's monistic metaphysics, apart from controversial departures in places, supports this organic, holistic conception of human nature.[9] It is only in his ethics that Aristotle pursues a different line of analysis. To be sure, this is understandable: We must follow right reason, first and foremost, which suggests that our reasoning faculty is of primary significance.

However, we should be careful to avoid an equivocation: Reasoning undoubtedly must be our means of serving our nature since we lack the instincts of other animals and thus need to think our way through life by understanding what is what. But the content or subject matter of our reasoning relevant to our practical lives must be whatever will enhance our nature, not just the theoretical content of thinking itself. Thinking is vital to living, but living does not consist of thinking alone, any more than one lives by bread alone. The standard for living well must involve whatever human life is, which includes not only our reason but all the rest that makes us human beings.

Why stress these points? Arguably it is with Aristotle, who follows and greatly modifies Plato, that we begin the journey of Western culture in developing a view of human life and society. Had it been left to Plato alone, we would likely have developed

8. Of course, it may turn out (see Machan, *Individuals and Their Rights*) that a central element of human nature is everyone's individuality, that to be a human being is in part being unique.

9. See chapter 1 of *Individuals and Their Rights*, where metaphysical monism is shown to be related to an ontological pluralism, that is, the indeterminate number of possible variations in kinds and types of beings in reality, provided they do not violate the basic laws of being Aristotle identified.

a simple and obviously untenable dualism and idealism. Shirley Robin Letwin explains the substance of this position as it pertains to the Western view of human nature:

> Each person is seen as an unstable compound of two warring parts. Insofar as reason dominates, order prevails. For reason is understood as a power to discover universal truths, laws, and patterns. It imposes uniformity. But order is threatened by the irrational element in human beings, which is a chaos of desires and aversions. Since these operate in no regular fashion, they produce an endless, disorderly, diversity in behavior.[10]

Clearly the implication is that the "irrational" element is bad, base, ignoble. Accordingly, the ethical substance of much of medieval theology and philosophy pointed human beings toward the supernatural, leaving most of humankind unsuited for earthly living. However, if the supernatural is a myth, or a mistake, such teaching would be misguided and misanthropic.

Aristotle modified the Platonic dualism and idealism by his monistic metaphysics, leaving us to strive for a natural life; but he construed it as owing loyalty to our supposed higher selves, as opposed to our supernaturally connected selves. He left a legacy that is ambivalent about commerce, allowing it a utilitarian and thus rather vague function in our lives: Retail trade satisfies only our intent on living, not on living well! But if our criticism of Aristotle is sound and he did unjustifiably demean the element of human nature served by commerce, it could well be that commerce must take its place next to other worthy professions that enhance human life, that serve us in our desire to live well.

The influence of Aristotle's legacy, especially in the era following his death, is beyond dispute. In Hellenistic Greece his attitude

---

10. Shirley Robin Letwin, *The Autonomy of Thatcherism* (London: Fontana Books, 1992), p. 338.

toward commerce held sway. As historian Herbert J. Muller observed, "They still regarded material wealth and power more as means than as ends, and spent a considerably larger proportion of their wealth on embellishing their cities and enriching their civic life than modern Americans are wont to do."[11] Not unlike most intellectuals, Muller shares the later Greeks' disdain toward wealth when it functions in any other capacity than in support of high culture. The legacy of such disdain carries down to the present, sometimes more pronounced, sometimes simply confusing.

Despite the prominent opinion of the classical world, which viewed commerce with suspicion and moral disdain, the institution of business kept expanding, as people traded more and more, taking trade from their markets all over the globe. We are now ready to examine the prevailing attitudes toward commerce and business in the era of Western culture guided largely by the Roman Catholic Church.

MEDIEVAL VIEWS OF COMMERCE

Our concern here is to identify the views of commerce promulgated to ordinary people, to the faithful citizens of various centers

---

11. Herbert J. Muller, *Freedom in the Ancient World* (New York: Bantam Books, 1964), p. 242. "The loveliest works of little Priene now embellish museums in Europe, but the bare remains of its public buildings and its streets enable one to visualize a gem of a city, well planned, beautifully built, and proudly adorned, that could hardly be matched in the much wealthier modern world. Its theater alone might humiliate any town of its size in America" (ibid.). However, to assume that material power and wealth are means in the old world but ends in modernity is just too simple. The nobility was by no means focused on noble objectives alone, nor are our contemporary efforts to obtain power and wealth unrelated to how we might use these to enhance our fullest possible appreciation of human living. What is missing, perhaps, though by no means necessarily a loss, is the effort to address some supposed higher reality, prepare for an afterlife, aim at an impossible ideal. But such struggles are probably the breeding ground for cynicism anyway.

of commerce, rather than the views of medieval theologians as found in their scholarly works. The origins of the widely disseminated ideas on commerce may well be innocuous, treating commerce as a decent and vital human activity. Indeed, there is some evidence for such a reading of many passages in the Bible. For example, consider 20 Matthew:

> For the kingdom of heaven is like a householder who went out early in the morning to hire laborers for his vineyard. After agreeing with the laborers for a denarius a day, he sent them into his vineyard. And going out about the third hour he saw others standing idle in the market place; and to them he said, "You go into the vineyard too, and whatever is right I will give you." So they went. Going out again about the sixth hour and the ninth hour, he did the same. And about the eleventh hour he went out and found others standing; and he said to them, "Why do you stand here idle all day?" They said to him, "Because no one has hired us." He said to them, "You go into the vineyard too." And when evening came, the owner of the vineyard said to his steward, "Call the laborers and pay them their wages, beginning with the last up to the first." And when those hired about the eleventh hour came, each of them received a denarius. Now when the first came, they thought they would receive more, but each of them also received a denarius. And on receiving it they grumbled at the householder, saying, "These last worked only one hour, and you have made them equal to us who have borne the burden of the day and the scorching heat." But he replied to them, "Friend, I am doing you no wrong; did you not agree with me for a denarius? Take what belongs to you, and go; I choose to give to this last as I give to you. Am I not allowed to do what I choose with what belongs to me? Or do you begrudge my generosity?" So, the last will be first, and the first last.

One interpretation of this passage would have the Bible affirming a free hand for commercial agents, leaving matters of trade to agreement rather than to preconceived propriety. Another reading might have this passage teaching that heaven is indifferent to the effort one puts into one's good works; whether one is early or late with one's faith, one will be admitted with equal welcome. In either case, the choice of this subject to demonstrate a point that gives some support for the view that the Bible is favorable toward freedom of trade, at least in the matter of labor.

Furthermore, the Bible is rarely overtly hostile to wealthy people. Indeed, the wealthy play numerous favorable roles in various dramatic events. As one scholar observes, "In the [Old Testament] the possession of wealth is generally regarded as evidence of God's blessing and so of righteousness."[12] However, in some sections of the Bible, for example, Ecclesiasticus, the problematic nature of the relationship between riches and the good life is considered, and throughout the Bible we find a vacillation between relating "righteousness and well-being" and "the necessity of complete detachment from wealth."[13]

Biblical doctrine concerning commerce by no means entirely determined medieval teachings. Indeed, Luther's reformation movement was largely intended to return the church to biblical doctrine. Yet Roman Catholic and other Christian theology rarely strays far from developing themes that are present in the Bible. If there are contradictions in such theology, it may be because there are ambiguities and contradictions in the Bible itself.

A simple illustration of this is to note the various Roman Catholic orders, some dedicated to the renunciation of nearly all earthly goods, while others freely partake of earthly blessings. There is also an evident difference between the Old and the New Testaments, mainly because the message of Jesus tends to be more negative regarding commerce. It was, after all, the money lenders who were chased from the temple, in the only display of outright

12. James Hastings, *Dictionary of the Bible* (New York: Charles Scribners Sons, 1963), p. 1031.

13. Ibid.

violence by Jesus in support of his objectives.[14] At those moments when Jesus appears more sympathetic toward wealth, it is a sympathy similar to that which characterizes our own culture.[15] Such sympathy laments poverty and deprivation while condemning and ridiculing the rich. Jesus can be seen as embodying the same contradictions as does our society, which gives us reason to think that the teachings of Jesus account for much of the ambivalence about wealth that is evident in Western cultures. Nevertheless, we do find in the Bible the following counsel:

> While the Lord realized that poverty brought sorrow, He also realized that wealth contained an intense peril to spiritual life. He came to raise the world from the material to the spiritual; and wealth, as the very token of the material and temporal, was blinding men to the spiritual and eternal. He therefore urged those to whom it was a special hindrance, to resign it altogether; and charged all to regard it as something for the use of which they would be held accountable.[16]

We can see here a close affinity between the Platonic-Aristotelian and the prominent Christian conception about wealth and commerce. In Colossians 3:1–4, we read also that "if you have been raised with Christ, seek the things that are above, where Christ is, seated at the right hand of God. Set your minds on things that are above, not on things that are on earth." In other words, while wealth may have a place in the decent life, that place

---

14. Jesus said that it is easier for a camel to go through the eye of a needle than for a rich man to enter the kingdom of God. In Luke 12, Jesus is supposed to find that the rich man occupies a place of torment beyond the grave, while the poor rests in Abraham's bosom.

15. Jesus told Zacchaeus, who only gave half of his wealth away, that he will be saved. And Lazarus, too, manages to lie in the bosom of Abraham, despite being a rich Jew.

16. *Dictionary*, p. 1032.

is lowly and of little significance in contrast with spiritual and otherworldly matters. This attitude has a serious impact on our moral outlook, rendering materialistic motivations, inclinations, conduct, and institutions morally suspicious since they may detract from, and create obstacles to, spiritual development. The temptations of the world, and the enjoyment of physical pleasures, can always pose an impediment to the enjoyments of the goods of the spirit. Whether this view is actually characteristic of popular medieval thinking is the question we need to investigate next.

We noted earlier that the messages from the Bible concerning commerce and wealth exerted an ambiguous influence in medieval times. Many people of this era were largely illiterate and thus encountered biblical thought through the mediation of religious leaders rather than directly. Even at that, the influence could be affected by individual interpretation not only by the priest but by members of the flock as well.

In addition, various sections of the Bible were written as records, not as instructions. Although parables clearly enjoin people to follow some teaching, the descriptive passages are historical accounts, not moral instructions. So medieval attitudes are not likely to be as homogeneous as one might expect, given the cursory references to the period that we find in many lectures and essays. Nevertheless, medieval religion, and the widespread opinion that it generated, was not generally favorable to commerce, especially not to its essential motivation, which focuses on worldly concerns and desires.

The earliest attitudes in evidence are so emphatically spiritual in focus that no explicit denunciation of commercial pursuits is needed to perceive hostility toward commerce. Plotinus, Porphyry, Saint Augustine, and many others deserve their reputation as distinctly otherworldly intellectual leaders in the fields of theology, philosophy, and political theory. Plotinus, for example, in his metaphysical view that reality is pure at its radiant and non-corporeal center, taught that the human body, which is dense, dark, and earthly, was shameful evidence of our separation from the One. The sins to which Saint Augustine profusely confesses are predominantly indulgences in the pleasures of this life. No doubt some of those sins are made possible by commerce, even if it does not necessarily force them on people.[17]

The details of the early Christian attitude toward commerce—for example, its view of money and interest, usury, miserliness, greed, and avarice—though informative, need not be elaborated here. The central and most significant point is that, at the ontological, most fundamental, level, the Christian holds as contemptible the very world that is attended to by means of commerce and business. For the medieval Christian, the worldly life is a mere means toward the real existence for which human beings ought to strive; and this way to salvation included, quite explicitly, resistance against the temptations and pleasures of the body. Just as Socrates had argued that life is a preparation for death, at which our souls are liberated from the chains of the body, Christian theology teaches that the afterlife is the proper object and determinant of our earthly existence.

Ironically, there is a preparation of sorts in this attitude for the secular view that living joyfully is our proper goal in life. If one accepts the ontological claim about the glory and bliss of the afterlife, then belittling life in this world amounts to a form of cost-benefit analysis. It is, after all, only common sense to give

17. Augustine himself first embraced the radical dualism of the Manichees, who regarded the lower half of the body as the disgusting work of the devil. But he later forged a Christian worldview that attempted to avoid radical metaphysical dualism. Still, he retained the stress on the dualism of worldly versus otherworldly virtues (e.g., in his *City of God*, 5th century B.C.), thereby continuing to foster the dichotomy between what fulfills our earthly lives and what secures the salvation of our everlasting souls.

up some few benefits to gain greater rewards in the future. There is nothing particularly self-denying about that. So the religious attitude of self-abnegation is somewhat disingenuous, for its true objective is nothing other than the enhancement of oneself. This is the old "it must make her feel good or Mother Teresa wouldn't do it" view. And indeed, Mother Teresa herself acknowledged that she was very selfish, for it brought her pleasure to help others.

Put more precisely, then, medieval Christianity was not opposed to happiness or pleasure as such. Rather, the highest-quality happiness and pleasure were not attainable in this world but could only be found in the supernatural realm. All attempts at earthly happiness were regarded as vain.

The resulting antipathy toward commerce and business was in some respects different from what the ancient Greeks felt. Christianity found it imprudent to seek happiness from the goods of this world, whereas the ancient Greeks found the highest goods of this world to be intellectual endeavors or states of mind. The precise form of happiness and bliss to be achieved in the supernatural realm is left unspecified, but it is safe to assume that, given the incorporeal nature of salvation, the issue of denying bodily desires is entirely moot. This is not the case for the Greeks, who believed that happiness is to be sought here on earth and attained in the context of living a corporeal life.

Interestingly, then, Christian morality is less self-denying than Greek morality, but this fact has had little impact on the Christian view of commerce and business.

MODERN VIEWS ON COMMERCE

In February 1992, the *New York Times* ran a review by Herbert Mitgang of Jonathan Franzen's novel *Strong Motion*, which, as the *Times* put it, "exposes the unethical practices of a recognizable group of entrepreneurs in the United States." The review describes what turns out to be the central theme of this chapter, namely, the modern view of commerce, which assumes that "a large company pollutes the earth, endangers people's lives, suppresses whistle blowers and covers up its activities to keep its greedy executives in corporate clover." Mitgang observes further that "muckraking American authors exposed such wealthy malefactors early this century; Henrik Ibsen, George Bernard Shaw and Arthur Miller created similar enemies of the people for the stage." We could add that Shakespeare was no kinder to people interested in making money, nor were Charles Dickens or Victor Hugo or a host of other writers for whom business was treated as at best a necessary evil.

In modern times, as commerce gained a much greater role in the life of culture, the attack on commerce also gained momentum. Thus continues the general cultural tension encouraged by dualism, the juxtaposition of idealism and materialism. The former elevated to the status of a noble vision, the latter relegated to the mundane.

Although these two worldviews are combined in dualism, they are in fact at odds, and it is not possible to live in accord with both at once. Those who have tried to avoid the reductionism of either of the dualities have favored, as did Aristotle, an ontological picture of considerable diversity. Such a view, which could properly be called monistic pluralism, sees reality as governed by certain basic principles (the law of identity, for example), while composed of an indeterminate number of types and kinds of beings, which are to be discovered rather than affirmed a priori.

This pluralistic view, in contrast with dualisms that divide reality into the ideal and material realms, has a practical advantage: It is more conducive to making progress in following standards by which to live. The dualist view seems to condemn human beings to constant guilt and disappointment, for it sets goals in terms of unattainable ideals. Western culture has produced numerous scientific and technological breakthroughs, allowing for increased enjoyment of the pleasures of this life, but that joy comes at the cost of regret and doubt over pursuing less than worthy goals. So the dualist ontology presents this dilemma: Whereas the ideals are worthy but unattainable, earthly pleasures are attainable but unworthy. To the extent that a human being strives to make the most of nature, his/her efforts are less than admirable. Our natural being must be pushed back to make room for our higher being, our supernatural form of life. Such is the logic of the dualistic view.

One could argue that the dualistic influence was not complete. Indeed, from the time of Machiavelli, through Hobbes, Hume, Mill, and other moderns, up to the positivists of the twentieth century, there has been a significant, influential turn toward reductive materialism. This is best exemplified in our time in the scholarly works of neoclassical economists, a profound effect of which has been to render human affairs subject to a kind of scientific study. Economics is arguably the field most affected by these developments. Scientific economics attempts to understand human commercial life in the language introduced by the natural sciences. Of course, psychology, sociology, political science, and other social sciences have felt the force of this reductive materialism as well.

In sharp contrast, the humanistic disciplines of the arts, including literature, music, and painting, as well as some schools of philosophy, offered a countermovement to reductive materialism. Perhaps the most illustrious representative of the countermovement is Immanuel Kant, who reacted vehemently to the demoralization of human existence implied by scientism.

According to scientism, only those substances are real which can be the subject matter of the natural sciences or the objects of scientific observation. This, of course, excludes all values and everything immaterial, including the human mind, except insofar as these can be reduced to material and, thus, observable and measurable entities and processes. Now Kant did not offer a naturalist alternative—for example, a revised Aristotelian pluralistic metaphysics. Instead, Kant fully embraced the scientistic claims about what science supposedly affirms of reality and the methods by which we ought to study it. Rather than challenging scientism directly, Kant offered a reformed dualism, whose impact was quite similar to the dualism of the past: the division of reality and human life into two incommensurable spheres, the phenomenal (which science can study) and the noumenal (which cannot be understood but which can be apprehended by spiritual awareness).

For Kant, the phenomenal realm included everything that scientism claimed for itself, namely, the world of experience, properly studied by means of empirical methods. The underlying assumptions of scientism, including universal determinism and the ontology of identifying the real with the quantifiable, were not challenged. To make room for morality and religion, Kant found it necessary to make an addition, the noumenal realm.

Scientism did not fully prevail, either as a true philosophy or as a widely accepted view, though many contemporary intellectuals, such as Stephen Hawking, still embrace the notion that what lies outside the scope of science (in particular, physics) is not real. Despite its ambitious beginnings and great confidence, especially in the positivist movement of the early twentieth century, scientism was more promise than payment, a hope for future fulfillment, similar to today's projections that the mind can be replicated without residue by a computer and so forth. There has, of course, been considerable progress in the direction of technology's promise, but scientistic reductionism still faces the nagging problem of the spiritual or supernatural dimension in terms of human choice, the distinction between right and wrong conduct, aesthetic experiences, and the like, which cannot be explained away or reduced to some other material/natural category.

From a historical perspective it could be said that the great genius of Kant was to make room for this part of human life by providing a palatable framework that would allow for both determinism and freedom, fact and value, matter and spirit. However, in doing so, Kant brought about a complete separation of nature and morality not found in either Plato or the medieval Christians. In particular, Kant exiled prudence from the realm of moral virtues, thereby precluding from commerce and business any opportunity for a noble and worthy reputation.

Absent a teleological view of human nature, the ethics of virtue cannot be understood, nor can one think constructively about what purposes would best serve people in life. The moral virtues are, among many other things, necessary means to certain proper ends in one's life. This may be obvious with respect to virtues such as courage and honesty, but, though perhaps less evident, it is no less true of prudence.

To call the virtues a "means" is not to separate them from their valuable ends, as though the virtues were "merely" means or as though nonvirtuous means could achieve the same ends. Virtuous conduct not only serves to achieve our proper goals— to live happily, to fulfill our human potentialities, to excel at living—but is itself a constitutive aspect of living properly. In short, such conduct is both a means and an end. It is precisely what it means to live well, not just an instrument for producing the result, a morally good life, as if these were in fact separable. Adam Smith, a contemporary of Kant, but with a firm loyalty to common sense, made the following insightful observation.

> Ancient moral philosophy proposed to investigate wherein consisted the happiness and perfection of man, considered not only as an individual, but as the member of a family, of a state, and of

the great society of mankind. In that philosophy the duties of human life were treated of as subservient to the happiness and perfection of human life. But when moral, as well as natural philosophy, came to be taught only as subservient to theology, the duties of human life were treated of as chiefly subservient to the happiness of a life to come. In the ancient philosophy the perfection of virtue was represented as necessarily productive to the person who possessed it, of the most perfect happiness in this life. In the modern philosophy it was frequently represented as almost always inconsistent with any degree of happiness in this life, and heaven was to be earned by penance and mortification, not by the liberal, generous, and spirited conduct of man. By far the most important of all the different branches of philosophy became in this manner by far the most corrupted.[18]

During the classical period, and even afterward, during the Hellenistic period, the time between the death of Aristotle and the birth of the medieval era, the objective of living virtuously was happiness, or *eudaimonia* (the good self or well-being). The goal or purpose of life was to live successfully as a human being, and the various philosophical schools competed over how this goal was best reached. The idea of living successfully as a human being was problematic for modern thinkers partly because of its teleological foundations. Teleology is a view of causation (Aristotle's famous Final Cause) that takes purposes—intentions about future states—as possible explanations for some (human) behavior. This was called into question by classical mechanical science, which excluded final causes or goals, recognizing only efficient causes as part of the universe, the kind of causes that we associate with the movement of balls on a billiard table. Galileo made it quite clear and explicit that, as a principle of modern

18. Adam Smith, *Inquiry into the Nature and Causes of the Wealth of Nations* (New York: Modern Library Edition, 1927), p. 726.

science, teleological explanation must be rejected and replaced by the language of efficient causes.

Also troublesome was the belief in some overriding, universal goal of human conduct. This seemed inconsistent with the evident diversity of human lives not only over time but also within the same region and community. A variety of ways of living could be regarded as honorable, proper, or, at least, morally unobjectionable.

Furthermore, it was nearly impossible to live the form of life that many ancient philosophers, and in particular the medieval theologians, thought proper for human beings. The aspiration to imitate Christ was implicit in Christian faith, and similar self-denying models represented the good human life for others. Some Christian and other religions went even further than Scripture in regarding our bodies as base and evil. And so morality came to mean something saintly, fitting for martyrs, and clearly impossible for actual flesh and blood human beings. The impact of the medieval ideal on the general attitude toward business, commerce, and our earthly existence was dramatic and tragic.

Kant and his influential followers were unable to integrate the moral point of view with a scientific understanding of human life and so introduced another dualism that divided the self (and all of reality) into two parts, the phenomenal and the noumenal. In practical terms this division is easy to appreciate: While our bodies necessarily and predictably obey the laws of nature, which drive us to seek food, comfort, pleasure, and the like, our minds are capable of guiding us to act in a principled, honorable fashion. Furthermore, this moral guidance need not aim at any earthly objective, for the phenomenal or earthly self is perfectly suited for these.

Examining the content of many early social sciences, including economics, one finds them holding that human nature is but a more complex version of animal nature generally. We are driven to eat, drink, and multiply by the same mechanisms as are chimps, mice, and foxes. In the end, human beings are just another, albeit more complicated, organism predictably responsive to the environment. On this view our behavior is the inevitable effect of natural causes and falls totally under the scope of science. Thus, for many of the social sciences, morality is a bogus discipline, a view forthrightly championed by B. F. Skinner in his famous books *Beyond Freedom and Dignity* (1971) and *Science and Human Behavior* (1953). These works represent the full development of the modern scientific view as it applies to human beings, a view in which prudence, industriousness, and similar virtues are reduced to the category of instinctual drives. Now, as Aristotle had discovered in his *Nicomachean Ethics*, a virtue must be a function of human choice to have moral significance. Thus prudence, formerly considered a virtue, is severed from morality and replaced by Skinner with drives or instincts. The instinct of self-preservation, the drive or motive of self-interest, accounts for our taking care of our bodily needs, leaving morality to aim for something higher and more noble.

The difference between the modern view and the medieval one is important to state explicitly here. Given our thesis concerning the sources of antagonism toward business and commerce, the fundamental problem with the medieval view is in its dualism, not in teleology. That is, goal directedness, purposiveness, was still inherent to the moral life. So while prudence was deemed a virtue, it was supposed to direct us toward preparing for the life hereafter. In contrast, the dualism of the modern view combined mechanistic materialism and idealism, resulting in a rejection of goal directedness altogether within nature. And so not only was the body demeaned but the very idea of morality as a guide to living was rejected.

It is easy to see how both commerce and business were part of the emerging culture yet lacked moral standing. Because of the body's urges, drives, and instincts, seeking wealth and prosperity was admittedly a part of human existence, but since these are involuntary drives, no moral credit could accrue from excelling at such pursuits. And so the moral life focused not on the objective of living well, achieving, and succeeding but rather on good intentions and the purity of will. (This may in part account for the emphasis on compassion, feelings of empathy, and considerateness in our own time.) Commercial pursuits came to be regarded as a kind of inevitable and unchosen part of life, as much of economic science sees it. We are driven to pursue the maximization of utilities since our private desires drive us to obtain wealth. This neo-Hobbesian view was embraced by the social sciences, whereas ethicists turned their attention to the problem of what to do if those drives should go unchecked. In effect, morality became a way to tame the beast.

Although commerce and business provided more of what we desired, practitioners in the field could take little credit for what they had achieved, and they were largely ignored by mainstream moral thinkers until they went overboard. The view that people in business could not help striving for profit, but when they transgressed some limit, they were blameworthy gained prominence. This gave people in their commercial roles and the professionals in business little hope and encouragement regarding their own moral qualities. The very culture that commerce and business were contributing to vigorously and dramatically essentially bit the hand that was feeding it.

CONTEMPORARY VIEWS ON COMMERCE

Business Bashing Today

It is hardly necessary to demonstrate that contemporary culture exhibits many tendencies to malign commerce, for the evidence is nearly everywhere. A typical example is *Blood Ties*, a television movie about vampires, which aired around Halloween in 1992. In this film the evil Eliah, depicted as "filthy" rich, has just managed to manipulate the city into condemning some housing for poor people so that he can build a colossal development. Not only is Eliah gleeful about this but he shamelessly bribes a jury to get his nephew off a serious criminal charge.

In one conversation that explores and develops his character for the audience, Eliah declares, "I am a free market economist." He adds, by way of clarification, that "everything and everyone can be bought." This view of the free market system is widely promulgated by those hostile to it, but the position is also espoused rather boldly and unabashedly by many free market economists themselves.

UNINTENDED COMPLICITY IN BUSINESS BASHING?

In 1992, Gary Becker won the Nobel Prize in economics for "having extended the domain of economic theory to aspects of human behavior which had previously been dealt with—if at all—by other social science disciplines such as sociology, demography and criminology." Becker is one of the earliest and perhaps most prolific of those economists who believe that what motivates people in the marketplace, the making of a good deal, is exactly what motivates them in all walks of life—when they make love, play with their children, attend church, or develop theories of social science.

The Nobel committee has been rewarding this viewpoint in economics for the last several decades. In 1986 the prize went to James Buchanan, who was credited for his pioneering work in applying economic, or "public choice," theory to an understanding of the political process. Soon after, George Stigler, also of the University of Chicago, received the award for his similarly oriented work in the area of government regulation. Even earlier, and perhaps most notably, Milton Friedman, the head of the "Chicago School," received the Nobel Prize for his work along more general lines that many thinkers credit for laying the foundation for subsequent economic imperialism. In his acceptance address, Friedman remarked that "every individual serves his own private interest. . . . The great saints of history have served their 'private interests' just as the most money grubbing miser has served his interest. The *private interest* is whatever it is that drives an individual."[19] Becker has echoed this sentiment in his most theoretical book, *The Economic Approach to Human Behavior*: "The combined assumptions of maximizing behavior, market equilibrium, and stable preferences, used relentlessly and unflinchingly, form the heart of the economic approach as I see it."[20] Stigler put it perhaps most succinctly: "Man is eternally a utility-maximizer—in his home, in his office (be it public or private), in his church, in his scientific work—in short, everywhere."[21]

All these economists believe that they are telling us something quite simple and true and that, to use Buchanan's words, all persons in society "are seen as ordinary persons." In other words, ordinary persons, all persons, are driven to advance their own lot on every front, as they understand it. Put bluntly, everyone is selfish. Thus, greed is no sin but is rather a fact of life, a natural drive motivating all human beings.

Given this way of thinking, there is no room for morality in human life, any more than there is room for morality in the lives

19. Milton Friedman, "The Line We Dare Not Cross," *Encounter*, November 1976, p. 11

20. Gary Becker, *The Economic Approach to Human Behavior* (Chicago: University of Chicago Press, 1976), p. 13.

21. George Stigler, Lecture II, Tanner Lectures, Harvard University, April 1980.

of dogs or giraffes. Everything is set: Stigler once argued precisely this point, that the world is just as it has to be, nothing wrong or right with it; it merely is.[22]

Although most of these thinkers are strong supporters of the free market system of economics as the most productive in human history, it is doubtful that this support is what the free market ultimately requires. The reputation of the free market itself has not gained much from what the economists have said, despite the Nobel Prizes. The collapse of socialism in Eastern Europe and elsewhere has done considerably more for enhancing the reputation of capitalism than has economic theory. In fact, the economic advocates of free trade and an unregulated marketplace have unleashed a backlash unfriendly to capitalism.

Outside the discipline of economics few academicians are supportive of capitalism. They are often disdainful of the "greed" that economists praise, a view familiar to the average American. One need only recall the protagonist of Oliver Stone's movie *Wall Street,* who espoused the doctrine "greed is good" and was thus roundly seen as a villain. Consider as well how the popular press has embraced the largely empty claim that the 1980s, guided by the free market rhetoric of Ronald Reagan (who in turn was advised by these economic imperialists), was a "decade of greed."[23]

It is an error with consequences of drastic proportions to ex-

22. He gave the talk at the 1980 meetings of the Mount Pelerin Society in Hong Kong.

23. When some economists make favorable references to *greed*, they do not have in mind some kind of mindless or obsessive pursuit of wealth but a dedication to prosper, to enrich oneself in those areas one prefers, to the extent one prefers. Indeed, for an economist the ancient concept of greed does not imply anything immoral but a natural propensity to strive to obtain as much of what one wants as one would like. In short, their meaning is something of a tautology: People will want as much of what they want as they want of it.

tend to every area of human life the approach that economists take. People do not calculate costs and benefits all the time, though we would certainly be better off if we did. Cost-benefit calculation is by no means automatic or instinctive, and to pretend otherwise invites complacency.

One reason the economic approach makes sense in its study of what people do in the market is that when we go shopping we often focus on making a good deal. That is, after all, only prudent and commonsensical: We would be (and sometimes) are foolish to ignore our economic well-being when we are spending money. Indeed, this seems more so in direct proportion to one's wealth, so that the more spending money one has, the less need there is to concern oneself with making an advantageous purchase.

Outside the marketplace other motivations are appropriate. Courage, honesty, generosity, justice, love, and so forth are also important virtues to practice in our lives. Economic imperialism demeans us by denying our freedom to choose from among possible motives. It dehumanizes us and creates the illusion that we all carry on as we do because we are driven by forces beyond our control and choice.

Despite the much-needed support of the free market that the thinking of these famous economists has generated, the right to individual freedom requires much more support than that provided by economics. However enlightening economics is, a view of human life limited solely to the economic perspective would be seriously incomplete and misleading. To understand our economic dimension is not to understand the whole of human life.

CHAPTER TWO

Commercialism versus Professionalism

PROFESSIONALISM

A common criticism of commercial society is that its dynamics undermine professionalism. This criticism merits attention.

To be a professional is not only to be a member of a profession (law, education, medicine, business, etc.) but to actually carry out certain specified tasks competently. Thus, a dentist is a professional in the task of taking care of teeth, an accountant is a professional in the minding of finances, and so on. The crucial point is that professionalism implies that a professional will be competent and focused with respect to relevant tasks.

The criticism we are investigating here is the claim that when one is concerned with making money, one tends to lose concern for competence. Thus, when everyone is incorporating as a business, aiming to maximize profits (as, for example, when doctors, dentists, dress designers, and others incorporate and give notice that they are now a business), it is doubtful they are able to keep a clear focus on the matter of professionalism, on being good at what they do. Instead, they will be looking out for what is marketable. This is the essence of the criticism: There is an inherent conflict between the demands of professionalism and the goals of business and commerce.

This objection has some merit. Certainly market forces will tempt those who are not fully committed to the standards of their profession to sacrifice quality or integrity for profit. A writer capable of a great novel may, for lack of a market in novels, decide to write pulp fiction. Someone who might otherwise be motivated to great scholarly ventures may, in light of the tastes prevalent in the market, write popular books. An artisan who crafts beautiful furniture may be unable to find a market for anything other than inexpensive rental wares.

Perhaps more to the point, and more significantly, there may be dentists, physicians, scientists, artists, teachers, and others who, though capable of doing excellent work, might lower their standards to capture a larger share of the market. Less carefully crafted work may generate greater sales and, thus, greater profit. Now, if one is tempted to increase profit in this way, then of course the high standards that define one's profession are likely to be compromised.

Some, such as John O'Neill, have criticized capitalism on similar grounds, arguing that it "produces in individuals a narrow conception of their interests including only interests in the pursuit of possessive goods such as wealth, status, power, and physical pleasure."[1] To develop his case that commercial or capitalist

---

1. John O'Neill, "Altruism, Egoism, and the Market," *Philosophical Forum* 23 (summer 1992): 282. A similar thesis is developed, in greater detail, by Andrew Bard Schmookler in *The Illusion of Choice* (Albany: State University of New York Press, 1993). The essence of this argument was advanced by Karl Marx, for example, in *Grundrisse*, trans. D. McLellan (New York: Harper Torchbooks, 1971), where Marx claims that the classical liberal or capitalist type of individual liberty "is at the same time the most complete suppression of all individual liberty and total subjugation of individuality to social conditions which take the form of material forces and even of all powerful objects that are independent of the individual relating to them" (p. 131). Marx's idea was so

society obstructs professionalism, O'Neill gives the example of a university urging its scientists not to squander their useful inventions by publishing the work that led up to them before profiting from them.

O'Neill's objection seems to emanate from a mistaken and overly narrow view of how human beings decide to act, a view that omits from consideration the various factors that actually enter into decision making. People are not necessarily simply prompted to action by their economic, cultural, political, or related circumstances; they often take responsibility for their choices, weighing these factors in the balance. Nor is it the case, as suggested by O'Neill, that a free society *requires* that people place their economic well-being ahead of other considerations such as professional competence.

PROBLEMS WITH
BLAMING COMMERCE

A closer look at O'Neill's example will show how a different understanding of human beings and human nature yields a radically different story. First, it is not certain that the university is being merely greedy in alerting its professors to potential loss of profits. Why not call this prudence rather than greed? After all,

---

influential that even after the evidence provided us by the closest to Marxist experiment in politics, the USSR, books in the West repeat this claim without any reluctance. See, for example, Wendell Berry, *What Are People For?* (North Point Press, 1987). And see Richard Farr, "The Political Economy of Community," *Journal of Social Philosophy* 23 (winter 1992): 118–39, in which the theme is unhesitatingly endorsed despite what one might have learned after the collapse of the Soviet Union. It should be noted, however, that Marxism is somewhat impervious to historical evidence. See Tibor R. Machan, "How to Understand Eastern European Developments," *Public Affairs Quarterly* 6 (1992): 24–34.

the university's students and faculty will benefit from the policy of minding profits, including the benefit of increased capacity for further research. Second, scientists are not "giving away free of charge" what belongs to them alone. The university's facilities have helped to make the research possible, and those who invest in the institutions ought not to be shortchanged. Third, it should be up to the university to decide when and whether and to what extent prudence should give way to charity. Only in a free market, that is, a context free of coercion to act in various ways regarding economics, can such a decision be made and moral credit given for the right choice.

It is interesting that O'Neill's discussion coincides roughly with a news item appearing in the *New York Times*[2] noting that singer Linda Ronstadt had just forgone making popular records in favor of music closer to her heart. Predictably, perhaps, her choice was not applauded by her record company, but it was her choice, made entirely on her own. She chose to use her talent, time, and skill in this way and, despite the pure capitalist nature of the record industry (in contrast with that of universities), acted on other than solely economic self-interest. That some human beings succumb to temptation is no reason to remove the temptation from their lives. Those who want to guarantee moral virtue in human affairs forget that morality is an achievement, not something that is forced on people.

FREEDOM IS NOT ALL FREE TRADE

A free society does not begin and end with a free economy. The essence of a free society is its emphasis on respect for individual rights to life, liberty, and property. Freedom of expression, association, religion, and numerous other liberties ought to be as

2. *New York Times*, "The Pop Life," September 9, 1992, C14.

valiantly protected in such a community as is freedom of trade. The free market is a but a constituent of a free society, not its definitive feature.

Finally, professionalism is partly a matter of habituation. Arguably, for the first few generations of commercialism and relatively unfettered capitalism, many people would pay more attention to their economic well-being than to some other matters of equally objective importance. But it should be understood that only recently have ordinary people (a) been able to enter nearly any profession, based on little more than openings and aptitude, and (b) been legally free to aspire to economic well-being and prosperity. Many people in near-capitalist societies can recall a member of their family, perhaps even themselves, suffering from poverty. And surely all of us know of poverty from the media. From this commonsense perspective, it is hardly surprising that economic security and prosperity should, at least for a while, concern us more intensely than it would in other circumstances.

The fact that some people will allow the virtue of prudence to reign supreme in their hierarchy of moral priorities does not mean that prudential motivations inevitably outweigh other virtuous motivations. Nor is it wise to ban conduct that is prudent, for that will likely drive it underground, as evidenced by the history of most command economies and dictatorships.

Otherwise legitimate commerce that is forced underground will emerge in a corrupt form. As with illicit drug traffic, so too with any illicit commercial endeavor; while no one can destroy it, the environment in which it survives will be hostile, generating hostile institutional arrangements and practices. The enforcer who substitutes for the law punishes violators of contracts. In the underground, the loan shark who cannot collect payments due has recourse to violence. This argues not against lending money for profit, but against making it a crime to do so.

THE FRIENDLINESS OF
"HOSTILE" TAKEOVERS

A villain of the Reagan era against whom many liberals love to unleash their moral indignation is the corporate raider, the financier bent on removing existing managers of firms by offering shareholders higher value for their stocks than what the current management is able to deliver. The new management then goes to work on squeezing all the profit out of the enterprise, usually to the benefit of the stockholders.

It should be explained here that corporations are not separate entities. They are individual human beings who have united voluntarily, aiming for some common goal and committing themselves to certain rules in pursuit of this goal. Corporations are not persons, anymore than orchestras or teams or families are, even if the law so treats them for certain purposes.[3]

Commercial corporate efforts can grow quite large, as can educational, athletic, or scientific corporate efforts. Corporations have been given special advantages by various governments in the past. For example, they have enjoyed limited liability protection against plaintiffs' attempting to collect damages for harm done to them in the course of conducting business. These special advantages, however, are not a sound basis for treating corporations differently from other voluntary collective efforts. The remedy for unfairness is to remove it, not to condemn the institutions that have been favored.

Critics of corporate raiding offer a host of complaints. They denounce the admittedly lamentable, but by no means permanently avoidable, lot of employees of these firms, whose jobs are

---

3. For more on this, see Robert Hessen, *In Defense of the Corporation* (Stanford: Hoover Institution Press, 1979).

often in jeopardy from a hostile takeover.[4] Then they bemoan the lot of the management running the targeted firm, as well as the suffering of some members of the community who have grown accustomed to the firm's presence. Other complaints concern the loss of tried-and-true products that the firm has provided to the market, the demise of old-fashioned business practices of the current management (e.g., being debt free), and the charming nepotism that often goes hand in hand with managing old firms. In fact, these complaints amount to refusing to accept the demands and consequences of living among free men and women whose patronage is never guaranteed and who are subject to a wide array of motivations, some of which are likely to be morally deplorable.[5]

Corporate raiders are now a stereotype, having been endlessly characterized by critics as greedy, ruthless, heartless, callous, and indifferent to tradition, quality, and true values. Raiders desire nothing but greenbacks; they are mere self-interested brutes living

---

4. Be it by way of voluntary market transactions or through democratic (or centrally directed) state planning, labor instability will never be eliminated. What the market does, as it were, through piecemeal processes, via the ebb and flow of responses to human preferences and the impact of this on employment, politicians do far less delicately, as when they order that a new highway be built, a fleet of submarines commissioned, or military bases shut down, thus eliminating commerce that rests on alternative demands.

5. Suppose Sally is producing health food, while Harry makes junk food, and potential customers flock to Harry's place, ignoring what Sally has to offer for sale. Suppose these customers really should eat health food. Such a situation may well be cause for legitimate lamentation, just as we find so many lamenting the past successes of tobacco firms in their efforts to attract customers (to which the reaction has recently been near prohibition). But if human beings ought to make the right choice of their own free will, not be forced to do so by other human beings, pertaining to matters about their own lives, this is a lament that may not be met with any kind of coercive remedy, not even one dictated by a democratic process. (If, however, fraud is involved, some kind of legal action is warranted.)

by the principle of social Darwinism, the survival of the financially fit and clever.

The prevalence of this attitude no doubt has contributed to litigation by various states attempting to prevent corporate raiding. Certain lawyers appear to be the greatest beneficiaries of these developments, attempting to gain advantage of the law while the market is prevented from operating freely according to the law of supply and demand.

What fuels the "anti–hostile takeover" sentiment is a form of moral outrage that is hopelessly one-sided. This sentiment has been nourished by innumerable books and magazine pieces, election rhetoric, and Hollywood movies such as *Wall Street*, *Other People's Money*, and *Barbarians at the Gate*. Employees and entrenched management are objects of sympathy, while stockholders are regarded as the unworthy beneficiaries of the process. But is this so? The popular view overlooks some basic human virtues and vices. Once these are factored in, the actions of corporate raiders appear far more just than they presently do.

Consider the possibility that employees of inefficient firms expect security without innovation. An inefficient firm is one that, given the potential of the total enterprise, fails to operate so as to pay a return on its shareholders' investment. Employees of such firms want to keep their jobs without adjusting to the unalterable fact of human change and development.

Consumers need protection, say the bureaucrats of the various government regulatory agencies, as well as "public interest" advocates such as Ralph Nader, Sidney Wolff, and, less stridently, Steve Kelman.[6] But with respect to corporate raiding, it is con-

---

6. Ralph Nader's and Sidney Wolff's work has, of course, some benefits, and there is nothing wrong, in fact, with organizations established to stand watch over various industries, were they to confine themselves to advocacy, instruction, teaching. Indeed, book and movie reviewers, theater and art critics, are often beneficial, without the power to impose their judgment on anyone.

sumers, including stockholders, who are totally neglected by the critics. Some scholars in the fields of business ethics and law have tried to make a case for this by introducing the category of "stakeholders." These are people who can experience the effects of corporate behavior, people such as employees, members of the community whose economy is connected with the firm, and neighbors whose residence and environment may be affected by the disposition of the firm. It has been argued that the concept of corporate responsibility should extend to include stakeholders to whom obligations of various kinds are due.[7] Thus, a stakeholder would be "any identifiable group or individual who can affect or is affected by organization performance in terms of its products, politics, and work processes."[8]

But Nader and Wolff make the mistake of agitating and testifying in behalf of government regulation and supervision of the market. Reviewers and critics, in contrast, remain part of the free market of ideas, with no power of censorship accruing from their work either to themselves or to some state agency.

Kelman, of course, is an advocate of certain kinds of government regulation and defends his views in prominent scholarly forums. See his "Regulation and Paternalism," in M. B. Johnson and T. R. Machan, eds., *Rights and Regulation* (Cambridge, Mass.: Ballinger Books, 1983).

7. Some of these ideas may be found in Thomas Donaldson, *Corporations and Morality* (Englewood Cliffs, N.J.: Prentice-Hall, 1982).

8. Anthony F. Buono and Lawrence T. Nichols, "Stockholder and Stakeholder Interpretations of Business Social Role," in W. Michael Hoffman and Jennifer Mills Moore, eds., *Business Ethics* (New York: McGraw-Hill, 1990), p. 171. It would be interesting to see if this criterion for what may be subject to government regulation would apply to, say, books, works of art, newspaper columns, films, and so on, all given firm protection against government intrusion by way of the First Amendment. Actually, some militant feminists argue that that is just what ought to be done when it comes to print or broadcast products deemed pornographic. See Catherine MacKinnon, *Only Words* (Cambridge, Mass.: Harvard University Press, 1994). Indeed, MacKinnon is more consistent than are those who make exceptions of the media while intent on subjecting business to involuntary servitude. (The very idea of such servitude

Just how broadly one can interpret the vague notion of "affect or ... affected" is suggested by the fact that some activists propose that every sizable corporation should be required to accept a consumer representative on its board. This would amount to a kind of in-house Ralph Nader, someone to represent the interests of stakeholders. In short, whatever such a representative deems pertinent will be pertinent. This defeats the function of private property rights in a society by blurring the distinction between "mine and thine," as well as the lines that demarcate spheres of authority.[9]

These views, then, which are gaining momentum in our society, are a direct challenge to the institution of private property rights, a challenge reminiscent of Karl Marx's platform for the abolition of capitalism: First abolish private property! Now all of this totally ignores the fact that stockholders have voluntarily invested (and thus risked) their own assets, intending to gain some future economic benefits and forgoing the use of these assets for other purposes in the meantime. By this act they have delegated to corporate managers the authority to act as a kind of financial manager, as well as the responsibility that comes with such a trust. Other persons who happen to take advantage of some of the side benefits of a firm's presence in the community are entitled

---

presupposes that there are human individuals with the right to their lives, liberties, and property that others may not violate with impunity.)

9. Despite what so many who follow Marx and Hegel have argued, the principle of private property rights predates modernity by several centuries. Aristotle defended it, as did William of Ockham. For a discussion of its role in human community life in the fourteenth century, see Cary J. Nederman, "Political Theory and Subjective Rights in Fourteenth-Century England," *Review of Politics* 58 (spring 1996): 323–44. As Nederman notes, "From individual property rights (including rights to one's own body and the fruits of one's labor) these early modern thinkers derived lessons about consent, governmental accountability, and resistance to abuses of power" (p. 327).

to nothing else from the firm than a conscientious respect of their individual rights to life, liberty, and property, rights protected by law.

However, no proprietary stake is held by such people, including the employees, who have signed up on condition of compensation for their skill and labor. They are not due any positive service beyond this and any other agreements freely negotiated between them and management. Anything else legally required of corporations in their behalf amounts to involuntary servitude, plain and simple.

This of course does not give corporations license to disregard the well-being of employees or anyone else affected by corporate policies. Moral considerations should never be overlooked in the decision-making processes of those managing firms, anymore than homeowners should disregard the sensibilities of their neighbors or the quality of their neighborhood.

But such a moral disposition must be for the homeowner to determine as a matter of personal ethical choice; otherwise, it lacks moral significance. Human beings who are forced to act ethically are not in fact acting ethically at all, for they are puppets whose strings are being pulled by government in the name of a good cause. Similarly, to force the corporation to act socially responsibly simply fails to make corporations morally good, quite the contrary; it contributes to the demoralization of corporate affairs, making them all a matter of government regimentation.[10]

---

10. For more on this, see Tibor R. Machan, ed., *Commerce and Morality* (Lanham, Md.: Rowman & Littlefield, 1988), especially the essay by Fred D. Miller Jr. and John Ahrens. See also John Hasnas, "Social Responsibility of Corporations and How to Make It Work for You," *Freeman*, July 1994, pp. 332–35. See also Douglas J. Den Uyl, *The New Crusaders* (New Brunswick, N.J.: Transaction Books, 1984); "Corporations at Stake," *Freeman*, July 1992, pp. 252–54; and "Corporate Social Responsibility," in Robert McGee, ed.,

In this instance the rationale for regimentation consists of remarkably weak notions. We are supposed to favor old technology
over advanced technology simply because workers don't want to
change and because members of the surrounding communities
are going to be inconvenienced, perhaps even brought to suffer
hardship. (This does not mean that a hostile takeover is the cause
of such hardship; the cause is to be found in the extensive dependence on the firm's presence or business that some people have
often carelessly allowed to develop.) We are supposed to revere
old firms instead of new ones because they preserve tradition and
entrenched community values.

Consider, for a moment, that all of this totally ignores the
rights of people who have joined together freely and with no
breach of obligation to anyone to secure a better livelihood and
enough wealth to help their children, fund their charities, purchase goods and services that they deem important, and so on.
In short, those who actually own the resources that enable firms
to operate and to create the values for which many people are
willing to exchange their own wealth are overlooked in favor of
others to whom no direct promise of service was made by the
corporation's officials. Thus understood, we can see a clear per-
version of the idea of fiduciary duty, of social responsibility itself.[11]

Business Ethics & Common Sense (Westport, Conn.: Quorum Books, 1992),
pp. 137–51.

11. In a widely discussed essay, Milton Friedman has argued that the sole
responsibility of corporations is to their stockholders, provided the rules of the
game are not violated (i.e., the law is followed). See, Milton Friedman, "The
Social Responsibility of Business Is to Increase Its Profits," *New York Times
Magazine*, September 13, 1970. Two problems arise: Actually corporate management has not only a moral but a legal responsibility to seek to make profits.
That is what they have contracted to do for stockholders; the rules of the game
could turn out, depending on prevailing political trends, to dictate some kind

Apart from this is the issue that the benefits of modern science and technology, which often translate into product safety and dependability, are thwarted, robbing consumers of advantages, commodities, and services that they might otherwise have enjoyed, including the very people in whose name the complaints against takeovers are made. This results in greater impoverishment and loss of values in contrast with the alternative. (It ought also to be kept in mind that money is the expression, in a common medium of exchange, of the fruits of one's life, one's skills, talents, effort, learning, patience, and industry.)[12]

Now, consider how insistent critics of capitalism are of the lack of exclusive attention to product and service safety and quality. Ironically, these are precisely what are sacrificed when tradition and old-fashioned community values are given moral priority. Corporate raiders demand the highest quality and safety standards. They demand an efficient operation, which results in benefits to stockholders and consumers. In the end, employees

---

of representation for stakeholders' interests, thus defeating the narrowing of the corporation's social responsibility Friedman favors.

Furthermore, see Miller and Ahrens in *Commerce and Morality* for why there is a larger moral scope, albeit uncoerced, for social responsibilities by business than merely that of making a profit. See, also, Tibor R. Machan, "Professional Responsibilities of Corporate Managers," *Business and Professional Ethics Journal* 13 (fall 1994), which is part of this book.

12. This is not to say that all of the values one may be able to exchange need be of one's own creation. Clearly a beautiful model, a seven-foot-tall basketball star, or a singer with perfect pitch have not produced on their own initiative some of what others are willing to pay them for. Yet these attributes are their own; no one else is entitled to them, any more than anyone else is entitled to take one's extra kidney or eye or good heart for uses to which the owner hasn't consented. The attitude that we owe to others whatever is of value about ourselves but we have not created on our own is reminiscent of the doctrine of slavery and involuntary servitude, even if it is proposed by a famous Harvard political philosopher (John Rawls, *A Theory of Justice* [Cambridge, Mass.: Harvard University Press, 1971]).

who are told the truth about the inefficiency of their firms are being treated with respect, not condescension. They do not need favors or special treatment; they deserve a return for their honest contribution to the production effort of the firm, as determined by what the free market will allow.

A fair and dispassionate look at this issue reveals that so-called hostile takeover efforts or corporate raidings are far more consumer and stockholder friendly than critics let on. It would also become clear that profits to a corporation are not, as the popular view would have it, more wealth to a few already rich, money-grubbing scum. Rather, the stockholders, the beneficiaries, are people preparing for the future by investing some of their hard-earned money or people drawing on retirement investment, living off of mutual funds, hoping to increase the value of their life insurance and pension income. Many of these millions of people are far from wealthy and anything but greedy and callous. The stockholders of the country are quite unlike the stereotype projected by the enemies of capitalism, those who caricature capitalists as avaricious misers. The higher value of shares that a "hostile" takeover creates will go to finance college, a decent retirement, a trip to Rome, some additional CD's for a classical music collection, payments on a health insurance policy, a car, a business venture, a donation, and so on. To sacrifice these for the sake of tradition violates justice and common sense. But this side of the story is never depicted on television dramas or in the movies, for that would seem to be siding with "big business," which makes for poor ratings and ticket sales!

The point here is not to defend corporate raiders by showing how helpful they are. Rather, we should honor people's right to and good judgment in pursuing a decent return on their investment. In doing so, they are also helping the rest of us by guiding firms to upgrade themselves as they seek our business.

WHAT'S ALL THE FUSS
ABOUT MONEY?

Nothing is more commonplace than the bad-mouthing about the rich we witness so often in our political environment. Not only are many of the literati railing against the rich, even while some of them eagerly urge their agents to negotiate hefty deals for paperback or movie renditions of their works (e.g., John Grisham, whose *The Pelican Brief* is a rich-bashing novel if ever there was one), but the right is making things worse by joining the chorus of money bashers.

Anxieties, uncertainty, and insecurity have no doubt prompted many people to seek instant scapegoats, which has often led to intensified denunciations of greed, avarice, the "me" generation, and the attempts of a few politicians during the past decades to contain government expenditures. The rich are blamed for it all—reminiscent of how the Nazis managed to turn so many German citizens against Jews, many of whom were closely associated with finance and banking.

But, in our Age of the Victim, the fault lies not in the men and women who engage in rash and destructive behavior. Instead, the responsibility for much of our social ills is placed on those who want to be thrifty with taxpayers' dollars or with their own. Even news reporters, who are supposed to be objective, refer to cost-cutting efforts by government as "Washington's cutting benefits," as if people have a basic right to be given other people's money.

It is now commonplace for many political candidates to refer to the horrible greed that pervaded our nation throughout its history but most dramatically and recently during the Reagan-Bush administrations. "The greedy 80s" has become something of a mantra, a repetitious theme for those whose only solution to social problems is to give more of other people's money to bureaucrats whose careers consist of giving that money to whomever the government has decided needs it. Not surprisingly, the myth that wealth is the root of all evil is perpetuated and supported by heavily intellectual tomes such as Daniel Bell's *The Cultural Contradiction of Capitalism*, which propounds the thesis that capitalism forces us all to become hedonists, people who care for nothing other than the satisfaction of their desire for pleasure.

By these accounts, money is at once evil and good. It is a useful instrument for facilitating market exchange, saving, and economic communication in general. But it is also a corroding influence because it encourages us to view everything in terms of a market price and tends to make everything a commodity. As Marx put it, with money a society becomes a *cash nexus*. It appears, then, that contemporary thinking about money is ambivalent, if not confused. A few points might shed some light and help to straighten things out.

First, it is worthwhile to recall that the famous biblical claim often quoted about money is not actually about money as such but about the *love* of money. It is said that the *love of money is the root of all evil*, not money itself or even a desire or preference or high regard for it. This is a crucial point: Love is proper for one's God, family, and friends, for one's personal intimates, not for anything else and certainly not for things. The logic of love requires a proper object, a worthy object. No wonder, then, that if one gets confused and loves money or golf or cars, thereby mistaking one's priorities, this paves the way to grief and ought to be resisted. None other than Saint Augustine, the medieval philosopher with deep insight into human psychology, offers an extended discussion of this in his notable essay "The Doctrine of Disordered Love."

Unfortunately, the warning against loving money comes within the context of the general admonition that we should lead

more spiritual lives and eschew pleasure and other material pursuits. We should note in response that there is *nothing wrong
with money* or with a healthy regard for its proper place in one's
life. Nor is it untoward to strive for as much wealth as is required
for living as well as one can. In the words of Emerson, "Money,
which represents the prose of life, and which is hardly spoken of
in parlors without an apology, is, in its effects and laws, as beautiful as roses. Property keeps the accounts of the world, and is
always moral."[13]

Setting aside the admittedly strong connotative force of the
word *money*, on analysis money is nothing more than a tool, a
convenient commodity used for purposes of trading other commodities and services. It is a convenient way of avoiding the
cumbersome process of barter, which once served small communities well but is far too inefficient for larger, more complex
communities.

Of course, money can itself be treated as a kind of derivative
commodity. Since money represents values for people, it becomes
a value, much like a ticket to a theater or sporting event. Many
items of derivative value exist. In this derivative state, such items
can gain or lose value, as, for example, concert tickets or claim
checks for pawned articles. Promissory notes are also of derivative value—no one would purchase them for the paper they are
written on, but they are extremely useful to us as means, making
possible more choices and more efficiency in our lives.

Even as a commodity the value of money derives from its utility
as a means to obtaining other ends that are in fact of substantive
value to persons. This being the case, what does all the hostility
toward money mean, and what might it reveal? Those who rail

---

13. Ralph Waldo Emerson, "Nominalist and Realist," in *The Complete
Writings of Ralph Waldo Emerson* (New York: Wm. H. Wise & Co., 1929),
p. 307.

against money cannot be arguing against using paper and metal as a means of exchange, as though the barter system were in some way better. So we have to look elsewhere to account for the hatred. A likely explanation, given the evident emotion of the money critics, is that the actual object of scorn is *living well*. After all, apart from its rather innocuous role as a means of exchange, what money, wealth, provides is the possibility of making one's life more comfortable, enjoyable, pleasant, exciting, and secure than it would likely be without money. What motivates the highly demeaning outlook on money is largely either misguided guilt about having achieved a decent standard of living while others are in need or common envy over others' wealth in the absence of one's own.

Either way, strong feelings motivate the attack on money. In the former case, the feelings border on compassion for the less fortunate; in the latter case, the feelings stem perhaps from the individual's own suffering and sense that life should be more pleasant than it is. In themselves, these feelings are perfectly understandable and healthy. The distortion comes from a mistaken underlying assumption, namely, that no one should or has a right to be happy so long as there is poverty, disease, misery, deprivation, hunger, and other regrettable human conditions in this world. It follows from this, of course, that no one has the right to the *means* to happiness (i.e., money) so long as others are deprived. This view has been forcefully argued by, among many others, contemporary utilitarian philosopher Peter Singer. In his book *Practical Ethics*, Singer offers the "greater moral evil argument," which says, in effect, that, so long as others are in need and I have more than I need, I am morally obligated to give of my surplus. Surely, anyone who believes this will (and ought to) feel guilty about having any wealth. (And those who believe this and are in need will feel that the wealthy owe them assistance.)

These are the puritans of the world whom H. L. Mencken described as being afraid that somewhere, someone might be happy. The humanitarian sentiment that we are describing here is dramatically illustrated in the following plaintive cry by the Reverend Martin Luther King Jr.:

As long as there is poverty in the world, I can never be rich, even if I have a billion dollars. As long as diseases are rampant and millions of people in this world cannot expect to live more than 28 or 30 years, I can never be totally healthy—even if I just got a good checkup at the Mayo Clinic. I can never be what I ought to be until you are what you ought to be. This is the way the world is made.

Critics of money tend to view the wealthy as an affront to the less fortunate. The critics resist drawing a distinction between those who have met with misfortune through no fault of their own and those who have destroyed their lives of their own accord. They also fail to distinguish between those who have honestly earned their wealth and those who have not. Without such distinctions, we are robbed of conceptual tools that are necessary for evaluating the thinking of different people on various topics, including this one.

To see the wrongheadedness of the antimoney view, we need only ask, "What would the poor like most?" If given a choice, would they choose for everybody being poor, or would they choose for themselves to be rich? It seems almost self-evident that the poor would like to have more wealth than they now have, to be more prosperous than they are. The unfortunate poor want to be well-off, and this is precisely what is so sad about their lives! And yet they disagree vigorously about the value and moral propriety of having money. Many both implicitly and explicitly approve of it; they would rather have it now, even before others do, than wait until the entire world is well-off. And who can blame them?

The confusion about money and the resulting injustice would not be so prevalent were people to start thinking more critically about the nature of money, rather than being guided by their feelings. Additionally, if people realized that the major difference between those with money and those without is their degree of *prosperity*, perhaps the wealthy would stop being stereotyped and seen as caricatures from the pages of the old *Pravda* or the *Daily Worker*.

It would also be helpful were it more widely recognized that many people's misfortunes have nothing to do with the fortune and success of others. Life is not a *zero sum game*, where all the good things that accrue to some have to be taken from others. Throughout the history of civilization there has been an absolute increase in wealth even as there has been a constant increase in the population. It is safe to assume that the quality of life of the average reader of this book, as it can be said with certainty of the authors, is measurably greater than that of nearly all the kings and queens who ever lived. Our life expectancy is longer, our food is fresher and more nutritious, our means of travel more efficient and comfortable; in short, the variety, availability, and quality of the goods and services available to us would stagger the imagination of even King Midas. Much of this is due to the development of commerce and business through capitalism; indeed, many of the advances in technology, which benefit us so greatly, were driven by the entrepreneurial spirit.

The amount of time and energy devoted to damning money and the wealthy in books, newspapers, magazines, and elsewhere is as abundant as it is unjustified. The fact is that money as such is innocent and to desire more of it is perfectly healthy and justified, provided that it is gained honestly and spent wisely and prudently. But even when these conditions aren't met, the grief that results is not the fault of money but of those who abuse it.

CHAPTER THREE

Used Car Dealers
as Heroes?

PREJUDICES AGAINST BUSINESS

There are several aspects to our cultural prejudice against business. In addition to the prevailing dualistic tradition of Western culture, which values one part of our being (mind, soul) over the other (body), the prejudice rests on a misconception. The error is the idea that the business professional is in conflict with the consumer, the ordinary person, and that business's gain must be Everyman's loss. And so there is a built-in suspicion that business is out to get the consumer, to take undue advantage since, after all, business is seen as pitted against the buyer. This is illustrated clearly in the paradigm of the used car dealer as petty crook. Another misconception arises from the fact that a large segment of the culture's resources is public, or "common," rather than privately owned; when businesses use public resources there is a tendency to think of them as parasitic on the public that supports these common areas such as freeways, parks, and forests. When individuals use these resources, they are seen as exercising a right; when a business uses them, it is freeloading and even worse, causing pollution, wear and tear, and so forth. This is no surprise, so the attitude goes, since business is already seen as far from the friend of the person on the street. This latter aspect shows itself clearly in the discussion concerning the environment. Because of the prejudice against commerce, business is subject to considerable regulation and restriction not imposed on other professions. Much of this restriction, as we shall see, is unnecessary and unjust. Examples that we shall explore are environmentalism and prior restraint. The overall thrust of this chapter, then, is that the prejudice against business, as with other prejudices, is born of misunderstanding and ignorance, which in turn leads to suspicion and fear, which results in scapegoating, mistrust, and restrictions.

USED CAR DEALERS AS SCAPEGOATS

Perhaps the favorite target of the commerce haters is the used car dealer, modern culture's epitome of the sleazy, two-faced, greedy capitalist out to cheat honest people of their hard-earned money by tricking them into buying damaged or inferior goods. As pointed out earlier, anyone engaged in making a profit is fair game for the critics, whether the profit earner is ultimately helping teachers to be more effective or showing someone how to retire in comfort. Whether Willie Loman's life is being reviewed, or the used car dealer is the butt of a yet another joke, the judgment is equally harsh; only the skill of the critical blows is different. From the fare found on commercial television to famous British or Australian imports, commerce is ever held in contempt.[1]

Despite the popular stereotype of the used car dealer as sleaze, these salespersons are engaged in a perfectly respectable endeavor that benefits millions of ordinary people. First, selling used cars

---

1. Examples of this abound, as has already been shown. It is worth mentioning yet another, though, from the television miniseries *Brides of Christ*, from Australia, featured on the Arts & Entertainment television cable network, in which a lay economics teacher at a Roman Catholic girls school remarks that economics is the study of money and the bastards who control it.

is a way for some people with certain skills to enhance their own economic well-being, to act responsibly and prudently in the maintenance of their lives. Second, used car dealers are providing a legitimate and much-needed service to many members of the public. Most of us have been involved in wanting to sell a car that we no longer desire to own. Some of us place a classified ad in the newspaper or post signs around the neighborhood. We may do some investigating to appraise cars comparable to our own to determine its market value. We may wait at home for calls or return calls to those who left messages. We may arrange for appointments to have our car inspected and enter into negotiations if the buyer is seriously interested.

Or we could shop for a new vehicle and trade the old one in, ending the whole process then and there. Those who make this possible, used car dealers, may turn around and sell our trade-in for a profit—or not! Clearly, their work is neither insignificant nor risk-free. What they are doing is of social worth. Many of us in society find it to be quite valuable. We can save time, avoid headaches, and sometimes even save money.

Those who have no clear grasp of the significance of this service may see the used car dealer as morally suspicious. If enhancing one's well-being, economically and otherwise, is not thought to be a worthy undertaking, and if enabling others to obtain something valuable is not well regarded, then the used car dealer and other sales professionals may be seen as reprehensible, mere exploiters who prey on human weaknesses.

Admittedly, it's possible to be crooked in any business or in any calling. But it is sheer prejudice to believe that because some task is motivated by the desire for economic advantage or for success as a commercial agent, the task itself is more susceptible to vice than others. Educators, motivated by the desire to convey their ideas, can certainly betray their profession and substitute indoctrination, entertainment, or something else for teaching.

Profit and the desire for prosperity are by no means exclusively capable of tempting one to corruption. Zeal can infest any ambition and drive it to corruption.

Some kinds of enthusiasm do not really qualify as zeal. For example, the financial speculator is often derided, but we would do well to understand such a person as a kind of adventurer, one who takes risks for the sake of possible serious financial gains, just as other thrill seekers such as mountain climbers, skydivers, and wilderness explorers are risk takers and adventurers. Additionally, for certain people—those who can afford it and ought perhaps to give it a try—the speculator is an indispensable financial surrogate.

The opposing view, that the goal of prosperity is more conducive to corruption than the goal of knowledge or artistic achievement, stems from the dualism we have been discussing throughout this work. The idea that our base appetites drive us to such conduct assumes that appetites are a more powerful force than our own judgments, more powerful than the desire to know. But isn't it more sensible to regard all of these objectives, and all of the natural desires and appetites that lead to the various tasks and professions in human life, as basically decent, yet corruptible? Certainly the desire to satisfy hunger is not base and ignoble, though one can become a glutton, just as the innocent desires to know and to create can lead to harm and ugliness. Desires and appetites are natural to human life and can be dealt with badly or well.

SOME OBSTACLES TO RESPECT

It hardly needs demonstrating that the used car dealer is not a cultural hero, except, perhaps, to those whose profession is to sell used cars and who have learned to fully appreciate this line of work. For nearly everyone else, the used car dealer and in fact salespersons in general are far from noble. This seems to be a widespread view.

Why are people in business such easy targets to disparage? The main reason, we contend, is that commerce has been associated with the pursuit of earthly material pleasure and thus cast in a bad light, in particular by much of philosophy and religion. If commerce could somehow associate itself with spirituality, it would likely get better press. Indeed, in certain epochs, when one or another religion (for example, Judaism and Calvinism) did embrace commerce, either commerce's reputation was elevated, or the religion was denigrated.

In addition to this major obstacle, other factors contributing to the low repute of commerce are worth mentioning. For one, commerce intrudes on the senses: People trying to sell a product or service must bring this fact to others' attention, so they tend to spread the word aggressively and seize every opportunity to do so. Thus, advertising in a commercial society such as ours tends to permeate the culture. Many of us who aren't in the market for what is being advertised react negatively to what strikes us as an intrusion. We consider junk mail, e-mail advertising, and telemarketing to be rude and bothersome; after all, we didn't ask for their stuff to be put in our mail boxes or e-mail bins, nor did we ask to be interrupted with phone solicitations. Both in our homes and in public we seem to be bombarded with messages designed to attract our attention to this or that product, and when we find this unpleasant, we tend to make up some damaging reason why we should condemn it.

It seems likely that people often condemn what they dislike since they do not feel comfortable about simply disliking things. It would be too egoistic to just turn one's back on something because it is unappealing, regardless of whether or not it has merit. It is more comfortable to make up something adverse about what is disliked, rather than just moving on, such as when we hear the familiar refrain "There ought'a be a law!" Thus, advertising that one dislikes is condemned as being somehow morally objectionable, rather than simply being annoying. As John Kenneth Galbraith complained in *The Affluent Society*, ads manipulate us to come to desire things, never mind that every invention does as well, as F. A. Hayek noted in his reply. Never mind, also, that we have the power to govern our desires. But this doesn't seem to be enough; we need to find fault with the pleas for our attention to justify not paying attention to them. Other reasons contribute to the hostility toward dealers and other salespersons. We discuss a few in the sections that remain.

THE VULNERABILITY OF THE HUSTLER

In communities with a great deal of public property, there is a good chance that those who are productive, trying to get ahead in life and to make things happen, will find themselves criticized and condemned as insufficiently public spirited or too selfish and greedy. In such communities, many concerns of the people are dealt with by means of government regulation, intervention, or provisions, including government contracts with private businesses to achieve public mandates. Thus, many enterprises and activities in the community take place in the public realm, subject to the legal edicts that guide governments (e.g., affirmative action, minimum wage laws, health and safety requirements, and the like).

Accordingly, those who own and manage businesses are more likely to encounter problems and criticism than those who don't because, in a community with a large public sector, people engaged in various projects face a constant risk of intruding on one another and having conflicting interests. As the economists put it, the danger of negative externalities is profuse.

Consider some simple examples. Someone using a public road

as he carries on in business may pass many others and drive over the speed limit in attempt to save time or meet a deadline. Or several people desiring to play may find themselves in a public park throwing a ball or a Frisbee and intruding on those who are there just taking in the sun. In a public school, an ambitious (or otherwise demanding) student may require greater attention from teachers, thus reducing the educational opportunities of less ambitious or needy students.

It would be helpful here to recall the central thesis of a famous essay by Garrett Hardin, a biologist from the University of California at Santa Barbara. In "The Tragedy of the Commons" Hardin argues that a common sphere will almost inevitably be overused, resulting in shortages and acrimonious struggles over what is left. That is, there will generally be great demand placed on this sphere by all of the members who have entitlements to the commons. Put another way, Hardin revives Aristotle's criticism of Plato's partial communism in *The Republic:* Those in charge of the public sector but also attending to their normal human ambitions will tend to be neglectful of their professional responsibilities.

Now Hardin's point is that individuals sharing a common property, say a grazing area for cattle, will tend individually to make as much use of the commons as possible if they want their cattle to do well. Absent any strict boundaries to constrain their behavior, the cattle owners will use as much as they can, not necessarily out of greed but in the ambitious pursuit of their goal. Additionally, even with strict regulations, it takes only one member of the commons violating those regulations to ruin the commons for everyone.

If there is a common pool of resources to which all are entitled, the various individuals or groups with their own purposes and goals will naturally try to draw from the commons what they can out of devotion to their projects. Consider the devotion of artists, scholars, and scientists, and what they would likely do if given unrestricted use of funds, materials, and the like. They would make as much use of these as their energies and time permitted, with pride, and no doubt without guilt.

It is not difficult to show that Hardin's (or Aristotle's) observation applies in other than ecological and environmental contexts (wherein Hardin's work has had its major impact).[2] If we assume that ecology includes everything, this becomes clear enough. Not just air, beaches, lakes, rivers, and soil but anything available for human use is subject to the tragedy of the commons.

In a community where private property rights govern nearly everything that people can use in pursuit of their diverse and various goals, what is available as a means to their goals is evident, namely, anything to which they have a private property right. However, in a commons, where there is no particular private property right assigned in the community, those intent on success will find themselves intruding on those who are less ambitious or who have conflicting objectives.

So it emerges that a good portion of the widespread hostility toward business is precisely because people in business try to get things done partly by using the commons. Such is the nature of entrepreneurial pursuits: To produce better cars, safer toys, fresher home-delivered pizzas, and so on, businesses make ample use of public roads, air space, public utilities, and other resources that are public commons.

There are a number of huge public sectors in our society, such as the air mass, lakes, and rivers. In addition are the public treasuries of our political communities, from which politicians dis-

2. Because of the focus in these disciplines on resource consumption from such public spheres as the air mass, ozone layer, ocean mass, and so on. Where private property rights can be reasonably strictly applied and protected, so that dumping and trespassing can be identified and dealt with effectively, the problem does not persist to the degree it does vis-à-vis public spheres.

pense benefits to their constituents, many of whom belong to the
business community. Given Hardin's principle, we could expect
that many ambitious entrepreneurs, in taking advantage of public
resources, will appear to be trampling on the welfare of other
people, even as they are also benefiting many of them. They will
certainly be seen as imposing large costs by those and on those
who are not enjoying the benefits.

The extent of such consequences is indeterminable. In a system
of property rights, how many people would be willing to work
hard enough to obtain the very things that the more ambitious
people are now making use of? Who knows whether and how
many people are benefiting indirectly from what they directly
provide for others? Just as there may be positive externalities to
extremely expensive ventures such as the space program,[3] so it
might be that when a company produces, say, computer parts for
some members of the public and in the process pollutes the air,
those who suffer the pollution but do not purchase the product
may still receive indirect benefits (e.g., a more developed technology for hospital equipment or education or personal comput-
ers).

With the commons it appears that everybody has an equal
entitlement to the public resource. Thus, those who are more
ambitious will appear to be rude, unfeeling, and greedy for so
aggressively and obviously making use of the public resource. In
a large commons nothing belongs to anyone, but all of it belongs
to everyone. So when people make use of things, they use what
everyone (else) owns. If I pollute the air I am depriving others
and being selfish; if I am spilling gasoline or oil into the ocean I
am invading our—meaning also, of course, your—ocean.

---

3. This line of argument was used in support of the public funding of such
projects when they were first being considered for government support (apart
from their military advantage).

This is not the case in a private property system because the ambitious will simply be regarded as having more, rather than as robbing from others. They will not even appear to be taking anything from others. Instead, they are making use of private property that at least in principle they can obtain without invading others, by means of *consent* via invention, exploration, inheritance, and purchase. A private property system encourages what economists call "full-cost pricing" and prohibits dumping. This is difficult to achieve in public realms.

But am I really *taking away what is yours* when I use public property? If it is a commons and I am doing my best at getting ahead within it, how can I be rationally blamed if other people are falling behind? Since I cannot know exactly what others want or where they wish to go, nor do I wish to meddle with them or to be a paternal political helper, it would seem best to leave others to rely on their own resources and ambitions. They are free to use or not use the commons, and it would be inconsistent with my goals to lie back and wait. There will always be those who will think that they haven't received their fair share since they *might have been* able to benefit from something that someone else used. Thus, there will always be complaints against those who are ambitious in a commons.[4]

This establishes another reason why there should be a greater degree of privatization in our society. With a greater private structure (the explanation and defense of which comes in chapter 7), people could become more benevolent and less suspicious of one another and would be much less likely to regard many of their fellows as "ripping one another off." The greater the com-

---

4. This sentiment of suspicion and envy is notoriously prevalent in communes and in socialist countries, as well as in public service industries where one person's gain is most often perceived as another's loss.

mons, the greater the opportunity for conflict, resentment, and political battle.

It is enlightening to consider the failure of socialistic and other collectivist political arrangements from the perspective of the "tragedy of the commons" argument. This consequence of any type of collectivism is not sufficiently appreciated by those who are trying to preserve collectivism by giving it more of a "human face" after its dramatic demise in Eastern Europe.

We should note here that by no means have Marxists and other collectivists admitted defeat. Their new story is that what we have seen for the last seventy years or so in the USSR and its colonies has been a major distortion and that we should now try the real thing. What is this "true socialism" like?

There are several versions. One is that true socialism is a system that places everything of importance in society at the mercy of the democratic process. A sure casualty of this would be the elimination of the right to individual liberty, the foundation of a civilized public life. Or "true socialism" is that which simply divides society into realms that follow principles of market economics and those of socialist planning. Or, again, "true socialism" is a system now called "communitarianism," with a good deal of life placed under the community's jurisdiction but "enough" left to personal management.

These various socialist ideals have been explored in depth elsewhere.[5] Let's address only one of them here. The democratization of nearly everything is a major threat to reasonable, limited democracy itself. In a wholesale democratic system, the minority are totally vulnerable to the majority's will, having no individual rights that provide principled protection against reprisals for op-

---

5. See Machan, *Individuals and Their Rights* and *Capitalism and Individualism*. For some briefer treatments, see *Liberty and Culture, Essays on the Idea of a Free Society* (Buffalo, N.Y.: Prometheus Books, 1989).

posing the mob. John Stuart Mill, staunch defender of democracy, warned against this possibility, which he called "tyranny of the majority." In any case, one ought to admire, and sometimes pity, those in our society who dare to be productive. They are on the front line, so to speak, taking risks and suffering rebuke and blame for not joining the passive masses who choose to remain safe, to complain about their lot, and to criticize those who succeed. In a society with an extensive public sector, producers and entrepreneurs are likely to be envied and derided for standing apart from the whining masses. Nor are they ever credited for the hard work that they do, for much of it goes unseen. Many of the activities of business—the planning, organizing, coordinating, buying, selling, shipping, and so on—are difficult to track just by looking. Few people are aware of these behind-the-store-front efforts, and so they remain unaware of the creative efforts of which they are the beneficiaries. Instead, the public relies on unflattering stereotypes found in television comedy skits and Hollywood movies to form its image of the business professional.

PRODUCTION AND PITFALLS

Simply being actively engaged in the world makes someone more susceptible to scrutiny and criticism. Thus, when one is as publicly visible as those in business tend to be as they navigate among other people—employees, customers, and the agents of the legal system—one's flaws are more open to view and more subject to condemnation, ridicule, and various other judgments.

Producers who market their product run a much greater risk of offending or upsetting others than do those such as artists who work in the privacy of their studio and later exhibit their work to an often appreciative audience or scientists, scholars, and even teachers who do much of their work free from public inspection. The point is that the temptation to do wrong is more likely to occur to those who do much than to those who do little and that the opportunity for wrongdoing with respect to other persons is more likely to arise for those whose profession naturally involves them with other persons. In the privacy of one's home, studio, lab, or classroom, one is under less public scrutiny.[6] Thus, for the artist, scientist, scholar, or teacher, doing wrong is generally less obvious or notable. Fraudulence in science or plagiarism in art or scholarship comes to light only rarely, not because of its infrequency but because of the much lower profile of art, science, and scholarship when it comes to public attention.

In our analysis, then, nothing about the professional in sales and marketing or, more broadly, in business excludes them from the traditionally honored professions. Educators, scientists, artists, physicians, journalists, and other professionals receive their more-elevated *moral* status partly because their circumstances generally shield them from constant public scrutiny. Consider, for example, the attention paid to the personal lives of Hollywood celebrities and the perceptions created about members of the film industry. In reality, there are likely no fewer divorces, affairs, and the like in the general population than there are in Hollywood. There are also likely no fewer crooks, cheats, liars, and such in the general population or among the honored professions than among members of the business profession. When those in business misbehave, however, their transgressions are more clearly perceived since they are usually acting in relationship to other persons who will complain, many of whom are predisposed by cultural prejudices to expect the worst from those in business and to look for it.

Consider, also, that when a company lays off a sizable number

6. It is noteworthy, however, that as members of households are more and more willing to air their grievances, household managers are coming under greater scrutiny and are not emerging always with a clean record.

of employees, the reaction is usually directed at the firm and its managers, rarely at the stockholders, and never at the customers who kept it going with their purchases but who may have changed their preferences and buying habits. Businesses cannot remain in business unless consumers patronize them. Even a well-managed company with a good product or service will fail if consumers do not purchase its products or services. And yet, though businesses are under the constant scrutiny and evaluation of a demanding public, they are also totally at its mercy. No one thinks that the consumer is under an obligation to patronize a worthy, but ailing, business. Should the company lay off employees for lack of profits, the owners and management are often criticized for being thoughtless and uncaring by the very people whose lack of patronage necessitated the layoff!

This is where many people would take issue with the theme of this book, arguing that "business (sales, marketing) appeals unabashedly to our appetites. There is nothing particularly noble about that appeal or satisfaction. The other professions, on the other hand, both appeal to the more noble element of our soul and require the virtues that arise out of those parts of the soul."[7]

This line of criticism will be addressed in chapter 9, "Dualism Disputed." Suffice it to point out here that there is something amiss in the notion that catering to human appetites is ignoble. This idea assumes that satisfying the needs and desires of human beings is something inconsequential, unimportant, unworthy of respect. This assumption is false.

However, many believe that their basic rights are being systematically violated by those who are trying to make money. Even

---

7. Captain Westhusing was a philosophy professor at the United States Military Academy, West Point, New York, during Tibor Machan's one-year visiting professorship there in 1992–93 and was kind enough to read and comment extensively on an early draft of this book.

in societies such as the United States, where commerce is relatively flourishing, there is a tolerance, indeed, a demand, for many laws and regulations that serve to offend the rights of dealers, merchants, brokers, investors, bankers, and the like. In the next section we discuss perhaps the most blatant instance of this.

GOVERNMENT REGULATION AND PRIOR RESTRAINT

Keeping the above in mind, we should now ask whether it is right that business be regulated by government while religion, the arts, and the press, among others, are, in contrast, remarkably free of regulation, at least in many liberal societies.

The idea of prior restraint within the context of Western law and, in particular, the First Amendment of the U. S. Constitution, is not difficult to grasp.[8] It is not a highly technical concept, nor should it be since every citizen is supposed to understand it.

Prior restraint essentially means acting to constrain or restrict the actions, or to otherwise burden someone in the profession of publishing or writing, before that person has been legally charged with some actionable offense. What may not be clear is why there should be civil libertarian objections to the practice of prior restraint. There are such objections and our legal system largely honors them. What is not evident from that alone is the prelegal justification for this prohibition.

Of great interest to our purposes is that our legal tradition has confined the prohibition to First Amendment cases but has allowed prior restraint in business, most notably by way of regulatory statutes. It can be argued that there is ample prelegal justification for extending the scope of the prior restraint doctrine

8. This topic is discussed in greater detail in Tibor Machan's *Private Rights & Public Illusions* (New Brunswick, N.J.: Transactions Books, 1995).

to include business and other activities in human communities. Let's briefly consider these matters.

Why is prior restraint limited to First Amendment–type cases? The main philosophical reason was suggested by the historic struggle for this prohibition waged by John Milton. Milton clearly represents those who wish to exempt from prior restraint members of the limited sphere wherein they operate, namely, men of letters. It is no surprise that those with the skills to work a trade and who also happen to be the most prepared to engage in political advocacy should stand up first and foremost for their own rights.

But this is not the whole story. Another aspect is that, as we have already seen, people whose work is theoretical have generally enjoyed greater respect than have others, especially those in business. Yet another factor, related to certain trends in metaphysics, is that intellectual activities have not appeared to be crucial to the workings of the world. Marx, for example, insisted that it is economic or productive forces, not ideas, that explain how the world works. Thus, it is more important to restrain and control such forces than to restrain ideas.

Perhaps the most fundamental philosophical explanation for prohibiting prior restraint once again goes back to Plato's idealistic philosophy. According to the standard reading of Plato, the actual world is an imperfect substitute for the ideal world of forms; what makes anything worthy of concern is its connection with this ideal world. Thus, human life itself is worthy only to the extent that it is connected with ideals such as the ideal of perfect humanity—the *concrete universal* that is the essence of the human being and is removed, metaphysically, from actual nature.[9] Put bluntly, the body is base, while the mind or spirit is

---

9. That is, an abstract idea that is actual or substantially real within the realm of abstract beings. In ordinary life this view is exemplified when people

noble. Sex and business are of this world only; theory, thought, and prayer are of the other, superior world.

Thus, our bodies are not of great worth, so there is little value to the practical, utilitarian concerns of life; and we should not treat them with the same moral respect that we pay to theory, speech, worship, and the like. This alone, of course, does not explain the absence of a firm concern for economic liberty in our culture and in others. Still, the dualistic view is a central philosophical reason for such a double standard. The pervasiveness of dualistic perspectives throughout the world's cultures is difficult to miss.

JUSTIFYING PROHIBITION OF PRIOR RESTRAINT

The foundation of our legal system includes the sensible belief (developed through the modern age but with origins in early Western thought) that human beings are sovereign, not the serfs or slaves of anyone.[10] From this point of view each individual is taken to be free and independent, not the inferior of another whose rule he or she must accept.

This belief has been most firmly adhered to in our country's history in connection with political activities. Thus, some thinkers, for example Judge Robert Bork, are inclined to understand

---

make reference to humanity or mankind or the race, using these terms to mean some concrete thing, as if there existed such beings over and above the individual persons who comprise them. For them humanity is to individuals as the human body is to its cells, limbs, or organs. For more, see Tibor R. Machan, *The Virtue of Liberty* (Irvington-on-Hudson, N.Y.: Foundation for Economic Education, 1994).

10. See, for some discussion of this point, Brian Tierney, "Origins of Natural Rights Language: Texts and Contexts, 1150–1250," *History of Political Thought* 10 (winter 1989): 615–46.

the First Amendment as properly applying only to "political speech." Even today, with scientific and artistic speech protected by the First Amendment, many legal scholars would deny that prior restraint is prohibited when it comes to commercial speech. Nevertheless, prior restraint is not prohibited when it comes to the practice of nearly every other profession. Government regulations restricting numerous business, manufacturing, and other processes are precisely what prior restraint would amount to in the context of the profession of publishing or writing. Many government regulations are equivalent to prior restraint: for example, when the Occupational Safety and Health Administration forces a firm to implement expensive safety measures in the workplace, even though no misdeed (i.e., no crime) has been done by the individual or company burdened with the regulation. This is analogous to forcing an individual to adhere to a curfew because at some hours of the day (night) someone might commit a crime (perhaps even worse, since curfews are typically enforced under conditions of martial law, which tends to be invoked rather more liberally in dictatorships than in free societies).

What is wrong here? Why shouldn't prohibition of prior restraint be limited to safeguarding the interests of those working with words, ideas, theories, and so on? Why expand it to cover all professionals, including those in business?

A quick legal answer is that such discriminatory application of the prohibition violates the principle expressed in the Fourteenth Amendment, that every citizen's rights must be protected by the law. However, this answer begs the question. It may be, as many have held, that the Fourteenth Amendment is misapplied when it is interpreted as referring to the treatment of different professions. It could be (and has been) argued that this amendment was not intended to hold that people must be treated equally under the law regardless of what activities they are engaged in.

Now, whatever the intent of the Fourteenth Amendment may

have been, the meaning of the words implies that, whether one is a journalist, a philosopher, a psychologist or any other professional, including a professional in business, the law should not discriminate in its treatment of the individual. But clearly the law does discriminate when some professions are regulated while others are protected from such regulation.[11]

More fundamentally, consider the substance of the meaning of the Fourteenth Amendment: No government is justified in violating the sovereignty of any citizen whose conduct is not inherently rights violating or not a clear and present danger to any other citizen. Accordingly, out of respect for individual rights, manufacturing and trade should be left unregulated even when they involve considerable risk. Legal attempts to guard against dangers should be by means of injunction, after demonstrating the clear and present dangers to be contained. Absent such a process, government regulation of business *or any other activity* constitutes treating some people not as sovereign citizens but as subjects.[12]

Thus, there seems to be no morally justifiable reason to treat professionals in business any differently from the way in which professionals in journalism or the arts are treated. All persons have the right to be treated by their fellows, and their govern-

---

11. An interesting recent development bears on this matter, although not directly related to business. Some philosophers have been embarking on what is referred to as philosophical counseling; it is a fact of many state legal systems, however, that psychologists need to be licensed in order to provide counseling. Will the philosophers also be subject to licensing? If so, will this not be a violation of their free speech, just as it is thought to be a violation of free speech to license journalists?

12. These points are developed in Tibor R. Machan, "Should Business Be Regulated?" in Tom Regan, ed., *Just Business, New Introductory Essays in Business Ethics* (New York: Random House, 1983), and "The Petty Tyranny of Government Regulation," in M. Bruce Johnson and Tibor R. Machan, eds., *Rights and Regulation* (Cambridge, Mass.: Ballinger, 1983).

ments, as sovereign individuals with rights to life, liberty, and property. Anything less is inhumanity and injustice in disguise.

LIBERTY AND RACIAL JUSTICE

Since the rejection of slavery and segregation as policies defended and imposed by government, there have been numerous political efforts to set things right in the area of race relations. Some of these, such as forced integration, mandated affirmative action, and forced quotas in hiring and promotion, have been divisive and themselves discriminatory. Others, such as the abolition of the separate but equal provision in public schooling, have been more sensible and principled: If the state is to educate our children, it has no business doing it by serving up different goods on the basis of color.

On its face affirmative action and similar measures conflict with the basic principle by which America is identified, the right to individual liberty. When applied in commercial affairs, this idea means freedom of trade. As one interacts with others in commercial exchange, no one, especially the government, is justified in setting the terms of the exchange process. Provided the right to liberty of all adult parties engaged in trade is not violated, government may not coerce anyone to do what he or she refuses to do. This, in short, is the right of free association applied to commerce.

How does this conflict with affirmative action or integration or quotas? The usual defense of such programs is that certain groups in society have had enormous advantage by way of oppressing others, including economic advantages yielding favorable terms of trade. So, it is argued, it is only fair and just that the tables be turned, at least until a level playing field has been achieved.

The focus of this line of reasoning is not the issue of individual

rights but of group advantages and disadvantages. Indeed, the
failure of government to protect the individual rights of blacks
and other minorities is a principal cause of group advantages and
disadvantages and the divisiveness and social tension that result.
To address consequences without regard to principle is to invite
further grief. Such is the case here, where much of the political
response to past discrimination conflicts directly with the principle of individual rights, especially the right to liberty and free
trade. The affirmative action approach imposes burdens on and
distributes benefits to people who may have had nothing whatever to do with slavery, segregation, or racism in our society. This
amounts to a novel rendition of racism rather than a just rectification of it.

Racism does not judge people on the basis of how they have
freely chosen to act, which is a feature of *moral* judgment. Instead, the racist judges people on the basis of group membership,
identified by reference to common traits that the members have
not chosen and that are irrelevant to choosing whether or not
one ought to interact with them. Blacks, Semites, Asians, Indians,
whites, and the rest are such entirely by circumstance, not from
any choice. To discriminate against anyone on this basis is gross
injustice. In commerce or in any other profession, race is (or
anyway ought to be seen as) entirely irrelevant and such discrimination is a violation of one's professional ethics as well as simple
decency.

How can racism be combated, then, without resorting to what
is now commonly known as "reverse discrimination"? How can
a legal system both oppose racism and respect individual rights
to freely choose, even if that choice turns out to be racist? Without
doubt, many people today still suffer from discrimination. The
challenge is to address this problem without compromising individual rights. An inherently discriminatory policy such as affir-

mative action, despite its good intentions, is bound to fail in practice because it is flawed in principle.

LIBERTY VERSUS
EFFORTS AT DECENCY?

If the classical liberal, libertarian, or laissez-faire ideas of individual rights to life, liberty, and property are sound, and if people in the marketplace would not practice affirmative action of their own accord, then no official opposition and coercion are justified. Instead, people are owed protection of their freedom to do what they want, just as a newspaper is owed protection, by way of the First Amendment, against any attack on it for printing unpopular or antisocial views.

Public policy and legal decisions in the United States are frequently guided by the goals of integration and restitution, as seen in policies such as affirmative action, hiring quotas, and so forth. Government has been undermining the right to liberty for the sake of these objectives. If a person does in fact own his/her home, he should be free to sell it to whomever he desires and to set the terms of the sale. Otherwise, ownership rights are seriously compromised. The owner of a business ought to be the one to decide who will be hired and fired, within the limits of the employment agreement. Hotel and apartment owners are not enjoying their right to liberty if the government has the power to tell them that they must rent to anyone who wants to rent from them. Schools that must admit everyone who seeks admission are not free institutions but are subject to the bidding of whoever imposes the policy. Yet, however valuable the objectives of fairness and decency that motivate such policies, when government uses force against racism, individual rights are violated.

Legal mandates such as government regulations that dictate to producers that they must hire certain persons because this rectifies a social injustice would be comparable to legally requiring consumers to patronize certain businesses in order to ensure fairness. Surely some people refuse to shop in certain stores for racist or bigoted reasons. The store may have what they desire to buy, but they irrationally choose not to shop there. Consumers own their money or credit and do not always use it to promote social equality whenever they shop. However, were the government to force them to shop or eat or play in places that they irrationally avoid, this would be a clear violation of their individual rights to liberty.

Or consider workers who refuse to apply for a job in a firm owned by a Jew or a black or members of some other group against whom they are prejudiced. They, too, have a property right to their skills and labor time, just as owners of firms and shops have a property right to their wares and services. Workers desire to set the terms under which they are willing to work, just as owners wish to set the terms under which they are willing to hire. Surely it would be a violation of the worker's right to freedom to coerce him to apply for a job that he shunned out of prejudice.

Now if such hypothetical cases involve violation of individual rights, so too must the actual cases that we are all familiar with, regardless of whether or not they aim to achieve important social or political objectives.

THE FAILURE OF
GOVERNMENT REGULATION

Current public policies aiming to abolish racial and sexual discrimination have been hotly debated, and there is considerable criticism of these policies on practical, as well as moral, grounds. Additionally, there are numerous local government regulations such as building codes and zoning ordinances that limit how business may be conducted. Now it is arguable that all of these are irrelevant since these kinds of laws were in place *before* federal laws against discrimination. It is also possible that such restrictions on market transactions that might or presently do exist would emerge from contract, not from legislation or regulation.

In any case, there are countless ways to evade compliance with the kind of federal legislation and regulation that aim to correct past injustices. For example, in higher education, there may be insufficient funds to fully comply with legal mandates for a national job search when there is a vacancy. So undertaking the legally mandated task of "affirmative action" is not possible. Thus, many institutions will hire late, when the law allows exceptions. Loopholes are exploited because it is too costly and cumbersome to take the measures that government has ordered.

Arguably, if the affirmative action route were the only available way to rectify past wrongs or prevent present and future discrimination, then perhaps it ought to be tolerated. Slavery and segregation are recent enough political and social evils that the demand for justice with respect to some people may be rightly exerted, however clumsily or imprecisely, if only to approximate the search for justice. But clearly, affirmative action is not the only means available to us. Nor is it a proper means since it sometimes involves forcing people to discriminate against innocent parties, creates widespread resentment, and requires enormous economic resources that diminish the nation's wealth and productivity. An alternative without these features would certainly be preferable for all.

RECONCILING LIBERTY
AND DECENCY

There is a way to both preserve liberty and abate racism and rectify past wrongs: compensation and full disclosure. Let's see how these would solve the problem of racial or sexual discrimination without intruding on the right to individual liberty.

Compensation for past injustices could be sought by victims through the courts when it is demonstrated beyond a reasonable doubt that certain other people have been the beneficiaries of slavery, segregation, or sexual discrimination. If no one can be identified as having benefited from the harm done to those victimized, then no case could be made. If the government is the culprit, rectification would be available, as when damages are awarded to someone whose civil rights were violated. This approach would rule out any complaints based on the overly broad claim of "collective guilt," where no one in particular is identified as responsible and where certainly at least some members of the "guilty" collective are clearly innocent. Let's now turn to a liberty-friendly approach to fighting existing discrimination.

FULL DISCLOSURE VERSUS RACISM

Consider a context where a business, in this case, say, a restaurant, is not burdened by national or local legislation and regulation related to discrimination. The restaurant owner makes her establishment available *to the public* for the specific purpose of dining, for a price. When an employment opportunity is announced, it is generally announced *to the public at large*. In a competitive, free market, opportunities at the workplace are usually announced *in writing* as open to all those who comprise the qualified workforce. Numerous similar examples could be offered where, in every case, there is an implicit claim that anyone is free to meet the offer and be considered according to terms pertinent to the potential transaction. A restaurant is open to people seeking to buy a meal, with some conventional requirements satisfied, such as a requirement for certain attire and the expectation of normal social behavior and so forth.

Thus, if no racial, sexual, or similar criteria are specified as terms of trade, none need be considered by those attempting to do business. Entering a restaurant, having sufficient funds to pay for the meal, and behaving such as to not be a nuisance should suffice to be served. If and when a proprietor tries to refuse service for racial or ethnic reasons, that would constitute a breach of clearly implied contract, or fraud, since it is a clear failure to live up to the implied terms of trade. Such conduct should be legally actionable in the courts of a free society. The same goes, of course, for all relevantly similar cases.

So, how does this differ from legislation that bars racism and sexism? In this view, it would be entirely legal to discriminate if one announces the policy up front and explicitly. "Whites only," "women only," "blacks only," "Catholics only," and the like could be made part of the advertisements for trade. There would then be nothing to which anyone, including government, could legally object to. Is this so outrageous an idea? Consider that in many areas of life such discrimination is accepted: for example, in church attendance, in hair salons or other establishments aimed only at women, men, or some other specific group, and in some clubs, such as the American Association for University Women, Parents Without Partners, and so on.

Many such "discriminating" organizations engage in decent and legitimate activities; others involve some activities that may be reprehensible; and certainly some organizations could be considered irrational, such as certain ideological, athletic, or religious groups, fraternities, some associations, and the like. Moreover, in an unregulated marketplace it is possible to have contractual relationships that contain restrictive covenants, some of them beneficial to social values, some indifferent, and some that may outright violate decency and goodwill. Now, in a society such as ours, democratic enough for the government to muster public support for public policies that aim to promote decency by way of legislation and regulation, it seems highly unlikely that businesses with viciously racist or sexist restrictive covenants would flourish and certainly not in any great numbers.

In any case, in a free society, discriminating policies that made clear sense and were announced up front would find little opposition. Irrational, unfair, pointless, or otherwise questionable policies would be exposed to the public, which could then take peaceful and voluntary measures of opposition, criticism, ridicule, rebuke, boycott, ostracism, and so on.

No doubt some pockets of discrimination would persist despite public scrutiny. But that is true now, along with the widespread violation of the individual right to liberty. By comparison, the full disclosure and compensation approaches would be far superior to the current policy. They would inspire remedies based on principles of compensatory justice or rational terms of trade implicit in market exchanges. These approaches would avoid the resentment now issuing from affirmative action and many regulatory policies that government has created and businesses only grudgingly comply with. Most important, these approaches would help offset the erosion of our basic right to liberty that certain public policies and legal mandates have created.

ENVIRONMENTALISM HUMANIZED

According to the literature of environmentalism, a major enemy of the environment is a doctrine known as anthropocentrism, the view that human beings are more important, more valuable than other aspects of nature, including plants and animals. Given this concept, the business professional is about as anthropocentric as one can get since business attempts to satisfy the desires and needs of human beings here on earth. It is relevant to our purposes, then, to determine whether there is any merit in the environmentalists' widespread criticism of business and whether there can be an environmental perspective that is not in conflict with the objectives of business. We want to argue, briefly, that there is.

Let us first summarize this position. To say that human beings come first in the known universe means that each individual is an irreplaceably valuable being, not to be sacrificed by another for anything or anyone else. A corollary to this is that there is no "human being" apart from individuals. Humanity as a collective unity is often mentioned, but no such concrete human entity exists other than the individuals who comprise the human species.[13] It should be noted here that none of this implies that individuals are unique; they do share attributes, contrary to the view of the nominalist, or what critics call "atomistic" individualism so influential in Western liberal individualism. A sensible anthropocentrism or human-centered worldview sees *individual human beings* as the most important entities in nature. (Since the context of our discussion is naturalism, we exclude possible supernatural entities.)

Thus, anthropocentrism holds that in environmental ethics, both theoretical and applied, the highest value must be attributed to measures, actions, and policies that enhance the lives of individual human beings.

THE IMPORTANCE OF BEING HUMAN

It would, of course, be absurdly circular to say that human beings are most important and valuable because we value ourselves as most important. So an explanation and convincing argument are called for. First we must analyze the concept of lesser or greater importance and determine how it gives meaning and validity to

13. For more on this topic, see Tibor R. Machan, "Environmentalism Humanized," *Public Affairs Quarterly* 7 (April 1993): 131–47. See also Tibor R. Machan, "Pollution, Collectivism and Capitalism," *Journal des Economists et des Estudes Humaines* 2 (March 1991): 83–102.

our discourse and conduct. We can then rank things in nature as more or less important. Finally, we can relate all this to concrete conduct and policy. If it emerges that ranking things as more or less important is a good way of making sense about (certain aspects of) the world, and if human beings qualify as more important than other features or beings of nature, then we have the beginnings of a reason we may—or, more strongly, ought—to make use of nature for our purposes.

Before we begin our analysis, we should make explicit something only hinted at previously. Many environmental advocates believe that when we make use of nature for our purposes, that alone shows that we are doing something wrong, that such conduct is parasitic, cancerous and that nature would be fine without us. This is the foundation of much of environmentalism today and from which much of environmental criticism derives. It also explains why so many environmentalists are unmoved by factual challenges and why they are often so intransigent and strident of tone.

Now even if it were not true that human beings were most valuable in nature, it certainly wouldn't follow that sacrificing us to other features of nature would be a sound, justifiable policy. Under those circumstances, very likely *no policy* could be shown to be sound and justifiable, for everything would be up for grabs. "Importance" would be arbitrary, a matter of who has the most power or screams the loudest. Further, we need not start from scratch here; there is plenty of evidence in nature of something being better, another worse. Botanists, zoologists, biologists, and others are all constantly ranking things such as the condition of a tree, some animal, or an ecosystem. We also know full well that one piece of rock is no better than another, one drop of water no better than another, or one planet no worse than another, except as they relate to other things of importance, usually the life and health of someone or something.

When we turn to plants and animals the process of evaluation or ranking commences quite naturally. First, we can speak of better or worse (i.e., more or less healthy) oaks, tomatoes, elephants, birds, and so on. So ranking is evident, and many environmentalists themselves engage in it when they ignore, say, the welfare of the tuna but fret about the dolphin, cry about the spotted owl but not about the cockroach.

This concern, which all environmentalists share, with preserving or saving one or another species or habitat or geologic/geographic item, implies that values, something being good or bad, arise with extinguishable beings, things that can flourish or perish, that can become "endangered." Among these things, the more complex and developed ones are more important than those that are simpler. If life gives rise to values, a life of greater complexity, creativity, and involvement with the world would be more important than one that is highly limited.[14] The quality of life establishes its importance.

IS NATURE HIERARCHICAL?

So far, all we have done is spell out something implicit in environmental discourse. When animal rights theorists lament the "inhumane" treatment of chickens and the "murder" of whales, with not so much as a moment of concern for the millions of flies and billions of bacteria that we kill daily, such talk, if it makes

---

14. The late Karl Popper makes this point succinctly: "I think that values enter the world with life; and if there is life without consciousness (as I think there may well be, even in animals and man, for there appears to be such a thing as dreamless sleep) then, I suggest, there will also be objective values, even without consciousness." (*Unending Quest* [Glasgow, Scotland: Fontana/Collins, 1974].) The point is developed in Ayn Rand, "The Objectivist Ethics," *The Virtue of Selfishness*, and *A New Concept of Egoism* (New York: New American Library, 1961).

sense at all, implies that higher animals are *more important* than lower animals!

Of course, many who are concerned about animals have in mind nothing more than treating them more humanely, even as human beings make legitimate use of them for their own purposes, such as nourishment. Others are more concerned about reckless, unnecessary destruction of entire species of animals. These are perfectly sensible concerns, and any viable humanistic ethics would insist on the humane treatment of animals, if only to cultivate human character in the direction of certain valuable sensitivities such as compassion and generosity.

But there are clearly those whose view is that nonhuman animals, even plants, have as high a standing in the scale of nature as humans do.[15] Some would even defend worsening the lives of millions of human beings to enhance the lives of some nonhuman animals such as the spotted owl or some other endangered species. For these people, the very idea of a development, a new housing project, or a road is an immoral, unjustifiable invasion.

In response to all this we need to show that there is a stable hierarchy in nature against which to check the message of the more radical environmentalists. What follows is an initial sketch of a view suggested earlier.

Some things, such as rocks, planets, and in general, inanimate things of nature, invite no evaluation. Other things, animate be-

---

15. For a very extreme position, see Christopher Stone, *Should Trees Have Standing* (Palo Alto, Calif.: William Kaufmann, 1975). For more moderate yet still quite radical versions of such positions, see Stephen R. L. Clark, *The Moral Status of Animals* (Oxford, England: Clarendon Press, 1977), Tom Regan, *The Case for Animal Rights* (Berkeley: University of California Press, 1984); and Bernard Rollin, *Animal Rights and Human Morality* (Buffalo, N.Y.: Prometheus Books, 1981). See also Thomas Palmer, "The Case for Human Beings," *Atlantic* 269 (January 1992): 83–88; and Mortimer Adler, *The Difference of Man and the Difference It Makes* (New York: World Publishing, 1968).

ings, invite evaluation but without any moral significance. A gazelle might be a good specimen and even more important than, say, a field mouse, yet no blame or praise is implied in that observation. Generally, beings known as persons invite moral evaluation because they presumably can choose whether to do well or badly at being what and who they are. With such beings it makes sense to praise or blame. Even positivists and subjectivists implicitly agree to this when they believe that their philosophical opponents are wrong about some things!

Now how does this relate to the issue of importance? Why is something to which moral classification applies more important than that to which it does not?

MORALITY IN NATURE

To begin with, only beings capable of moral values are able to make practical use of the idea of importance: Environmentalists know this too, since they talk to *us*, *to other persons*, not to the spotted owl. More fundamentally, human beings have the kind of life that engages nature more fully than any other kind. Human life is considerably more involved in the world in creative and responsive, sometimes destructive, ways than other kinds of life. Thus, one can implore or urge human beings but not tuna or leopards. Human beings are also highly individualized, extending themselves in myriad ways into nature and capable of making choices concerning the best way to live one's life and to relate to nature. Among the values that arise from the diversity of human response to living in nature are things such as art, culture, science, religion, and, ironically, environmental science.

People can employ concepts such as "value" and "importance" in various ways, some useful and some rather misguided and entirely divorced from their logical and historical origin. A good example of the latter is the use made of these concepts by some environmentalists, in particular the more militant ones who say that all living beings have intrinsic or innate value or inherent importance. Nearly all environmentalists would value a bird over a rock or a fish over a log. But the very idea of valuing implies gradation or ranking, which means that some things must be of lower and others of higher value. The very kind of reasoning that identifies a bird as more valuable than a rock logically entails that human beings have more value than other animals. In the scale of nature the best candidate for the highest value is the individual human being since human beings introduce into nature additional values, in particular, moral values. This does not mean that every individual is good or always acts in a morally praise-worthy way. Rather, it means that the potential value or impor-tance of a human being is greater than that of any other being in nature known to us.

As clear and simple as this is, certain trends in the history of ideas make a rational assessment of what is and is not valuable problematic. In particular, the classical liberal intellectual tradi-tion has, to a significant extent, embraced value subjectivism, which precludes the idea that nature itself can serve as a standard for determining value and importance. Unless this subjectivist view is refuted, environmentalists and many others in our culture cannot rationally assert the value and importance of anything. What well-grounded theory of value makes the spotted owl more important than the job of a lumberer or carpenter or developer?

Some might answer, "Well, it's intuitively evident." But it is not at all self-evident or intuitive that the snail darter is more important than better irrigation. Is it known in everyone's heart, as a matter of self-evident fact, that the purpose of making a profit (i.e., promoting human prosperity) is clearly less valuable than that of preserving an endangered species? The ongoing de-bate in itself would suggest that the answer is no, and if anything seems clear and evident, if not intuitive, it is that the measure of importance is precisely whether something enhances human life.

It might be objected that most environmentalists do not value animals over human beings, but they do value life over money. This objection trades on a simplistic distinction and creates a false dilemma. Money is merely a means to life, a medium of exchange by which human beings in complex societies manage to obtain goods and services that enhance their lives. To juxtapose money and life is like juxtaposing blood and life or breathing and life. These are not opposites, except to those who demean others who live by means of money or who find human life on earth unimportant, base, and tawdry.

A full development of these kinds of discussions would require offering more historical support than would serve our purposes here. The present effort cannot, on its own, carry much weight. It is but one entry in the dialogue between those who see the value of business and those concerned with the environment, perhaps at a basic philosophical level. However, when coupled with other relevant discussions, it may turn out as vital that we know beyond a reasonable doubt that human beings are the most important beings known to us in nature. At very least, this knowledge is vital in the search for a sensible approach to dealing with the problems addressed here and by environmentally concerned persons.

WHAT DOES THIS MEAN FOR THE ENVIRONMENT?

Individualist humanism is a strict environmentalist stance consistent with nature since, as a political stance, individualism is justified by reference to human nature itself. Natural rights individualism, the view that every human individual has basic inviolable rights to life, liberty, and property, implies the kind of environmentalism that seeks solutions in privatization and "internalization of negative externalities," "full-cost pricing," and tort and property law, rather than in restrictive legislation and regulation.

As things stand, ours is a polity of what might be called democratic fascism. It is not primarily individual rights, but the will of the community (i.e., those who manage to be most influential) that serves as the standard of legal justice. In such a legal climate whether the environment is handled prudently is determined by the highly volatile winds of public opinion and participatory, unchecked democracy.

Under democratic fascism, as distinct from plain fascism or democratic socialism, politics involves the legal fiction of individual sovereignty, private ownership of property, and the reality of extensive government regulation based on the shifting tides of public opinion. In such a system, nothing is safe from the meddling hands of politicians, yet there is a veneer of justice via the pretense of democracy.

A genuine and informed concern for the environment would leave policy matters in the hands of private individuals and the system of justice based on individual rights. Those who run the firms that interact with the environment most intensely have no less at stake in how the environment is treated, provided this stake is properly delineated by the legal system. Here, as in any other area of human community life, any problems ought to be adjudicated in the courts, not regulated by bureaucrats appointed by zealous politicians whose personal ambitions should not be allowed to ruin human lives. The alternative seems nearly certain to be the politics of the proverbial lynch mob that condemns people whose ideals differ from those of their own (e.g., the environmentalists), an alternative forgetful of due process.

CHAPTER FOUR

What Is Morally Right
with Insider Trading

In this chapter we will examine one area of federal regulatory law that is under the clear influence of business bashing. In many professions, initiative, savvy, and seizing on an advantage are generally encouraged, as, say, when journalists are prompted to scoop their competitors. In business when someone gets a tip and moves on it, this is often considered unfair and in some instances is even forbidden by law. It will be useful to examine the case for this attitude toward insider trading and to consider it critically in light of our understanding of the cultural prejudice against commerce.

Insider trading is obtaining information from nonpublic sources, such as acquaintances, friends, colleagues, and using it to enhance one's financial advantage. As Vincent Barry explains, "Insider dealings refers to the ability of key employees to profit from knowledge or information that has not yet become public."[1] Sometimes such a practice can be conducted fraudulently, as when one who has obtained the information has a fiduciary duty to share it with clients but fails to do so or when the information

1. Vincent Barry, *Moral Issues in Business* (Belmont, Calif.: Wadsworth, 1983), p. 242.

itself was stolen. These are not, however, features of insider trading as such, as understood in the context of business ethics. In fact, in the enforcement of government regulations relevant to insider trading, it is *fraud* that is cited as the illegal conduct.[2] This suggests that much of the relevant law concerns "justice as honoring of contracts" rather than "justice as fairness," the latter being the concern of many in the business ethics community who discuss insider trading.

The focus of the ethics discussion on insider trading is that the information on which trade is based is not known to others within the interested trading community, aside from the insider. In other words, the information is not "public knowledge." Thus, the trader has an advantage over the rest of the market participants who are on the outside, and this advantage is taken by many to be unfair.

This chapter will argue against the view, common to business ethics discussions, that insider trading is unjust because it is unfair. We will argue that it may well be one's good fortune, or

---

2. Rule 106-5 of Securities Exchange Act of 1934. See also *SEC v. Texas Gulf Sulpher* (1968); *U.S. v. Chiarella* (1980), and *U.S. v. Newman* (1981). Both definitions and sanctions vary somewhat from state to state and case to case. *Black's Law Dictionary* (St. Paul, Minn.: West, 1991), p. 547, states that insider trading "refers to transactions in shares of publicly held corporations by persons with insider or advance information on which the trading is based. Usually the trader himself is an insider with an employment or other relation of trust and confidence with the corporation." Pub. L. 100-704, Sec. 7, Nov. 19, 1988, 102 Stat. 4682, provides that there be a study and investigation of, among other things, impediments to the fairness and orderliness of the securities markets.

While the language of securities law does mention the fairness that is most often the concern of those discussing insider trading in the field of business ethics, it seems that the main focus of the law and the regulatory bodies fine-tuning and enforcing it has to do with fraudulent trading in insider information or its misuse by those who have fiduciary duties not to disclose and use it until it is made available to the general trading public.

personal achievement, to learn of opportunities ahead of others and that this does not constitute moral transgression. In fact, acting on such information can be prudent and indicative of good business acumen, so long as it does not involve the violation of others' rights. The conventional view assumes that others have a right to information that one has honestly obtained ahead of them and that it is wrong to withhold such information. As we shall see, there is no sound moral principle to support this assumption.

There are numerous occasions where we make morally permissible use of special information, despite the fact that others might also benefit were it available to them, and where requiring that this information be shared would be ludicrous: for example, when someone first learns of the presence of a potential dating partner, a good buy on a used car, or a house coming up for sale in a preferred neighborhood. Taking advantage of such special opportunities is an exercise in good judgment, not unfairness or deception. So too with insider trading.

Those who claim otherwise confuse the marketplace with a game in which rules are devised with the special purpose of giving everyone an even chance, as in golf, when handicaps are assigned, or in professional football, when the lowest-ranked team gets first choice in the draft of new players. The market more resembles life itself, where different persons enter with different assets—talents, looks, health, strength, economic circumstance, and such. Given our differing talents, interests, and situations, we must do our best to make our way successfully in life. Apart from occasionally benefiting from the generosity or charity of others, all that each of us has is a fighting chance, not necessarily an "even" chance. Children of musically proficient parents will likely benefit "unfairly" in obtaining musical opportunities. Those born in poverty in Bombay will face harder times than those born in Beverly Hills to movie star parents. Each of us is aware of others more fortunate and less fortunate than we. Many of us should also assist the less fortunate by charitable means. However, no general moral requirement exists for strangers to "even out the playing field" of life, if indeed that were even possible. But we are morally required to refrain from imposing obstacles on others, from violating their rights to liberty as they attempt to make the best of things for themselves.

The marketplace, too, is a setting where different persons face different circumstances. People do not have a natural obligation to perform involuntary service to strangers, which is another way of saying that we are not obligated to be altruistic. The market provides opportunities by way of demands that can be met by means of voluntary compensation. In competing with others for these opportunities, and avoiding fraud and coercion in the process, one is treating others with the respect they deserve as potential traders. Exceptions exist, of course, as when one trades with family or friends, which may give rise to moral complications. However, the norm is where people treat each other as competitors seeking opportunities for trade, nothing more. There can be parallel human relationships side by side with trade, but we can keep the commercial ones distinct enough to understand the ethics that ought to govern us as we engage in trade. Let us now develop some of these points.

WHAT IS INSIDER TRADING?

The concept of insider trading that is employed in business ethics discussions has a broad meaning: It includes anyone's ability to make deals based on not yet publicized knowledge of business opportunities. As such, insider trading involves making financial investments on the basis of knowledge others do not have and may not be able to obtain in ordinary ways. For example, Jones knows the president of a firm, who tells him that the firm is thinking of expanding one of its divisions or has struck oil in a new field, so Jones buys a block of stock in advance of the knowledge becoming public so that he can enjoy an increase in value. Jones is neither deceiving nor defrauding anyone. He is not taking anything from others that wasn't freely given to him. Jones is simply acting on special, "insider" information.

Now it is conventional wisdom to treat this version of insider trading as morally wrong since it supposedly adversely affects others because it is unfair. As one critic, John Hetherington, has put it, "What causes injury or loss to outsiders is not what the insider knew or did, rather, it is what they themselves [the outsiders] did not know. It is their lack of knowledge which exposes them to risk of loss or denies them an opportunity to make a profit."[3] In other words, that the outsiders do not know what the insiders know constitutes harm to the outsiders since they are unable to make use of opportunities available to the insider.

But consider the reasoning here: What kind of causation is it that fails to make a difference when it does not exist? If someone's having certain information has no impact on what another does,

---

3. John A. C. Hetherington, "Corporate Social Responsibility, Stockholders, and the Law," *Journal of Contemporary Business*, winter 1973, p. 51; quoted in Barry, *Moral Issues*, pp. 242–43. In business ethics discussions of insider trading and other normative topics, little attention is paid to the distinction between ethics and public policy. Thus, even if there were something ethically objectionable about some business practice, this does not ipso facto warrant rendering it illegal or subject to government regulation. An analogy might help here: When we discuss journalistic ethics, it is clear enough that journalists may engage in unethical behavior that should not be made illegal. This same distinction is not generally observed when it comes to the profession of business. For an exception, see Tibor R. Machan, ed., *Commerce and Morality* (Lanham, Md.: Rowman & Littlefield, 1988), especially "Ethics and Its Uses." For a business ethics perspective hospitable to viewing business as a morally honorable profession, see Tibor R. Machan, "Professional Responsibilities of Corporate Managers," *Business and Professional Ethics Journal* 13 (fall 1994), on which chapter 7 of this book is based.

it can hardly be said that one caused harm to the other. Certainly, had the outsider known what the insider knew, he or she could have acted differently, but this does not show that the insider *caused* any harm. Unless we assume that valuable information known by one person ought, morally, and perhaps legally, to be distributed to *all* parties (since one cannot know in advance who *might possibly* benefit from it), there is no moral fault involved in insider trading or any causation of harm.[4] After all, such information is hardly on a par with, say, learning that a certain widely used product had an unknown life-threatening property. Such an assumption would, of course, beg the most important question here. It also bears the burden of proof. Indeed, if one *were* to learn something of that kind, one ought to make it public.

The widespread but mistaken view that insider trading is wrong accounts for the support of its legal prohibition by conventional wisdom. Of course, even if morally wrong, it does not follow that the practice should be *legally* prohibited. But there is good reason to think that the moral objections are groundless and that the opposition to insider trading is more likely the result of the long-standing prejudice against gaining economic prosperity without sharing it. Clearly, in our era there is considerable belief in the view that a level playing field is morally mandatory when people embark on commercial or business endeavors.[5]

4. If someone does not do what he or she ought to do, the causation involved may be the kind that consists in taking away a supporting feature of an action. Someone who steals a part of my car engine causes it to fail to operate properly by removing what such an operation needs. That is how stealing can cause the ensuing harm. Fraud produces harm similarly: Something one owns, namely, what another has legally committed to one, is in fact withheld. But without such commitment, or even a moral duty to provide, no causation of the lack of desired advantage can be identified. For more on this, see Eric Mack, "Bad Samaritanism and the Causation of Harm," *Philosophy and Public Affairs* 9 (summer 1980).

5. The most prominent is, of course, John Rawls, *A Theory of Justice*

WHY INSIDER TRADING IS RIGHT

Without doubt anyone lacking information that others possess can put one at a disadvantage, and in fact nearly everyone in the marketplace is in that position to some degree. Now, this might be called "unfair" in the sense that good fortune puts some people at an advantage relative to some others. However, to be careful and precise, the concept of fairness does not apply in this context, despite what many people believe. For someone to act fairly, there must have been a prior obligation to distribute benefits or burdens among a given number of persons in some suitable proportion or in line with certain specified procedures. But acting fairly is not a primary moral duty: For example, someone who wins the lottery is not morally obligated to redistribute his winnings to everyone else! Nor are thieves, who may be distributing their loot fairly, thought to be acting morally in doing so. Only when one *ought* to treat others alike does fairness have moral significance. This occurs in special circumstances such as teachers being professionally obligated to pay attention to all the students in their classes or parents being obligated to give equal care to all of their children.

Applying this to insider trading, if one has a prior obligation to share information with certain others, such as a fiduciary duty

---

(Cambridge, Mass.: Harvard University Press, 1971). One main problem in Rawls's defense of justice as fairness is that Rawls believes that no one can deserve his or her advantages or assets in life—it's all a matter of luck. As he puts it, "No one deserves his greater natural capacity nor merits a more favorable starting point in society." The reason? Because even a person's character (i.e., the virtues he or she practices that may provide him with ways of getting ahead of others) depends in large part upon fortunate family and social circumstances for which he can claim no credit (p. 104). If one rejects this deterministic account of virtues, then a trader's prudence cannot be discounted as one assesses whether he or she deserves to gain from how trade is conducted.

to clients or associates, then what makes one's dealings morally and possibly legally objectionable is that it is *owed to others*, not that the information is "from the inside." Only in such cases is fairness obligatory, as a matter of one's professional relationship to others, established by the promise made or contract one has entered into prior to the ensuing duty to be fair. Only then does one cause injury by not doing what one has agreed to do, namely, share information before using it for oneself. Accordingly, Hetherington's objection to insider trading is without moral force. What he ought to have criticized is the breaching of fiduciary duty, which may occur on occasion with failure to divulge information (possibly gained "from the inside") that has been promised to a client.

Furthermore, if one has stolen the information by spying, bribing, or extortion, once again the moral wrong comes from its having been ill-gotten, not from its being inside information. And if the information was acquired accidentally, such as its having been overheard in the lavatory or at a bar after alcohol has perhaps loosened some tongues, here again the issue is what one owes to others. We do not have a natural obligation to share good fortune with just any, unrelated other people.

In emergency situations, when others are in dire need or have met with some natural disaster, virtues such as generosity and charity are usually binding on those who are able to assist, though these are not obligations that the law must enforce. Indeed, enforcing generosity or charity is impossible since the moral significance of a virtue is destroyed if it is practiced at the point of a gun! Additionally, in the context of the normal hustle and bustle of life, no such virtues are called for toward strangers, only toward those one is related to by prior commitments, intimacy, and love. In the ordinary course of life one ought to strive to live successfully, to prosper, to make headway with one's legitimate projects, not embark on the tasks of emergency crews during a disaster.

From the viewpoint of commonsense ethics, the idea that there is something morally amiss with insider trading seems groundless. One clearly has no moral, let alone legal, obligation to share with strangers information that might benefit one in other familiar circumstances. Imagine, for example, that an appealing eligible single man moves into a neighborhood wherein also live several single women, all of whom would be interested in meeting the man. Suppose that one of the women happens to get (inside) information about the man's impending arrival and is able to introduce herself to the man first and possibly secure a dating advantage over the others. Has she done wrong? Few would think so, and yet most people would agree that the prospect of a successful romance and possibly serious relationship was more important than the prospect of a successful investment. Or suppose, again, that one learns of a good music teacher who is moving to town and is thus first to contact her for lessons, before her calendar is full. This would hardly be morally wrong. Of course, were the person in no great hurry to find a teacher but had a friend who was, it would be generous and thoughtful to tell that person about the impending arrival of the teacher. This would be thoughtful but not obligatory.

THE BAD REPUTATION OF COMMERCE

The reason these situations do not invite widespread moral rebuke, in contrast with insider trading, is that we tend to consider objectives such as finding a suitable mate or learning a musical instrument something benign, morally untainted. But with respect to economic gains, in many quarters there is an initial moral discomfort and suspicion about it. The shadow of greed looms large and may even overwhelm prudence, the first of the cardinal virtues.

WHY INSIDER TRADING
SEEMS WRONG

The intellectual source of moral disdain for insider trading, at least among moral philosophers and many of those in the humanities, is the more general disdain for economic or commercial self-enhancement. There seems to be no end to how fiercely commercial success is demeaned among many of those who preach and reflect on morality. But, as we are seeing, this attitude is totally misguided.

Becoming prosperous can be a means to attaining numerous worthy goals and should thus itself be deemed a worthy pursuit. Nor need the pursuit of prosperity be obsessive. Indeed, any goal can be pursued immoderately, either in excess or in deficiency. An artist can be overambitious by pursuing her art to the neglect of family, friends, community. Even truth can be pursued fanatically. The chances for corruption in pursuit of economic advantage are no greater than through other pursuits. This disdainful attitude toward commercial professionals is entirely unjustified. It is a prejudice as much deserving of study as prejudices toward racial, religious, or ethnic groups.

Now what about the fact that we encourage fairness in athletic competition, as when we impose handicaps in golf and horse racing or when baseball and football leagues utilize player drafts to even out the advantages of teams? Does this not indicate an emphasis on fairness beyond what our analysis has so far allowed? Isn't fairness heavily stressed in the allocation of chores in families, fraternities, teams, and a host of other human social groups?

BAD ANALOGIES

These examples are misleading. It isn't fairness per se that is stressed in golf and horse racing; what appears as such is actually an effort to foster games and races that capture and keep the interest of spectators as well as participants. Similarly for the policy on player drafts—if a team wins repeatedly, interest will begin to wane and the sport will lose its fans.

As to families and such, there exists a prior obligation to share burdens and benefits among the members proportionately, if not equally. Parents have, so to speak, invited their children into the family, and when benefits (or burdens) are reaped, all those invited should share them.

Among people who are not in such relationships no fairness principle operates. No doubt, we sometimes make a mistake and transfer the attitudes we have acquired handling family matters to other areas of our lives, but this is an illogical extrapolation, a category mistake, a faulty analogy. This is evident by considering that someone born to a family with, say, musical talent, or some other advantageous genetic inheritance has no duty to see to it that those born without these somehow share in the advantages. Neither is one doing the right thing in imposing burdens on members of families who do not suffer as his does. That sort of policy seems suspiciously born of, and conducive to, envy and resentment, not moral decency.

THE MORAL MERIT OF INSIDER TRADING

Seeking to benefit through ingenuity and shrewdness is good business, and good business is as important an activity and skill as good medicine, good law, good education, good engineering, and so on. Professional ethics ought not condemn that which is in accord with ethics in general, such as the virtues of fortitude and prudence. Competence and skill, even excellence, at managing the material progress one might be able to make in life ought not be treated as less important than competence and skill at managing artistic, scientific, educational, or other activities.

Some people defend insider trading because it contributes to the overall efficiency of market transactions. They argue that those trading from the inside send signals to others whose reactions then help propel the market to its new level of efficiency.

There may be something to this line of defense, although it comes perilously close to arguing that the end justifies the means. Unless the actions of individuals who engage in insider trading can themselves be shown to be justified, such arguments do not advance the cause of commerce as a *noble* venture. One may be able to show benefits to society at large based on theft, even murder, yet these are by no means justified by such reasoning.

Since many people regard fairness, equality, and a "level playing field" as the most important criteria for a morally decent marketplace, insider trading is held to be morally deficient. But, as we have seen, these are not the proper criteria for evaluating the morality of trade. The proper criterion is respect for individual rights and the principles that derive from those rights. Within the framework of such respect, insider trading is entirely unobjectionable. More strongly, it can even be morally commendable, as a matter of prudence and commercial savvy, both of which should be readily recognized and encouraged as virtues by anyone who must work for a living.[6]

6. We wish to thank Professor Clifton Perry, the editors of *Public Affairs Quarterly*, and George Childress for the help received from them in the preparation of this discussion. We are, of course, fully responsible for the use made of this help.

CHAPTER FIVE

Business Ethics: Texts and Teachings

MISEDUCATION ABOUT BUSINESS

Ambivalence is a common feature of contemporary life. We are told by experts on one side that our children need more discipline, by the other, that they need more love; by one major political party that government must provide for the needy and disadvantaged, by the other, that government assistance creates dependence. We may believe that criminals ought to be punished but hear persuasive arguments in favor of rehabilitation and so on. The origins of this ambivalence are no doubt complex. Ours is a highly industrialized, pluralistic, technological, commerce-driven democracy. We are called on to make decisions on a daily basis and often face a multitude of competing choices. We seem to be bombarded by messages from all sides concerning what to purchase, how to dress, what to eat, how to vote—in short, how to live our lives. On almost every social, political, and economic issue there are experts on both sides. Even among our trusted friends there may be considerable differences of opinion about a good many matters. Such conditions naturally tend to create ambivalence in us, especially in moments of crisis. We want to make appropriate decisions, to do the right thing, but we are often torn. Ironically, in contemporary society strong beliefs and convictions are often taken as signs of inflexibility and closed-mindedness, which contributes even further to ambivalence. Perhaps the most telling tension of all concerns the key to happiness: We are torn between convictions that promise happiness here on earth and those that hearken to another world and call on us to renounce this earthly life. As the title of a newspaper editorial suggests, "We Praise Mother Teresa and Then Hit the Shopping Mall." We want it both ways but sense a contradiction.

This tension is not inherent in our nature, despite what some thinkers have argued. We are indeed unique but not necessarily separate from nature. Birds, as flying creatures are unique; so too are fish. So uniqueness in itself should pose no insurmountable problem. It is possible for human beings to live harmoniously and happily in this world. In our case, however, there is the possibility of going wrong. Human beings must learn about the world and themselves, and sometimes we learn poorly or are taught the wrong things. This is especially the case when it comes to our attitude about business, as taught in our colleges and universities.

BUSINESS ETHICS MISCONCEIVED

Some time ago, in a "My Turn" column[1] in *Newsweek* magazine, Professor Amitai Etzioni of George Washington University lamented that the Harvard Business School students whom he had been invited to teach showed little interest in the subject he was trying so hard to explain to them. Etzioni, author of, among other works, a book[2] highly critical of neoclassical economics, com-

---

1. Amitai Etzioni, "Money, Power & Fame," *Newsweek*, September 18, 1989.
2. See, again, Etzioni, *The Moral Dimension*.

plained that he "clearly had not found a way to help classes full of MBA's see that there is more to life than money, power, fame and self-interest." More specifically, Etzioni expressed disappointment that the MBA students were fond of business, including advertising. Some endorsed the idea of "consumer sovereignty," meaning that consumers have the power to make up their own minds as to what they will purchase, even in the face of persuasive advertising. In evident exasperation, Etzioni responded with the rhetorical question, "But what about John Kenneth Galbraith's view, [which] argues that corporations actually produce the demand for their products, together with whatever they wish to sell—say male deodorants." (The implication is that the idea of consumer sovereignty is a myth, that people are made to buy things by advertisements, not by their own considered judgments. In short, people are powerless against the forces of advertising.)

Etzioni further complained that the Harvard MBA's did not wholeheartedly welcome his "ethical" criticism of corporate PACs, political action committees, often established by organizations such as corporations, labor unions, and educational associations. He notes that "scores of corporations encourage their executives to form political-action committees, and use the moneys amassed to influence both Congress and state legislators. . . . One student said he liked PACs: 'Last summer, I worked for a corporation that has one. Its PAC allowed me to advance my economic interest. And I could use my vote in the ballot box, to support those who agree with my international ideas.'" After informing us of this lamentable state of affairs, Etzioni asks, again, rhetorically, "So, it's OK for corporate executives to have, in effect, two votes, while the rest of us have one?"

Etzioni's editorial is remarkable for two reasons: First, it illustrates a mainstream negative attitude against business by academics; second, the typical substantive criticisms, when examined, are far from telling. For example, although the professor never mentions it, there is a famous response to Galbraith's debunking of the consumer sovereignty doctrine.[3] In a now well-known piece, yet rarely used in business ethics texts, F. A. Hayek argues that while desires are in a certain sense created, this occurs naturally with all innovations—artistic, scientific, religious, and otherwise.[4] When a new symphony is composed, it may "produce" a demand by becoming a potential source of artistic enjoyment, especially if people find it preferable to other music. Certainly, every service or product aims to meet someone's desires, someone's judgment that it has merit for her. Even male deodorants, a product Etzioni denigrates as an obvious case of trivial consumption, may have a point for some people who are not, perhaps, as biosocially gifted in this respect as the critical professor.

Admittedly, there are market failures, wrongs that can occur within the system of free exchange. For example, no doubt there are consumers who will buy things simply for the thrill of the purchase and perhaps even waste their money on a product or service that is bad for them. They may even have been "talked into" these purchases by a clever salesperson or persuasive ad. But, surely, one may doubt Galbraith's (or even a business ethics teacher's) general competence of judging what is the right thing for others to buy. In general, such decisions are best made by, and ought to be left up to, the consumer. It would be an especially hard judgment to make in the ivory towers of Harvard or George Washington University.

Consider also the PAC case. Etzioni's complaint seems inconsistent with the well-respected American public policy tradition

3. John Kenneth Galbraith, "The Dependence Effect," in T. L. Beauchamp and N. E. Bowie, eds., *Ethical Theory and Business* (Englewood Cliffs, N.J.: Prentice-Hall, 1983), p. 360.

4. F. A. Hayek, "The Non Sequitur of the Dependence Effect," ibid., p. 508.

that guarantees citizens the opportunity "to petition the government for redress of grievances" such as repealing the double taxation of the corporate capital gains tax or being singled out as the villain in the fight for a clean environment. Where does Professor Etzioni's lament leave all the special interest groups that eagerly lobby in Washington for such causes as the protection of the snail darter, animal rights, and the vigorous, relentless and constant redistribution of the "nation's" wealth? What about all the various Naderite public or consumer interest groups or the Sierra Club's constant pleadings? Their enjoyment of tax exemption, as those of other 501(c) "nonprofit" corporations, gives them extra leverage, not to mention the cloak of moral righteousness, in their efforts to secure benefits for their constituencies.[5]

In short, unless we wish to exclude businesses from participating in the democratic process, which hardly seems democratic, Etzioni's criticism of PACs is, at best, unjustifiably selective. Finally, to Etzioni's concern that corporations get two votes while every citizen gets only one, it should be noted that corporations are also taxed twice; they are indeed treated as *persons* in much of our corporate law.

UNDERSTANDABLE DISLIKE OF BUSINESS "ETHICS"

Judging by Professor Etzioni's own account of how he went about teaching his business ethics course, it is small wonder that his students responded with little enthusiasm. Evidently the professor did not teach business ethics; rather, he engaged in that fa-

---

5. The idea that such public interest organizations are actually concerned with everyone's interest is a sham. For more, see Machan, *Private Rights and Public Illusions.*

miliar academic pastime, business bashing, only this time to an audience who knew better than to take it seriously.

Etzioni's approach to the teaching of business ethics is fairly typical, and his dismay is shared, in varying degrees, by many teachers of business ethics. The underlying failure of this approach is not so much that it is biased, which it certainly is, but that it does not actually cover the topic that names the course. What occurs in the great majority of classes and texts in this field is not the teaching of business ethics but the denigration and attempted taming of business. They are concerned not with the subject matter of ethical conduct within the profession of business but instead focus on the advocacy of public policy to reform it, as though business were particularly corrupt and out of control. The ethics that is taught is elementary, involving mainly the laying out of some standard ethical theories and proceeding to show that those in business have no chance on earth to satisfy any sensible conception of moral behavior.[6] This contrasts strikingly with how other profession-specific ethics courses are taught.

6. A typical example is William H. Shaw, *Business Ethics* (Belmont, Calif.: Wadsworth, 1991). This book, written by a self-professed Marxist, is (1) published by one of the foremost textbook publishers in the field of philosophy and (2) spares no space in arguing against the very possibility of ordinary business being ethical. Shaw, for example, discusses the nature and historical origins of capitalism, citing the analysis of Robert Heilbroner, himself a neo-Marxist (until the fall of the USSR) and mentions the role of such early entrepreneurs as Anton Fugger, who "established weaving as a mass production industry and lent large sums of money to the Hapsburg emperors to finance their wars" (p. 123). We do not learn of the achievements of Fugger in areas such as making the livelihood of hundreds of weavers easier and having the ambition to develop his enterprise to nearly everyone's economic benefit.

Shaw bashes nearly every aspect of business, from its environmental record to employment practices, advertising, you name it. And this is a typical book, albeit with a few dissenters beginning to make some inroads. Finally, Shaw repeats the biased presentation of advertising found in Etzioni's column, mentioning only Galbraith's charge that advertisers create desires and manipulate

In medical ethics, as well as in educational, legal, or engineering ethics, a major course objective is to take general ethical theories and show how they might apply to the problems that arise within these special disciplines. What would a utilitarian say about surrogate motherhood or the problem of honest communication in the diagnosis of fatal diseases? How do we apply the tenets of Christian ethics, or of ethical egoism, to the problems of risk aversion in the design and construction of high-rise apartments or automobiles? These are typical examples of problems that are explored in various branches of applied ethics.

Just as the study of ethics generally presupposes that human beings want to live morally good lives, the study of applied ethics presupposes that people want to be decent human beings in the conduct of their various professions; what they need is some enlightenment, some guidance, about what the special problems in these areas might require of them. It is the task of applied ethics to provide this guidance. The idea that is prominent in academia and elsewhere, that "decent" means one thing in business and something else in the other professions, is an unfounded prejudice, arising from a metaphysically biased account. This account, as noted earlier, reduces business to a lower-order profession, assuming that the aspirations that give rise to business are somehow lowly, base, cheap, uninspiring, ignoble. The metaphysical presupposition underlying this double standard will be examined shortly.

Teaching professional ethics, then, amounts to taking the gen-

---

consumers so as to gain leverage, with no mention of the Hayekian reply. (Some collections of articles in the field of business ethics do, however, reproduce both discussions side by side!)

For a discussion of the nature of advertising, why most critics grossly misunderstand it, see the essay by Douglas J. Den Uyl on the topic in Machan, *Commerce and Morality*.

eral moral principles that human beings should live by and considering their implications for the various professions. The instructor does not simply take a stand and badger students into believing what he or she believes, as though the classroom were an indoctrination center.[7] Indeed, the professional ethics of teaching would vigorously reject such an approach. Ironically, many of those teaching business ethics are violating their duties as professors, as trainers of young minds. In a professional ethics course, the teacher ought to help students examine the tenets of the major ethical systems and their implications for the special areas of human conduct being explored.

At an advanced level of teaching a professor may, without violating professional integrity, present and defend her or his own convictions since in such courses students may be assumed to be reasonably independent thinkers capable of taking issue. The professor has a duty to encourage and assist students in doing so, despite his or her convictions. This is not because there are no correct ethical answers but because a professor's duty is not to indoctrinate but to clarify, familiarize, explain, and provide a just treatment of a subject by considering major viewpoints on it. This dual respect for the subject and for the student is at the heart of the time-honored Socratic method. Its ultimate aim is the discovery of truth. The ethics of education would bring this home to the many teachers of business ethics who violate the very

---

7. An element of contemporary moral theory does, however, aid and abet this approach to teaching applied ethics, namely, intuitionism, the view that our moral convictions are ultimately firmly embedded, gut feelings about right and wrong, not capable of being defended by argument, not subject to logical, historical, and factual scrutiny. A good deal of academe embraces this view, or some version of it, when it accepts the positivist notion that ethics is but a datum, something expressing how people feel, not a cognitive discipline at all. The insistence on being value free contributes to this attitude and intuitionism is certainly complicit in what results.

principles of their own profession as they denigrate the profession of business.

Admittedly, teaching applied ethics is problematic. The idea behind the initiative, which began in the early 1970s, was that those preparing for various professions should be taught not only the content and skills of their field but some understanding of how to conduct themselves, how to carry on decently, consistent with broad, generally accepted ethical standards. However, college and university teaching does not easily accommodate that impulse. In the academy, only the sciences are taught by means of providing reasonably straightforward answers to questions and solutions to problems. In contrast, the humanities, liberal arts, and social sciences are generally taught by means of the dialectical approach, which stresses the Socratic method of comparing and contrasting different answers and solutions rather than delivering the one right answer.

This poses an apparent dilemma, for ethics is precisely about doing the right thing, choosing the best course of conduct from among alternatives. How can one teach applied ethics, as distinct from ethical theories (which are discussed in courses on moral philosophy), without becoming doctrinaire?

One answer is to consider competing moral theories and then note that considerable agreement does exist among them all, concerning at least the range of ethical virtues that human beings ought to practice. No moral theory denies that one ought to be honest, just, courageous, prudent, generous, kind, and so forth, even if they differ about how these virtues are to be prioritized. So one can always focus on the application of these virtues to special cases that arise in various professions, setting aside some of the conflicts that face one in the field. When these conflicts are confronted, for example, when one must decide between honesty and kindness or prudence and generosity or justice and loyalty, the ways that different moral systems handle the problem can be explored. Here some measure of thoroughness and even-handedness in the presentation and discussion is about all than can reasonably be achieved. It is improper to avoid this difficulty by simply becoming an advocate of one's own position or even the position that is most widely embraced in one's culture.

THINLY DISGUISED BUSINESS BASHING

Business ethics courses as actually taught and discussed in textbooks and journals quite often, if not typically, involve demonstrating to the student that the very objective of the profession is less than noble. One need but notice how disdainfully Etzioni recalls his student's justification for joining a PAC organization: It "allowed me to advance my economic interest." Etzioni evidently sees no moral value in this justification. Indeed, he is a well-known critic of any consequentialist or teleological ethics, where good and right are identified by reference to some valuable results, including, perhaps, the well-being of the moral agent. For such philosophers and ethicists, the pursuit of prosperity is in itself simply amoral. This despite the long tradition of moral teaching wherein such pursuits were construed as a species of the *virtue of prudence*, a trait of character that has, after all, been regarded as the first of the cardinal virtues.[8] Prudence, broadly defined, is the intelligent living of one's life; it is the virtue of being careful to consider one's choices, in particular the so-called practical choices that bear on the quality of one's life. So it is prudent to exercise financial self-discipline by, for example, saving money for emergencies, prudent to pay attention to one's diet so as to maintain health, and so forth.

---

8. Recall Adam Smith's observations about the problems of modern moral philosophy (chap. 1, note 18) and what impact this has had on the prominent conception of business ethics.

Instead of our culture seeing business as the institutional expression of this virtue—the good deeds people engage in as they carry out economically beneficial endeavors—business itself, as a profession, is generally distrusted and maligned. By implication, the only way to be moral in business is essentially to abdicate. Short of that, one is at least required to redeem oneself after one has left the executive suite. Is it any wonder that Harvard's MBA students were unreceptive when this kind of "business ethics" was taught to them? In essence, they were being taught that their chosen profession was morally suspicious.

As business ethics is conceived in many classrooms and in most textbooks, a decent, moral person in this profession must demonstrate to others that one is not really serious about this business stuff and that the only reason some people carry forth in the field is that it is a necessary precondition for doing some truly good things in life. That is, to help others, one must have the products and services that commerce makes possible. In and of itself, so the story goes, commerce has no moral value. This attitude, when applied to, say, medicine, would see medicine to be no more than a necessary condition for keeping people fit to save their souls. Thus, a decent person in business cannot gain moral worth by paying attention to making money or earning a good return on investment; rather, one in business must rectify social ills and be socially responsible, over and above doing a job well.

This idea that business is somehow the handmaiden of more noble purposes may have as one of its sources the tradition of mercantilism, which most teachers and authors in this field apply to corporate commerce: Corporations are entities created by the government to serve some public purpose. Richard DeGeorge, author of numerous texts and articles in business ethics,[9] adheres to this view, as does no less a critic of business than Ralph Nader.

9. Richard T. De George, *Business Ethics* (New York: Macmillan, 1982).

Both see business professionals as entrusted with some public purpose to which achieving economic success must be subordinated. But this view is founded on an intellectual base that is itself misguided and antiquated. Robert Hessen[10] examines the idea of business corporations being entities created by the state, tracing it back to a conception of the state within the feudalist and mercantilist tradition. In the era ruled by that tradition, citizens were viewed as subjects and thus lacked personal, individual sovereignty. Many contemporary intellectuals, with their contorted critiques of individualism—claiming that individuals are inventions, that those who affirm their existence are advocating that everyone is some kind of isolated, "atomic," individual—are trying to revive this perverse tradition.

This widespread view should be exposed for what it is, an unjustified elevation of some persons to a superior status over others. The implication of the "government-created entity" view of corporations is that citizens are essentially servile, even in their economic endeavors. In truth, business corporations are actually best understood as voluntary associations, where people employ professionals to perform economic tasks aimed at making a profit, as a means by which to prosper in life.[11]

ECONOMICS IS OF NO DECISIVE HELP

Admittedly, when business ethicists who denigrate commerce look to economists as the moral defenders of business, they generally find little that is of moral substance. But this is hardly

10. Hessen, *In Defense of the Corporation.*

11. For a more detailed analysis of the profession of business and of commerce in general along these lines, see the various contributions in Machan, *Commerce and Morality.* Essentially the idea is that commerce is one manifestation of prudential conduct in large social systems and the profession of business emerges as the institutional result of such prudential conduct.

surprising since economists, as students of business, seek technical and theoretical understanding of the processes of business, making only a few assumptions about what generates business in the first place. Economists do not focus on moral issues, a trait they share with other social scientists who, until recently, attempted to remain value free and "scientific" about their subject. Rather than looking to the economists for why business might be an honorable activity, business-bashing ethicists should look to fellow ethicists: ones who see business activity as a perfectly legitimate form of prudential behavior, aiming at the prosperity of the agents or their clients. Then they should try to come to terms with the arguments that are offered to establish the moral propriety of such prudent conduct.

Instead, business ethicists tend to argue with those in a different field, with people who are generally not prepared to debate the fine points of moral philosophy. It then becomes a simple matter to discredit the moral foundations of genuine business, making it appear that the field is nothing but an arena of naked greed and, thus, sheer vice.

As noted earlier, business ethics textbooks and courses are typically preoccupied with the notion that business needs to be tamed by government intervention, regulation, or litigation. A host of invented new "rights"—consumers' rights and workers' rights—are then owed government protection, the way that basic rights are viewed in our political system.[12] For example, it is

12. For a good collection of essays debating the issue of workers' rights, see Gertrude Ezorsky, ed., *Moral Rights in the Workplace* (Albany: State University of New York Press, 1987). See, for a detailed defense of the workers rights' view, Patricia Werhane and H. Persons, *Rights and Corporations* (Englewood Cliffs, N.J.: Prentice-Hall, 1985). For a detailed bibliography of books and essays in the now burgeoning field and subfields of business ethics, see Donald G. Jones and Patricia Bennet, eds., *A Bibliography of Business Ethics 1981–1985* (Lewiston, N.Y.: Edwin Mellen Press, 1986).

claimed that there are workers' rights to decent wages based on comparable worth (by some intuited standard), rights to fairness, job security, safety and health protection on the job, and so forth. It matters little what the market (i.e., the freely choosing consumers and the existing supply of goods and services, including labor) enables the employer to pay and do or what workers agree to do of their own free will. Once these rights are "established," business ethicists then advocate a deluge of regulatory measures that force those in business to comply, go under, or suffer serious penalties. This alone should explain why PACs have become vital to the business community.

Behind this push for the regulation of business is the notion that the motivating force of business activity, profit, is not an honorable objective. We simply should not allow people thus motivated to run free; they should be kept under strict supervision and stringent controls: thus, the proliferation of government regulatory bodies at all levels of government, bringing entanglements and obstacles that often stifle what little chance human beings have for economic solvency. Denying that there is moral value in the pursuit of profit clears the way for demanding that professional objectives be sacrificed for the "greater good" of workers and consumers, even at the risk of insolvency!

This is admittedly a rather bleak picture. No doubt there are teachers of business ethics who offer a more balanced approach. Yet if we consider the literature in the field, including major scholarly books and articles as well as textbooks, the negative scenario is justified.

THE FALSE ETHICS OF
MOST BUSINESS ETHICS

A survey of business texts will support the claim above that professors of business ethics themselves poison the well in their teaching and writing and thereby perpetuate a negative, often cynical view about the nature of business and commerce.[13] For example, in the discussion of employment, the major objective of most business ethics authors and professors is to demonstrate that there should not be *employment at will*. Instead, it is held that employers ought to be constrained forcibly, by government regulation or litigation, in their judgment about whom to hire or fire or promote. Nor may employees make certain kinds of decisions: for example, to work at higher risk than what the regulations (e.g., OSHA rules) allow. Regardless of employees' desires to take the risk for higher pay, they are forbidden to do so because of punitive restraints placed on every business by government. In effect, certain otherwise morally acceptable (commercial) behavior among consenting adults is forbidden by government regulations! In no other area of social and public life (except perhaps the area of certain sexual practices and the use of nonprescription drugs) do ethicists take such a strong and widely voiced stand against individual judgment and liberty.

In another area, most business ethics professors argue that the subordinate role of employees ought to be changed because employees have rights that should diminish the position of management. The employer is viewed as a tyrant, an oppressor, and an exploiter who should be restrained by legislation and court action.[14]

On this view, it is irrelevant that some employees may prefer working for those who are willing to take bigger risks in exchange for greater returns, irrelevant, also, that different kinds of commercial enterprises might require different organizational struc-

13. Douglas J. Den Uyl and Tibor R. Machan, "Recent Work in Business Ethics: A Survey and Critique," *American Philosophical Quarterly*, April 1987, pp. 107–24.

14. See J. E. Chesher, "The Ethics of Employment" in Machan, *Commerce and Morality*.

tures for efficiency and perhaps even for worker safety. All this is subordinated to the will of the state, with the fervent approval of many who teach our college students the ethics of business.

In the academic community there is a fairly sustained attack on the profession of business, abated only here and there by a few dissident texts and teachers. In the main, the very texts and courses that ought to guide students through some of the particular ethical difficulties of their field are actually a message to prospective members of the business community that their chosen profession is morally bankrupt.

MISDIRECTED VENOM

The academic mistrust of business can be illustrated with a particularly apt example, the "documentary" film *Poletown Lives*. The film concerns the discontinuation of production at a manufacturing firm that had made promises in return for government favors. The treatment of the case is so clearly one-sided as to count as propoganda rather than documentary. This film, a Blue Ribbon winner at the American Film Festival in New York in 1983, has been vigorously advertised and marketed as excellent study material for the classroom. Business ethics teachers are among the targets of this appeal. A number of disturbing issues arise. For one, there is the assumption by the promoters of this material that people who teach courses in business ethics, anthropology, communications, economics, history, political science, social work, sociology, urban studies, and the like are willing to use materials that are essentially propaganda. There is also the assumption that what merits a film prize is thereby worthy education material. But something even more serious is at issue here, something more fundamental. We need to dig below the surface.

In "The Poletown Dilemma," a 1985 *Harvard Business Re-*

view essay, Joseph Auerbach points out that General Motors Corporation was able to make use of the *eminent domain* law to secure land in Poletown for an assembly plant. None of the promotional literature calls attention to this fact. Instead, what the film and the promotional literature stress is the immense power of General Motors (and, by implication, "big business" generally) to influence politics.

Consider, now, the real issue underlying this case. The *eminent domain* law concerns *government's* "taking private property for public purposes." Now this law is entirely perverted when the purpose for which private property is taken is private, such as General Motors' economic advantage. Nothing in the Fifth Amendment of the U.S. Constitution authorizes such use of the "takings clause." When interpreted honestly, the *eminent domain* tradition concerns the need of governments to do their business: build courthouses, police stations, prisons, military facilities, roads, and so on. *None of this implies the government's right to use eminent domain to favor special groups, especially at the expense of other special groups* (as when it was, in this case unsuccessfully, used by Donald Trump to obtain, in 1998, a private home in Atlantic City the owner of which didn't choose to sell to Trump who wanted to build a casino on the site).

Those who complain about the Poletown incident are not likely to object in principle to the use of *eminent domain* in this way by the government. That is, those critical of the Poletown incident would not object to the government's taking private property for such *private* uses as building museums, swimming pools, parks, and so on. What they deplore is the use of *eminent domain* that favors business! After all, business is not among the privileged groups that supposedly have the "right" to such special favors.

A genuinely free society that conformed to the spirit of the Fourteenth Amendment to the U.S. Constitution would guarantee all citizens, including their various associations, clubs, corporations, teams, and the like, equal protection under the law. It would follow, then, that no particular group(s) would be entitled to special assistance, subsidies, exemptions, and so forth. This would be possible, of course, only if the law protects only our negative rights—to life, liberty and property—rather than protecting such entitlements (i.e., special privileges) as funds or property that will enhance our private projects. But once such positive benefits are collected from citizens and made available for distribution, there is no logical, rational limit that could be placed before any group seeking to obtain them. Now those in business certainly see themselves as having significant goals that should qualify them for some of the benefits of wealth redistribution. Once the doors are open to special pleading, they should be open to all, including those in business. But opening the doors at all is a violation of due process and an invitation to abuse.

Without question, General Motors should not have been allowed to make use of the Fifth Amendment takings clause for its economic purposes. Nor should others be able to for their particular objectives, whether these are scientific, artistic, educational, or athletic (think of the costly stadiums erected by cities at other people's expense). Yet no one makes movies about how evil these groups are when they act precisely as General Motors did in Poletown!

To show the Poletown film in a business ethics class as an example of the political power of corporations (and, by extension, of the corruption of American business generally), without offering a principled and fair-minded discussion of the issues involved, amounts to shallow, uncritical, and unscholarly propagandizing. It is not worthy of being called "education." Those producing and disseminating such material are complicit in the undermining of the free market system of economics, the most productive and just method of providing much of what human beings need and want from life. It is hardly surprising news that businesses take advantage of the opportunity to secure special favors from government: What group does not?

This is not to say that the practice of seeking and gaining special protection from government is acceptable since in principle it is not, even if it is in fact a common practice. The point is that those who criticize business for doing this voice no objections whatever to other groups of citizens who are doing exactly the same thing! Do the critics protest when educators seek government funds for projects the public evidently does not wish to finance? What about artists, including museums, community theater and symphony groups, painters, poets, and so on who clamor for state help for their projects, even though such "help" consists of funds expropriated from citizens, not gained from voluntary giving?

The problem with the academic spin on the Poletown affair isn't that General Motors acted innocently but that the matter is presented in such a lopsided manner, as though General Motors (and business generally) is in some sense uniquely guilty of taking advantage of *eminent domain* and wealth redistribution.

WHY BUSINESS IS MALIGNED

Why is business bashing such a common phenomenon in university departments of philosophy and even in business schools? Why does business get such bad press?

Some people say that the reason is envy: Business succeeds at making life enjoyable for many people, especially those who read the market right, something others begrudge. This is the view expressed in Helmut Schoeck's famous book *Envy* (1957) and Ludwig von Mises's *Anti-Capitalist Mentality* (1956). Others point to the dislike and distrust of economic power, which can often be used to exploit innocent and helpless folks. There is also the view that business brings this on itself by using a double standard—appealing to free market principles when engaging in commerce but then calling on the state for assistance in times of hardship, as when Lee Iacocca asked the federal government to bail out Chrysler when it faced economic disaster.

These explanations are not fully convincing. The envy premise, for example, ignores the many areas of life wherein people are excellent and successful but are not so righteously envied and denigrated as are their counterparts in the business world. Without suffering the spiteful envy aimed at those who excel in business, people win Nobel Prizes, become top entertainers and champion athletes. Rather, the public tends to recognize them as morally legitimate accomplishments, as admirable, rather than bad-mouthing them and singling them out for higher taxes. The economic power premise overlooks the fact that power has many sources, some more and some less popular than others.

In lamenting economic power, we are already betraying our distrust of economics. What kind of power is this? Generally, it is power gained from others having found one's products or services sufficiently valuable to part with their own wealth so as to obtain them. If the wealth gained is not used criminally, it should not be reproached. But when politicians are induced to dispense special privileges, so that the money contributed to their campaigns buys not goods or services but decisions made against others in one's own favor, then economic power becomes corrupt.

Consider the power that comes from being famous in the various nonbusiness areas of life, such as entertainment, athletics, news broadcasting, television hosting, and so: Oprah Winfrey, Phil Donahue, Cindy Crawford, Michael Douglas, Walter Cronkite, and Michael Jordan, to name but a few. No one complains that these people have power, evidently because they came by their power in worthwhile, morally acceptable ways. In short, they are perceived as having earned their power, as somehow deserving it.

In contrast, business is suspect because its objectives and means are thought to be questionable: seeking wealth outright by "exploiting" people's desires, wishes, dreams, and, worst of all, their hopes for some pleasure in life. These desires and so on are themselves viewed with considerable disdain. Thus, the power of business is under a cloud, and it is widely believed that public policy ought to be forged to curtail it, regardless of whether the power is exercised for good or ill—consider the treatment of Microsoft, as an example.

Concerning the willingness of business to turn to the state, though this is deplorable, analyzing the present-day context in which this occurs can be enlightening. Nearly every identifiable group in our society today appeals to government for assistance with its special interest project. If government advances ecological interests, this is deemed honorable. If artists are given support, few ethicists object. Nor are the ethicists themselves disdainful of taking a few thousand dollars in support of their next ethics book (e.g., from the National Endowment for the Humanities). Since business cannot continue without making a profit, if public policy is such that brokers, money managers, investors, and so on will lose unless they heed the policy, business is effectively coerced to operate according to government policy. Thus, antitrust suits, subsidies, protection measures, and the like are nearly unavoidable means of remaining viable in business, despite their corrosive effect on the integrity of the institution.

On examination, then, the standard explanations for why business is not respected are not fully satisfactory. There is a more fundamental reason, an ancient one, which comes from some of the most honored philosophers, Plato in particular and, to a lesser extent, Aristotle.[15] Plato's Socrates is otherworldly in his view of

15. We have considered earlier that it is Plato's and Aristotle's explicit

what is truly noble in reality, while Aristotle merely singles out the intellectual parts of human life as deserving of high honors. This suggests that things associated with the satisfaction of our animal nature, or physical selves, should be regarded as a means, not an end.

We have seen that many of the major philosophers and theologians in the history of Western philosophy are largely responsible for promulgating the dichotomy of human existence and the denigration of our worldly nature. The attitude that motivates business bashing is intellectually rooted in that form of dualism, which subordinates so-called worldly matters to the ideal realm of reality. We should briefly reiterate this point.

In idealism, ideas, spiritual things occupy a higher, more important, and even separate realm than do the things of nature. According to dualism, reality consists of two major elements: the natural, or material, and the spiritual, or intellectual. Many of the major philosophers who embraced dualism placed the intellectual or spiritual on a higher plane. This is especially so of those who have devoted much of their philosophical energies to ethics or morality. In part, the reason for this is that, since the sixteenth century, a predominantly naturalist philosophical system would have excluded free will, an essential presupposition of ethics.

To the extent that they believe human beings to be composed of both the intellectual (spiritual) and the physical (natural) elements, these philosophers usually honor the intellectual element of human life. Indeed, in Aristotle's ethics, the truly happy life is

---

questioning of the merits of wealth and, indeed, commerce itself, that is largely responsible, given comments in Plato's *Republic* and Aristotle's *Nicomachean Ethics*. That seems a minor source of lamentation about these issues. Far more important is Plato's (wholesale) and Aristotle's (partial) denigration of the kind of human life that seeks the kind of happiness that is achievable on earth. Both philosophers, not to mention subsequent followers, especially in theology, seem to consider success in a merely natural life either base or lacking significance.

one lived entirely in terms of one's intellect.[16] This is the contemplative life. In Plato's moral and political philosophy, it appears that those people with highly developed intellectual skill are the superior, more ethically worthy ones. Others acquire moral standing in proportion to how much their work is related to ideas or ideals. Thus, scientists, soldiers, and statesmen would be higher on the chain of being than those involved in trade. The latter scarcely qualify for moral praise since their work mainly concerns the crude appetites; they are, as it were, servants of our drives and instincts, our lower or beastly selves. However, the others are regarded as excellent and accorded the role of leadership and guidance in society.[17]

Subsequent Western philosophy followed this lead. It is arguable that, because of this attitude, the biblical claim that a camel can more easily pass through the eye of a needle than a rich man can enter the kingdom of God has been interpreted as a denigration of wealth seeking per se. And Jesus' extreme anger and violence toward the moneylenders using his church also makes good sense in this context. Although one may be sure that churches were used by other professions or were home to the practice of other vices, including various irreverent and irrelevant conduct, we have no evidence of Jesus striking out against these.

These popular religious readings express a denigration of prosperity and wealth seeking. Consider, as well, the long-standing prohibition against usury, those acts of financing that laid the economic foundation for modern near-capitalist Europe. The attitude was, and continues in some circles to be, that making money lending money is against human nature and contrary to our true selves.

16. Aristotle, *Nicomachean Ethics*, book 10, 7, 1177b 18–21.

17. This, of course, is the general substance of Plato's *Republic*, as ordinarily interpreted.

Generally speaking, at only one time in Western philosophy did we escape this way of thinking. A radical swing in the opposite direction took place with Thomas Hobbes's utter materialism. An enthusiastic follower of Galilean physics, and a spokesperson for science in general, Hobbes basically denies the spiritual or intellectual realm.[18] According to Hobbes and his followers, everything is matter in motion and everything can be explained and understood in terms of physics. Hobbes's philosophy, embraced by many others of that era, including Francis Bacon, was a reaction of sorts, swinging from idealism and dualism over to pure materialism.

Assuming that we take reality to be of two spheres, and that we designate one to be divine or spiritual, it is no surprise that those who attend to our natural wants and needs, to our earthly existence, would not be highly honored, and may even be held in moral suspicion, for diverting our attention from the truly important. This parallels the kind of suspicion aimed at human sexuality throughout the ages. It has been thought of as a base activity, necessary but ignoble.

In our time, an additional factor relevant to the centuries-long prejudice against business must be considered. Given the brief uplift afforded by the materialist philosophy of Hobbes and his followers, including the political economists of classical liberalism, the reputation of business has actually made some gains, at least on certain practical fronts.[19] Commerce has at least become legitimized: Some of the severe disdain toward it, which once

18. The history of this is widely discussed. See, for example, Wallace I. Matson, *A New History of Philosophy* (San Diego, Calif.: Harcourt Brace Jovanovich, 1987).

19. Hobbes and others, including Bacon and Machiavelli, ushered in a serious and nearly exclusive concern for human life in the material realm, fostering those intellectual disciplines concerned with practical matters such as political science and economics.

took the form of an outright ban on much of what now passes for business, is no longer institutionalized. What remains is a moral suspicion toward business, which, unfortunately, has fed into the legal mechanism such that business has descended nearly to its earlier status of disrepute. From an initial flirtation with laissez-faire systems that promised to establish the principles of freedom of conduct within commerce, we are now witnessing a slow reactivation of the earlier mercantilist systems whereby business must be carried out or guided by the state.

WESTERN LIBERALISM UNDER ASSAULT

Ironically, this attitude toward business weakens the West's ability to teach the newly emerging Eastern European and many African countries how to recover from the horrors of socialist (or colonial) economic mismanagement. The possibility of a moral high road for capitalism has been undermined, and only half-hearted support can be heard from Western leaders.

None of this is new. It isn't just today's *Newsweek* or tomorrow's rerun episode of *Dallas* or next term's business ethics courses that perpetuates this rather sorry rejection of business as a respectable enterprise. Rather, such an attitude arises from the fundamental confusion that human nature can be divided, that one part of our being is far nobler than the other, and that our lower nature must be pushed back so that we can flourish as the fully spiritual beings that we truly are.

Not every major ancient philosopher adhered to this radical division. (Aristotle begins, perhaps, a trend toward moderation in this area, and Democritus actually leans very close to Hobbesian reductionist materialism.) But with the rise of Christianity the idea of the divided self becomes predominant in Western culture. Socrates expressed the theme of this fundamental confusion by saying that all of life on this earth is really just a preparation for death and that death is when we join our truly spiritual selves as we abandon our natural, material selves.[20]

In this kind of intellectual atmosphere, those who strive to make a prosperous, successful, material, natural living possible for us, those who serve us in shops, markets, and warehouses, rather than churches, universities, or museums, are bound not to enjoy honor and respect. It does not matter that some of them seek their own self-improvement in this regard—after all, many saints strove for personal salvation, many artists, for self-expression, and many scientists, for knowledge of truths that interested them alone. The difference here is that business aims at well-being here on earth and in this life.

It is interesting to note, finally, some of the practical policy consequences of the widespread scorning of business. Consider how throughout history the people who have been alien to a culture, and thus could not participate in their own traditions, often had little recourse but to join the business or financial class. In Europe, these were very often Jews, though elsewhere other ethnic or racial groups played the same role.[21] At first, these aliens were demeaned, and, later, when the practical value of their work was undeniable, they became the object of hateful envy. In some cases, their final end was extermination.

ANTIBUSINESS FROM RIGHT AND LEFT

Thus far, the thesis being offered is that, though many factors contribute to the shabby treatment of business in our culture, the

20. See Plato's *Apology*. Some argue that in Socrates' view this idea is but a myth, not to be taken literally. Yet its influence cannot be underestimated.

21. See again, for a good historical sketch, Thomas Sowell, "Middleman Minorities," *American Enterprise*, May/June 1993, pp. 30–41.

most fundamental relate to our basic ideas about human nature and moral ideals. These ideas are more influential in the shaping of our lives than, for example, our economic motivations or ethnic loyalties. No doubt there are some difficulties with the thesis being advanced. For instance, one might argue that the left's contemporary doctrine, Marxism, is an exception to this analysis; after all, isn't Marxism a materialistic philosophy that simultaneously denigrates business? This challenge deserves a response.

Marxist materialism is a peculiar kind—it is *dialectical* materialism, which adheres to the notion of a firm hierarchy of nature. In Marxism, as in more explicitly idealistic philosophies, intellectuals tend to be at the top of the hierarchy of social human life. Those who engage in intellectual labor are regarded as of higher caliber than those who do menial work. Indeed, one of the functions of capitalism in Marxist philosophy is to eventually eliminate menial labor and to prepare us for pure intellectual labor in a communist society.

Furthermore, according to Marxism, until humanity is rewarded for its labors sometime in the future, we are supposed to wait and be servile. Despite its historical association with violent revolutionary action, Marxism actually confines individuals to actions determined by the dynamics of their class membership. When the promised future does arrive, most of the work of humanity will be intellectual, for capitalism will have created the machinery to do tedious work. Marxism also holds that capitalists produce for the masses what those masses ignorantly want, thus engendering market anarchy rather than a rational economic order. However, a rational order would produce what is "right," aside from basic necessities: those goods and services arising from our intellectual talent, such as musical composition and philosophical criticism.

What we have seen thus far is that the widespread denigration of business has underlying intellectual roots that are historically deep and culturally pervasive, extending to how business ethics is treated at our colleges and universities. The fundamental mistake of this intellectual view is the division of human nature into separate selves and the resulting failure to think of a human being as an integrated unity, an entity that needs to be cared for and honored in its entirety.

From a moral point of view, to be prudent or conscientious about one's life involves seeing to one's complete well-being. Clearly, this is acknowledged in our care for the many aspects of our health as we champion the well-rounded individual. Strictly speaking, the flaw is not that our predominant intellectual view is completely mistaken; rather, it is one-sided: our attitude is not uniformly anticommerce or antibusiness but fundamentally ambivalent. In the main, because of our schizophrenic intellectual heritage, we tend to both welcome and demean commerce in human life. In general, as we grant the health professionals honorable standing (possibly because they derive from *theoretical* science), we withhold it from business, though our reason for honoring health professionals applies equally to business. Professionals in business attend to some of the legitimate purposes of life, generally construed as the securing of prosperity. Although this may not be sufficient to a fulfilled and successful life, it certainly seems to some degree to be necessary for happiness. Thus, since their profession addresses the various aspects of the essence of human life, it deserves all the honors extended to educators, doctors, scientists, lawyers, and politicians.[22]

22. Arguably, though, since commercial and business endeavors tend to reap their rewards directly in the marketplace, public acknowledgment may not be missed very much. It is more a matter of the general moral psychology of the situation that is of importance, even though this is not without its particular impact for those embarking on commerce and business, whose general sense of what they are doing tends to be cynical, self-mocking.

When we teach business ethics to students who aspire to the profession, we ought not denigrate their goals or make them feel ashamed. Rather, they should be guided in how to perform this honorable activity in a way fully compatible with the basic moral requirements of a human life. Further, it should be made clear to them that when some moral point of view appears to denounce their profession, that moral point of view may be in error. Students should be encouraged to struggle with these difficulties, to accept them as challenges, rather than being indoctrinated to believe that business must be at fault.

There is nothing peculiar about telling businesspeople that while they are engaged in business they ought also to be responsible, to be concerned with being a good parent or citizen. Such reminders do not denigrate the profession. But if the message is "Well, you may do business, but only because it's a necessary evil," we do everyone a great disservice. Yet this is precisely the message conveyed all the way from TV sitcoms to the classrooms of the Harvard Business School. Such is the confusing moral climate in which we live.

Consider the paradoxical and disturbing result of all this. In such a climate of ambivalence, it is difficult to induce people in business to seriously concern themselves with behaving properly, given how utterly confused they must be about moral issues and the mixed messages that our society is sending about business and commerce. Since business professionals tend to be viewed in many contexts as exploiters, misers, greedy callous people who lack the capacity qua professionals to act morally, it's no wonder that business ethics courses often resemble preaching to sinners, admonishing them to repent and change their ways.

Once an activity is deemed inherently wrong, one can hardly hope to upgrade it or ennoble it; the best one can do is to attempt reform and to issue stern warnings. This explains much of why business ethics courses are typically taught as they are, with an emphasis on the evils of commerce and a suspicion of behavior motivated by pursuit of profit. Students of such courses thus enter the business world with a sense of moral confusion about the very nature of their profession; the well from which they are about to drink has been poisoned. How can business professionals take pride in their accomplishments when the culture they serve does not honor their practice? This is most clearly evident, ironically, when a business professional excels: The very fact of success within business is itself suspect, often taken as proof that one has cheated!

Business is thought of as a rather shady practice, different in degree, not in kind, from trading in the black market or participating in "organized" crime. Oddly enough, some members of the business community itself contribute to this perception. Business-bashing television programs such as *Quincy, Dallas*, and *ER* are sponsored by corporations. Consider also the popular prime-time sitcoms, often with antibusiness themes or characters who play bosses or managers who lack compassion and generosity and are otherwise of questionable character. Rarely, if ever, is the hero or heroine a sympathetic employer whose employees steal from the company, are undependable and generally disreputable, though in reality more than a few employees are exactly so. Again, major corporations fund these programs, evidently without realizing that they are paying to have their own reputations smeared! The same can be said of many publishers (businesses) that publish textbooks and other works depicting business as morally bankrupt, a common character being the corporate executive or business magnate who is shown advancing his economic objectives without moral concern for others.

Would hospitals employ people whose explicit aim was to undermine health? Do universities openly champion ignorance and stupidity? Do priests, rabbis, and ministers usually preach sermons favoring atheism? And yet business often acts without regard to its own well-being and moral reputation. Some would say that this is because such ventures are profitable, thus proving how morally shallow the business mentality is since it sacrifices its own reputation for the almighty dollar.

All this no doubt has had disastrous implications beyond what we have suggested, affecting our society psychologically, morally, culturally, and economically. On the one hand, judging from the considerable attention devoted to commerce, business, and the economy by the news media alone, business is undeniably a significant aspect of our lives. On the other hand, the very people on whom this attention is focused, the ones who figure prominently in these news stories, cannot take full pride in their activity, unlike their counterparts in the other professions.

BUSINESS CAN AND SHOULD
BE ETHICAL

Those relatively few professors of business ethics who discuss all these issues in class without an antibusiness bias no doubt have a different experience from that described by Etzioni, who deplored the response of his students at the Harvard Business School. Etzioni took his experience as evidence that those inclined toward business lack moral concern. On analysis, what it actually shows is that treating students disrespectfully (by, in this case, denigrating their career choice) is bound to backfire. It is understandable that these students found themselves resisting "business ethics," given how it was presented to them.

Consider how MBA students would respond to a business ethics class were the instructor to treat their profession as respectable and, with that assumption, to go on to explore the various problems of ethics that might arise in business. Within this perspective, there would be nothing untoward in raising the possibility of unjustified dishonesty in advertising, in unjust discrimination in employment and promotion, in the possible problems and injustices related to nepotism, in the moral complications involved in trading with foreign colleagues who adhere to morally insidious standards, or in the responsibility of business professionals to consider the moral implications of the environmental consequences of commerce and industry. Indeed, in the proper scholarly context of unbiased investigation, business students, as do students of other disciplines when they are encouraged and feel free to think, will (and do) respond intelligently, thoughtfully, and with appropriate moral seriousness.

It is hardly a surprise that the Harvard MBA students found Etzioni's approach to teaching business ethics offensive. His message was that their goals were basically contemptible, that their chosen profession is lamentable and by its nature precludes the possibility of leading a decent human life. This quasi-Marxist notion, that capitalism is a necessary evil, a deplorable but passing period of humanity's development, has unwittingly overtaken our universities as an outcome of much of Western intellectual history.

BUSINESS VERSUS
PROFESSIONAL ETHICS

One of the standard charges aimed at commercial newspapers and magazines is that their reliance on advertising prevents their being objective in reporting on and discussing matters related to business. Less noticed, but logically equivalent, is that noncommercial educational, scholarly, and scientific enterprises are just as vulnerable to bias. If they accept support from the government or other subsidizing agencies, how can they report objectively or critically on matters relating to public policy, government regulations, political activity, and other related matters? Organizations such as PBS, National Public Radio, and our public schools and universities, all funded by taxes and grants from various government agencies, are vulnerable to possible conflicts of interest.

The ethics of journalism and publishing requires honest and unbiased reporting on matters of significance to readers. This seems to be a fundamental ethical principle inherent in the purpose or function of journalism. Anything less would be a violation of professional duties.

Scholarship is equally constrained. Of course, in some cases journalistic posturing is mere sham, as in trade publications such as the education profession's *Chronicles of Higher Education* and IBM's in-house magazine *Think*. But these publications are so patently partisan, propagandistic, and given to special pleading that few people expect adherence to the standards of journalistic ethics. They may be unexceptionable in their own right, bound perhaps to the ethics of advertising or advocacy but hardly guided by the ethics of journalism.

Nor do we normally regard government publications as models of objectivity, even those of the U.S. Information Agency, which is supposedly dedicated to informing the deceived of the truth about America. Here, something akin to propaganda is clearly at work, making a breach of journalistic ethics a moot issue.

In contrast, responsible professional conduct by bona fide journalists and scholars has its obstacles. In particular, advertisers are generally thought to be capable of intimidating a paper or magazine by threatening to withdraw their advertising. But there is a further charge: When a publication is owned by some huge corporation, one involved in international business or political affairs, it is argued that the publication will not be free to objectively report on and discuss matters of vital global, diplomatic, or military interests in print. Indeed, those who attempt to justify censorship in countries such as Israel, Mozambique, and China usually claim that the idea of a free Western press is a myth since corporate ownership skews journalistic focus. One cannot effectively defend freedom of the press simply by denying this claim; a sophisticated political analysis is required to rescue freedom here.

However, nonprofit publications face a similar conflict of interest. Such publications are supported by foundations, among which many are well-established and less-than-neutral private groups such as the Ford, Rockefeller, Earhart, Olin, or Carnegie Foundations, which are overseen by numerous prominent individuals, some of whose ideological and business commitments are far-reaching. Influential organizations such as government bodies include the navy or the National Endowment for the Humanities.

It is not difficult to imagine the emergence of a news item or topic of significance involving a foundation that supports a magazine or broadcast project. The well-known interview program *Firing Line* is sponsored by several major corporations, and its host, William F. Buckley Jr., could well find himself with a guest whose book is a sustained, serious, and telling attack on one of these corporations. *Ms.* magazine receives foundation support, as do various progressive, libertarian, conservative, and other publications, programs, and projects. Indeed, virtually all centers or institutes devoted to the study of professional ethics, business ethics, values and society, and the like receive support not only from foundations and corporations but very often from governments as well. Countless scholarly papers devote their first footnote to expressing gratitude to the Lilly Foundation, the Rand Corporation, the National Science Foundation, the National Endowment for the Humanities, or some other private or government body for funds that made possible the research that led to the piece. Consider the troublesome conflict that could arise for the scholar in some instances were he or she to focus attention on the source of the support. In fact, and fortunately, anything along these lines is quite rare.

There is a telling distinction between private and government support. The presumption is that private support is voluntarily given and not expropriated from the donor; the opposite presumption attaches to government support. For the moment, let's ignore arguments favoring the view that tax-supported projects are voluntarily financed.[23] For our purposes, it is enough to note the origins of taxation: the extraction of wealth from people denied the right to own property, with no alternative but to rent and work the land of others and paying for this from their meager income. In short, taxation is a feudal institutional arrangement that largely negates or undermines private property rights, even as it evolved into the modern era.

In any case, the distinction between taxes and voluntary funding has an interesting ethical dimension. Special problems arise associated with the advocacy of government funding, a form of incitement to state violation of individual rights. These problems are issues of political ethics and as such are not our concern here; our focus is on the professional ethical problems related to corporate and foundation funding of journalism and scholarship. We should now examine the charge that these create conflicts of interest and other thorny problems.

The main response has two parts. First, the most important thing for consumers of publishing (in journalism or in scholarship) is the existence of a free, competitive market. Since practitioners of these professions will doubtless often refuse to undermine their own enterprise so as to scrutinize the misdeeds of their funders, the consumer has to rely on the existence of an open

23. During the Clinton administration's reign in Washington, around April 15, 1994—the filing day for income tax reports—the commissioner of the Internal Revenue Service made such a claim.

market of ideas. It is reasonable to assume that the various members of the free press are not altogether at liberty, if they wish to remain alive. Even that impeccable organ the *Wall Street Journal* would have some trouble directly attacking Dow Jones, even if its editors felt journalistically justified. The *Journal* is required to print all of the parent company's news releases—verbatim![24] One might have expected such an eminent and secure publication to enjoy more autonomy than that.

In any case, the consumer is clearly best off in a free, capitalist society because competition ensures a variety of sources. If one broadcast network will not report a damaging story about, say, its parent company's president, another likely will. In this context, the main danger to the consumer, then, is a legally protected monopoly or oligopoly. And, as an elementary knowledge of economics will reveal, monopoly and oligopoly are much more likely in an economy with extensive government intervention than in competitive or free markets.

The second point concerns practicing scholars and journalists. That the consumer is protected from monopoly does not permit a professional succumbing to pressure. If a major funding agent for the scholarly or public policy foundation does something relevant to the concerns of the scholars or researchers, should not the organization study and report on it?

We should note here that although professional ethics, narrowly focused, is just as objective a code of conduct as one should expect of a sound ethical system, it is not at the same level of fundamentality as the basic ethical principles that everyone should invoke. A principle of professional ethics is not on the order of an absolute moral principle or categorical imperative. For instance, professional ethics are contingent on the impact

24. This information came from someone who was employed by the *Wall Street Journal.*

that adherence to the more general and fundamental moral principles will require of a person.

This may be illustrated with business ethics, wherein the defining purpose and moral responsibility of an executive is to further the economic well-being of his or her firm. But since this executive, as a person, can also be a citizen, a friend, a parent, and a spouse, other moral responsibilities and concerns should also guide his or her conduct. Exclusive devotion to work would be irresponsible since parenthood requires attention to one's children, as do friendship, marriage, and other personal and social nonprofessional relationships and commitments pose responsibilities. Put generally, and perhaps somewhat commonsensically, living well requires, among other things, finding the proper balance among one's concerns, needs, desires, and responsibilities. This principle can be found in all of the wisdom literature of the world.

The same applies to journalism or scholarship. One may find an interesting story concerning a major supporter, but if publishing it would be suicidal to one's livelihood, it would be prudent to refrain. However, should the story be sufficiently vital, wisdom may call on one to inform a competitor. Total silence could be immoral, especially if the story itself involves immorality: for example, the funder is betraying someone or violating a moral value, an ethical precept, or a just law. In other words, at a certain point one may have to forgo the benefits of support for moral reasons, including reasons directly related to the performance of one's profession (e.g., if one discovers that the funder has embezzled the funds that it contributes or is making demands on the journalist or scholar that would require betraying professional ethics).

As with most ethical problems, the difficulties presented by an actual conflict of interest are often complex and made up of unique and subtle details that would require reflection, analysis, and deliberation before a proper moral solution were found. We can only speak generally and offer hints in an abstract discussion. To assume or expect otherwise and to think that real moral problems can be solved apart from the actual concrete situations within which they arise is ignorance at best and irresponsibility at worst. Some formal and general considerations are relevant to all real moral problems, but these abstractions alone are rarely sufficient for solving any but the most simple moral conflicts. One ought always to consider the details.[25]

It should be stressed here that the principles that apply specifically to professional ethics are not the general and fundamental principles that a sound moral theory will propose for virtually every situation encountered in life. Rather, these principles are hypothetical: If you are in these situations, then act in such a such a way! Principles of professional ethics, such as those of journalism, are not like the general prohibition against murder or theft; they more resemble edicts about therapist-client or doctor-patient relationships. In most cases, the right thing to do will require examining a rich context of background information. The charge that a potential conflict of interest makes the practice of a profession inherently problematic is false. It is a reckless charge often issued by business bashers whenever economic interests are involved in some undertaking. But conflicts of interest are an inevitable part of any ordinary person's life, and economic interests are relevant to virtually every aspect of life, not just to business professionals.

Thus, even from this brief and necessarily sketchy discussion, it can be seen that conflict of interest cases may be properly

25. There are too many to list, but among the often discussed ones we find exposing smoking hazards in the face of heavy advertising revenues from tobacco companies; discussing sugar monopolies when one's publication depends on their support; television magazines' failure to discuss Sunday morning children's programming in the face of the networks' dependence on revenues from advertisers; and so on.

approached in a variety of ways, depending on the details, including simply shelving the problem or passing it on to those who can address the issue more effectively with less risk. The idea that martyrdom is morally necessary and necessarily noble is highly questionable and inconsistent with the goal of being successful at living a human life. From a moral point of view, it would be wrong to seek out and perform actions that lead to the destruction of one's values and projects, unless something fundamental were at stake. In such a case, one is still preserving the overriding personal value: one's integrity.

Journalistic or scholarly ethics requires no suicide. Certainly, courage requires taking some risks, weighing values, and choosing sides when conflicts occur. But courage is not the only virtue; prudence, moderation, thrift, honesty, and the rest are virtues as well. In general, an action cannot be regarded as courageous if it is performed in disregard of other virtues. With respect to living a life, each virtue must be given due consideration. Being successful in that undertaking is the ultimate moral responsibility of every human being and comes before the more specialized ethical responsibilities related to one's profession.

CHAPTER SIX

Individualism and Corporate Responsibility

CORPORATIONS AND RESPONSIBILITY

We may now be in a position to meaningfully ask the question, "What are the special ethics of business?" We needed first to see that business is not inherently corrupt, that it is a decent, upright profession, for an activity that is corrupt cannot possibly be carried out ethically. Thus, as long as business is deemed to be basically worthless or a necessary evil, there can be no such thing as business ethics, which explains the joke that "business ethics" is an oxymoron.

We can now raise the serious question of the social responsibility of business. Accordingly, we may conceive of the moral responsibility of business as including the practice of numerous virtues, including prudence, which implies the conscientious pursuit of profit, prosperity, commercial success. Professionals in business assume this responsibility partly as a matter of their job description but also as human individuals living in human communities.

In addition to prudence, business professionals are responsible for practicing all the other virtues that are applicable to human social life generally, such as generosity, charity, liberality, courage, civility, though prudence would naturally be the dominant virtue in their role as business executives.

In the context of commerce, prudence is referred to as "profit making"[1] and is the only virtue that Milton Friedman, prominent economist and founder of the Chicago School of Economics, acknowledges as the corporate officer's moral responsibility to stockholders or clients. This is implicit in his claim that the only moral imperative in corporate business is to earn a good return on the investments made in behalf of shareholders or clients. "In his capacity as a corporate executive, the manager is the agent of the individuals who own the corporation or establish the eleemosynary institution, and his primary responsibility is to them."[2] Now, if it is the case that executives ought to honor the promise that they make to the individuals who own the corporation, it follows that the purpose that gave rise to soliciting and to making the promise is morally acceptable. What purpose is this? None other than to prosper economically, to profit from the undertaking. Why else would anyone *invest* in a commercial enterprise?

1. This point is not noted by Friedman but is implicit in much of post-Kantian, contemporary moral philosophy wherein prudence is contrasted with disinterested moral motivation. Yet, from a non-Kantian (e.g., Aristotelian) ethical perspective, prudence is a moral virtue, albeit not the only or even primary one. In the jargon of economics much of prudential conduct pertaining to doing well in one's (earthly) life amounts to profit making. Another characterization of such conduct is the pursuit of prosperity or the maximization of utility. Unfortunately, within the literature of academic economics the concepts of profit, prosperity, and utility tend to be defined purely formally and in the framework of a subjective value theory. Prudence is admittedly tied to an objective conception of human well-being.

2. Milton Friedman, "The Social Responsibility of Business Is to Increase Its Profits," *New York Magazine*, September 13, 1970, p. 33. See also Milton Friedman, *Capitalism and Freedom* (Chicago: University of Chicago Press, 1961), pp. 133–36.

So the moral imperative of an executive ultimately stems from their clients' and their own prudent choices.[3]

Friedman has been criticized frequently for his narrow conception of the responsibility of corporate executives.[4] His critics argue that executives have much broader responsibilities than Friedman identifies.[5] Further, most critics seem to hold that such broader responsibilities conflict with Friedman's position and its implicit radical, Hobbesian or "atomistic" individualism.[6]

Admittedly, Friedman's atomistic individualism is radical and inadequate, but the broader understanding of corporations envisioned in this book does not support state regulatory enforcement of such responsibilities, contrary to what some critics of Friedman would expect. The alternative view that we propose would thus buttress the framework of the free market system that Friedman champions. It would also make a better case for the free market because it would demonstrate not only that free

---

3. Friedman does not explicitly connect the moral responsibility to prudence, only to the promise. But presumably the reason the promise needs to be kept in economic relationships is prudential. It was prudent for the two parties to have entered into such a relationship. In any case, we will be exploring the view conceived along such lines, regardless of what Friedman might say about the basis of the choice made by corporate executives for making their promises to shareholders to reap them financial benefits and the shareholders' promise to pay them for such work.

4. For a succinct example, see Norman E. Bowie and Ronald F. Duska, *Business Ethics* (Englewood Cliffs, N.J.: Prentice Hall, 1990).

5. Usually these involve so-called social responsibilities of corporations, although there need be no unanimity about what in particular these are. Among those often mentioned are the responsibility to care for the environment, to benefit employees, to consider the broader interests of customers, to enhance the local culture by various means, and so forth.

6. See, for example, Etzioni, *The Moral Dimension,* or Robert Bellah et al., *Habits of the Heart: Individualism and Commitment in American Life* (New York: Harper and Row, 1984). Of course, there is a long history of debate about whether American individualism is of the Hobbesian variety or not.

markets are efficient vehicles for prosperity but also that the pursuit of prosperity is *morally* commendable.

The alternative case may be summarized as follows: Instead of the narrow individualism implicit in Friedman's and many other economists' analyses (where individual interest is defined as maximizing one's utilities),[7] one may adopt a broader type of individualism that can appropriately be called "classical" individualism. Here is a brief description of that view, as expressed by Aristotle scholar E. Zeller:

> To [Aristotle] the Individual is the primary reality, and has the first claim to recognition. In his metaphysics individual things are regarded, not as the mere shadows of the idea, but as independent realities; universal conceptions not as independent substances but as the expression for the common peculiarity of a number of individuals. Similarly in his moral philosophy he transfers the ultimate end of human action and social institutions from the State to the individual, and looks for its attainment in his free self-development. The highest aim of the State consists in the happiness of its citizens. The good of the whole rests upon the good of the citizens who compose it. In like manner must the action by which it is to be attained proceed from the individual of his own free will. It is only from within through culture and education, and not by compulsory institutions, that the unity of the State can be secured. In politics as in metaphysics the central point with Plato is the Universal, with Aristotle the Individual. The former demands that the whole should realise its ends without regard to the interests of individuals; the latter that it should be reared upon satisfaction of all individual interests that have a true title to be regarded.[8]

7. A point that is in the end very difficult to render nonvacuous since perusing one's utilities can refer to nearly any activity, given the subjective utility theory most economists embrace.

8. E. Zeller, *Aristotle and the Earlier Peripatetics*, trans. B. F. C. Costelloe and J. H. Muirhead (London: Oxford University Press, 1897), pp. ii, 224–26

Once its details as a moral position are elaborated, classical individualism supports the idea that the dominant responsibility of economic agents, including corporations, is to flourish financially. And it does this without denying that many subsidiary responsibilities ought also to be fulfilled, some of which would benefit the community.

ANTI-INDIVIDUALISM IN BUSINESS ETHICS

Professional ethicists—especially those who teach business ethics—have often targeted ethical egoism (also known as classical individualism) for criticism. This is because most ethicists take the neo-Hobbesian position toward neoclassical economics as "the ethical individualist or egoist" foundation of the private property–based capitalist society that they find morally deficient.

Furthermore, neoclassical economics, which underpins free market capitalism, has always been closely associated with individualism. These economists argue that a society organized so that individuals may pursue their chosen goals and desires will produce the greatest good. This brings to mind Bernard Mandeville's motto "private vice, public benefit," echoed in Adam Smith's work as well as in much of the nontechnical renditions of neoclassical economics. Economists in this tradition argue that the overall social good is most efficiently promoted by means of the unimpeded selfish behavior of individuals.

(quoted in Fred D. Miller Jr., *Nature, Justice and Rights in Aristotle's Politics* [Oxford, England: Clarendon Press, 1995], pp. 200–201). For an individualist understanding of Aristotle's metaphysics, see Emerson Buchanan, *Aristotle's Theory of Being* (Cambridge, Mass.: Greek, Roman, and Byzantine Monographs, 1962). As he puts it, "in identifying ousia (Being) with [what it is for each thing to exist], Aristotle is asserting that the fundamental reality on which everything else depends is the existence of the individual" (p. 2)

Friedman's thesis about corporate social responsibility is indebted to this view. Thus, a belief in the compatibility of the public good and individual selfishness (meaning the fulfillment of one's desires and satisfaction of one's preferences) relies on a specific view of the human individual. We find it first spelled out in the individualism of the seventeenth-century English philosopher Thomas Hobbes, the first major modern materialist philosopher and forthright nominalist. Hobbes held that human nature does not exist independently of our minds and thus cannot be known objectively.[9] Rather, we have a metaphysics consisting of raw, barren, radical, or "atomic" particulars or individuals. Only particular things, not kinds or general classes, exist in reality. Thus, contra the classical view, there is no "human" nature, only pure particular individuals seeking gratification.

Hobbes's individualist social analysis was widely taken to be the application of the laws of mechanical motion to human life. Self-advancement or self-aggrandizement would occur mostly successfully if left unimpeded, just as classical physics holds that motion advances best in frictionless space. Applying this to social life, Hobbes believed that the laws of motion would initially lead to conflict, whereupon human intelligence would introduce social rules. This would improve on the "state of nature" by greatly increasing the chances of survival. Individuals would thereafter behave in an orderly fashion.

Echoing Hobbes, Milton Friedman holds that, so long as corporations "play by the rules," their responsibility is limited to fulfilling their promise to shareholders to invest their wealth prudently and profitably. This promise itself grows out of self-interested motives.

---

9. In our own time this doctrine is closest to the pragmatism of Richard Rorty. See Rorty, "Solidarity or Objectivity" in *Objectivity, Relativism and Truth*, pp. 21–34.

But Hobbesian individualism is not the only type that makes sense and also supports the classical liberal social order, including its economic system of laissez-faire capitalism. An alternative is classical individualism.[10] In this view an objective human nature provides moral guidelines to human conduct in all spheres: social, political, personal, and professional. Whereas Marx claimed that "the human essence is the true collectivity of man,"[11] classical individualism holds that *the human essence is the true individuality of every human being.*[12] This kind of individualism, or egoism, is plausibly sound and may be the best answer to the ethical question we all ask, "How ought I act?" or, "What responsible conduct am I to engage in?" or again, "How ought I live my life?"

If this individualism is sound, and if it supports the free market system, the case for capitalism will have been made. Classical individualism escapes the kind of objections that are leveled at the neo-Hobbesian individualist approach usually found in the economic defenses of the free market and its ethical dimensions. Friedman's position could be amended along classical individualist lines without greatly altering its implications, while allowing for a different ethical perspective on the issue of the responsibility of corporations.

The essential tasks of business are fully congruent with the

10. This idea develops Ayn Rand's initial sketch in her *The Virtue of Selfishness: A New Concept of Egoism* (New York: New American Library, 1964). See also Tibor R. Machan, *Classical Individualism* (London: Routledge, 1998).

11. Karl Marx, *Selected Writings*, David McLellan, ed. (Oxford: Oxford University Press, 1977), p. 126.

12. The most developed version of this type of individualism is found in David L. Norton, *Personal Destinies: A Philosophy of Ethical Individualism* (Princeton, N.J.: Princeton University Press, 1976). Earlier, Ayn Rand sketched a similar position in her various novels and in *The Virtue of Selfishness: A New Concept of Egoism* (New York: Signet Books, 1961).

general tenets of a sound professional ethics. By "professional ethics" is meant a code of conduct pertaining to a specialized field of activity and justified by sound ethical theory. By "business" we mean, of course, the organized endeavors and enterprises that have economic enhancement as their dominant end: in short, profit-making institutions.[13]

Many ethicists find it problematic to regard business as morally upright because of the profit motive or the economic self-interest that drives the profession of business. Consider, for example, the book mentioned earlier, *The Moral Dimension* by Amitai Etzioni, which advances a deontological ethical perspective on commerce. Deontological (post-Kantian) ethics takes an action to be morally proper only if it is motivated from pure duty, by a belief in a basic principle or goodness conceived as altogether unrelated to personal objectives, purposes, or desires.

WHY DEONTOLOGICAL ETHICS?

The deontological view of morality likely emerged because, under the influence of scientism, the objective of self-enhancement had been understood to be pursued automatically, instinctively. Such psychological egoism, as it has come to be called, originated with Thomas Hobbes. It views self-interested, profit-yielding conduct as innately driven, not as a matter of free choice or initiative. In exploring the nature of morality, Kant discovered that there is no room for significantly moral conduct within the framework of such mechanistic behaviorism. So Kant conceptualized—some might say invented—the noumenal realm, beyond the natural world, in order to make room for freedom, thereby making mo-

---

13. Here again by "profit" we do not have in mind some technical term defined in tax law or economics but the commonsense idea of prospering in one's ability to obtain goods and services for purchase in the marketplace.

rality possible. Kant thus advanced the quintessentially deontological ethics, in which only conduct unrelated to objectives, goals, or consequences can be morally significant. As a result, prudence was philosophically deprived of its status as a moral virtue, prudent conduct became morally irrelevant, giving birth to a conceptual contrast between prudent and moral motivation.

Additionally, when contemporary moral philosophers recovered substantive ethics, they rested it on intuitions. As it turns out, the intuitions of the bulk of academic philosophers have been altruistic and egalitarian. Among those who have professed to have such intuitions, John Rawls is perhaps the most prominent figure in philosophy and political theory.[14]

It is impossible to divorce commerce from its goals. People buy and sell to further their objectives, including their own enrichment or that of those they cherish. In the last analysis, commerce is clearly a self-interested practice, aiming at enrichment, whether at the individual or corporate level. In turn, the special occupation of business aims at providing the service of commercial expertise to those willing to pay for it. One invests in stocks, shares, partnerships, and other enterprises so as to increase one's wealth, to prosper. Business professionals provide the expert skills to facilitate these goals. They are thus professional profit makers.

It is not possible to reconcile this professional objective with a deontological ethics. The alternative ethics, the (Aristotelian) teleological view, is not deemed to be metaethically sound by many who work in applied ethics because of difficulties that they claim inhere in identifying any natural purpose or end in human life.[15]

---

14. See Machan, *Individuals and Their Rights*, where it is argued that intuitionism is methodologically deficient in part because it varies with the times and cultures and is likely based on prior education and osmosis.

15. This is itself probably related to the prominence of empiricist views of what counts as having correctly identified some general purpose. It is related even more fundamentally, to the very strict criteria for what it takes to know

Nevertheless, the teleological perspective is sound and supports the view that the profession of business is morally legitimate. This teleological view of moral rightness is comparable to how we regard a physician, attorney, teacher, scientist, or statesman as embarking on morally worthwhile tasks that further certain goals in life. The profession of business is similarly morally legitimate in serving a valuable goal that morally we ought to pursue, namely, prosperity.[16]

Deontological metaethics is deficient precisely because it rejects the connection between right conduct and certain natural ends such as happiness, well-being, and prosperity. There is simply no basis for divorcing ethics from our practical, goal-oriented human lives. Ethics is nothing else but a set of standards for trying to live a good human life, and a good human life must be identified by an understanding of human nature, one that is inescapably goal directed. Throughout life we are in search for guidance

---

something, that one has to be certain beyond a shadow of doubt before one can justifiably claim to know. Once these two elements of moral epistemology are altered, there is no problem with teleologically based ethics. See, for example, Machan, *Individuals and Their Rights*.

16. Perhaps one reason other professions than business can be viewed as having moral standing is that they are not directly or immediately related to self-interested objectives. Medicine or science in general, or education or art, can be viewed as having some kind of principled grounding, apart from its value to human individuals.

We should note here that having moral standing is different from being recognized for its utilitarian or practical value, even though morality itself cannot, in the last analysis, be in conflict with what is of utility or practical. But the latter are more limited: One can find utility in a good getaway car for the purposes of robbing a bank! What many fail to see is that having some admiration for business is not the same as having moral respect for it. And that the moral respect is lacking is obvious even on the part of the general public, which, after all, indulges in the offerings of writers of pulp novels and TV series in which people in business are invariably the bad guys.

as to which goals we should pursue, how we should pursue them, whether those we are inclined to pursue are worthy, and so on.

This understanding is not without controversy, but we contend that the classical definition of a human being as a rational animal is still fully defensible.[17] The idea that each person is a rational animal implies both that each of us has moral responsibilities to fulfill and that the standard of such responsibility is that everyone is a human individual. This supports the classical individualist position, in which the dominant goal (i.e., normative ideal) of everyone is to succeed as a human being, an individual.

IS BUSINESS MORALLY LEGITIMATE?

Before we apply this to professional ethics and more specifically to business ethics, we should note that any profession's moral legitimacy is open to scrutiny. Pacifists protest what they believe is the immorality of the military profession; Christian Scientists hold that physicians do the wrong thing; pro-lifers argue that abortionists are morally corrupt; many environmentalists condemn the practices of science, in particular animal research; and so on. Some professions seem to be at the brink of immorality, such as espionage, the questionable aspects of which are exploited to full measure by John Le Carré in his numerous novels, most notably *The Spy Who Came In from the Cold.*

Commonsense morality, the framework that tends to guide most people within a culture and that requires philosophical assistance only when dilemmas arise, views the profession of business as based on the virtue of prudence. Since classical times, prudence has been identified as the first of the cardinal virtues. It

---

17. Machan, *Individuals and Their Rights* and *Classical Individualism.*

requires that we take decent care of ourselves; recklessness, care-lessness, inattentiveness, and such are moral shortcomings.[18]

Two things are missing in the commonsense ethics. One is a clear idea of what the "self" is that requires prudence, that we ought to care for. An idealist (and dualist) conception of the self understands by "prudence" something less concerned with pros-perity here on earth than does a naturalist conception. If one sees human beings as essentially divided into two parts, one tied to this world and the other yearning for a supernatural dimension, then prudence will have different implications from a view that conceives of the self as part of nature alone.

Despite the promise of a life beyond our earthly existence, to see human beings as divided in the fashion envisioned by idealists and dualists is fraught with difficulties, both philosophical and practical. Suffice it to say here that persons are part of the natural world and that neither reason, observation, nor the common daily experiences of mankind attest otherwise. To place an uni-dentifiable part of human beings in some other realm of being defies common sense, and to offer "faith" as evidence seems at best to beg the question, if not to admit that evidence is lacking altogether. At very least, it makes little sense to disparage the natural, temporal, earthly life that we are certainly experiencing simply because one desires or hopes for or has faith in another life.

The second feature missing from commonsense morality is that it does not allow us to rank the moral virtues in terms of common sense alone.[19] This is where an ethical theory is required. Just as commonsense physics alone will not allow us to generate elec-tricity—a theory is required—so too in ethics, where challenging

18. Den Uyl, *The Virtue of Prudence.*
19. This is akin to our not understanding the structure of the physical world from simply experiencing that world by way of the normal use of our senses.

cases aren't decidable without a systematic ethical viewpoint. Classical individualism succeeds at serving this purpose of assisting commonsense morality when the going gets rough.

A moral perspective has a significant ontological feature that is applicable to evaluating the various professions people embark on; contrary to mechanistic materialism and its variants, there is no basis for precluding the possibility of free will in human life. Indeed, there is both philosophical and special scientific justification, beyond a reasonable doubt, to believe that human beings are able to initiate mental activity, to govern themselves.[20]

Furthermore, the neo-Hobbesian idea that we pursue our ends automatically, a view employed mostly in neoclassical economics and in behaviorist psychology, is riddled with difficulties, not the least of which is that applying this view to itself renders it meaningless. Instead of this reductionist approach, it seems more sensible to adopt a pluralistic ontology, which allows for different kinds and types of entities in nature. Within such a perspective the moral dimension of reality arises only in connection with certain kinds of entities. In particular, morality begins with living entities that have the faculty of choice and thus can govern their own conduct. This kind of entity brings into nature the problem of how such a being should act, how its living ought to be carried out.

Assuming that there is promise in classical egoism, what are its implications for professional ethics and for business ethics in particular? What a person ought to do in life includes taking care of his or her economic values, those objectives that enable one to obtain worldly goods, pleasures, joys, delights, and the like. Un-

20. Sperry, *Science and Moral Priority.* See also Tibor Machan, *The Pseudo-Science of B. F. Skinner* (New Rochelle, N.Y.: Arlington House, 1974), and *Individuals and Their Rights.*

like the familiar egoism seen in many ethics textbooks,[21] in classical egoism one strives to become as good a human being as the individual one is and doing so *involves many capacities to be realized in addition to economic ones*. Although it is vital to serve one's economic (more broadly, prudential) goals, even these can extend far beyond the mere satisfaction of desires. Given the classical individualist outlook, rather than being driven by desire, one's desires should be shaped by the vision one creates of oneself as the human being one can and would ideally become.

PROFESSIONAL AND SOCIAL RESPONSIBILITIES

The discussion in this section should not be confused with the Friedmanite thesis concerning the social responsibility of corporations. Rather, our focus is on the community and political dimensions of the individual that may require enhancement even in the course of conducting one's professional tasks. In the case of corporate business, for example, one may be morally responsible not only to reach one's economic objectives but also to realize various objectives associated with being a member of one's community. A business professional's life is, after all, no more or less compartmentalized than that of the other professions. Individuals are multifaceted; their lives include a wide range and variety of interests, objectives, desires, and so on, some of them overlapping, some conflicting. To think otherwise is to make the same mistake that the kindergartner makes when he is surprised to learn that his teacher doesn't live in the classroom.

Professional ethics involves determining the responsibilities

21. For a survey of these, see Tibor R. Machan, "Recent Work in Ethical Egoism," in Kenneth J. Lucey and Tibor R. Machan, eds., *Recent Work in Philosophy* (Totowa, N.J.: Rowman and Allenheld, 1982).

and restraints one needs to observe in relationship to the profession one has chosen to pursue. Yet, apart from one's professional responsibilities, there are other standards for conduct that may not be breached, standards that apply to living as a human being per se, as well as fulfilling various other roles one has in one's life and community. Accordingly, the conduct of corporate executives, managers, stockholders, and employees can be evaluated by the standards of ordinary morality as well as by the ethics specific to the profession of business.

As a case in point, it is clear that in advertising one could violate professional ethics as well as ordinary human morality by way of misguided promotional campaigns. For example, one could arguably criticize corporate officers for knowingly or carelessly targeting vulnerable, gullible groups of people with advertisements. If a cigarette company recklessly or deliberately aims its ads at teenagers, whose capacity for judging what they ought to purchase hasn't developed well enough to make an informed choice about whether to smoke, it is arguable that this is morally objectionable. So, too, if beer, wine, or spirits manufacturers or retailers target children or others who are especially vulnerable to influence and would be harmed by the purchase.

As we will see, none of this implies that such practices should be subject to bans or prohibitions but, rather, to criticism, social protest, and moral entreaty. It is one thing to identify some conduct as morally objectionable, quite another to prohibit it. Prohibition deprives the agent of the choice to do the right thing on her or his own initiative. Prohibition should be reserved for those actions that are directly injurious to others, for the more we prohibit, the less room there is for individual morality.

The point of Friedman's discussion is that no other moral "demand" may be made on those in corporate business than to fulfill their implied promise to their clients, a promise to secure for them the greatest possible economic benefits consistent with the law. This view accords quite well with the radical individualist conception of the human being, so that beyond the mere imperative of keeping a promise made in the service of one's self-interested goals, there is nothing one ought to do in one's capacity as a business professional.

Critics rightly see this as an impoverished conception of the bounds of professional ethics. However, the same critics then often go to the other extreme to embrace deontological communitarianism or altruistic ethics, suggesting that business can become moral only if it severely restrains itself from the pursuit of profit. This position narrowly conceives of making profit as the exclusive goal of business and then argues that business should be subordinate to whatever alternative need is evident in the community. Business ought to be tamed so as not to be pursued with the kind of rapaciousness that one associates with an innate drive for selfishness or profiteering.

In vivid contrast, the classical egoist position understands professional ethics to require that the dominant objective for a member of any profession is the conscientious performance of one's professional tasks. But this is not an exclusive objective, nor is it inconsistent with paying heed to other goals and commitments, such as the enhancement of one's community, the improvement of the environment, and the development of quality political institutions.

Interestingly, there is a dimension to the classical egoist ethics that resembles deontological ethics in terms of an absolute, universal, and inviolable element. This is the inestimable value of individual moral sovereignty, the role of the choices of the moral agent in the determination of conduct. Here is where fundamental individuality or selfhood enters the moral arena, by recognizing that it is the person, not others for that person, who chooses morally significant conduct.

Given this, the scope of legally enforceable moral responsibility within the classical individualist ethics is far more restricted than in alternative ethical and political systems. This perspective does not identify individuals as being naturally *connected* to society, in the way that, say, a team member is tied to the team or a business partner to the partnership. According to classical individualism such ties, even when essential and proper, must be chosen, not imposed by law. The law enters only when citizens are intentionally or negligently deprived of their sovereignty by others.

Thus, while the moral demands of classical egoism on those in various professions are greater than the demands advanced in Friedman's position, the political framework of business conduct implicit in this ethics is close to that advocated by Friedman, in that legal coercion is vigorously resisted. Thus, for example, although business ought to support the neighborhood so as to maintain or improve its quality, it ought not be forced to do so, any more than an individual ought to be forced. Such is the power and value of individual sovereignty.[22]

22. See Tibor Machan, *Individuals and Their Rights*, for a detailed explanation of why the moral dimension of human nature requires the classical liberal political framework. For a treatment of negative externalities such as air or water pollution, see Machan, "Pollution, Collectivism and Capitalism," *Journal des Economists et des Etudes Humaines*, pp. 83–102. For a treatment of the political status of children, see Machan, "Between Parents and Children," *Journal of Social Philosophy* 23 (winter 1992): 16–22. Some of the issues of this chapter bearing on the philosophy of the social sciences and the moral foundation of the free market system are discussed in Machan, *Capitalism and Individualism*. See also Machan, *Classical Individualism*.

CHAPTER SEVEN

The Right to
Private Property

On pain of living a life that's seriously immoral, a typical well-off
person, like you and me, must give away most of her financially
valuable assets, and much of her income, directing the funds to
lessen efficiently the serious suffering of others.
                                        —Peter Unger, *Living High and Letting Die:*
                                                Our Illusion of Innocence

WHY THE CONCERN WITH
PRIVATE PROPERTY?

The institution of the right to private property is perhaps the
single most important condition for a society if it is to be hospitable to business. There is no mystery about why Karl Marx put
the abolition of private property at the top of his list of revolutionary changes leading to his communist utopia.[1] Under communism we are all deemed to be one. Privacy has no place in a
system that holds, as we earlier noted Marx proclaiming, that
"the human essence is the true collectivity of man."[2] Thus, privacy is ruled out *by definition*. Stealing, robbery, burglary, em-
bezzlement, trespassing, not to mention borrowing, bequeathing,
giving, and the like are precluded where everything is the property
of everyone all at once! Instead, with respect to property, nothing

---

1. Marx emphatically denied that communism is a utopia or ideal. "We
call communism the real movement which abolishes the present state of things,"
a scientifically discoverable end of humanity's development. See Karl Marx,
Selected Writings, ed. D. McLellan (London: Oxford University Press, 1970),
p. 171.
   2. Ibid., p. 126.

would be untoward except the failure to share, to distribute fairly what is needed.

However, if we are fundamentally individuals, then communism is not right for us and the system of private property rights could well be the best system of political economy for human beings. It would be helpful here to reiterate a somewhat novel defense of property rights as understood within the framework of classical liberal political economy. Any work that attempts to establish the moral legitimacy of a profession must also show that the sociopolitical or legal preconditions of that profession have moral and political standing. For example, in order to defend espionage, one would have to show that secrecy is not always morally wrong; if one wanted to argue that soldiering is a morally defensible profession, one would also have to argue that some kind of military establishment is itself morally defensible.

This issue is crucial in a discussion of the moral status of commerce and business, as well as in the field of business ethics. Generally, free trade is predicated on the existence of a basic human right to private property: If one cannot own anything, one certainly may not trade anything. One would lack the authority to set terms of trade, prices, and so on. Furthermore, if all persons in society have this basic right, and if someone (or a group, a *company*) chooses to exercise that right by establishing a business firm, certainly many actions of the owner will be legally, if not always morally, justifiable. Thus, although it may be morally wrong for an employer to fire an employee at will, without cause, such conduct will not be subject to government regulation since that would amount to the violation of the right to private property. The only rebuke could be some form of peaceful protest such as a boycott, strike, public condemnation, and so on. In short, the employer's capricious conduct could not be officially censured, any more than could be the conduct of a pornographer or other perpetrator of some vice or, indeed, the conduct of an employee who quit at will without prior notice, leaving the employer at a great and perhaps undeserved disadvantage.

WHAT IS PRIVATE PROPERTY?

Karl Marx understood well the nature of the right to private property. In his essay "On the Jewish Question," Marx said that "the right of man to property is the right to enjoy his possessions and dispose of the same arbitrarily without regard for other men, independently, from society, the right of selfishness." This is correct but far from the whole story. The right to private property, whether it be a toothbrush or a factory, authorizes persons to use what they own as they see fit, without regard for other persons. This use may be reckless as well as prudent, provided it does not invade the rights of others.

The right to private property as a *natural* right was not discussed in such direct terms until the eleventh century. William of Ockham characterized natural rights as "the power of right reason," the power to make one's moral choices on one's own, free of others' intrusion. Since such choices are made by human beings within the natural world, it follows that one of our natural rights would have to be the right to private property, as John Locke later made clear.

Ockham's use of the term *natural rights* followed several centuries of unsystematic references to basic rights, which usually meant some area of personal jurisdiction, a sphere of privacy where the agent has full authority to choose what to think or do. Clearly, within an increasingly secular understanding of reality, the extension of basic rights to include private property rights was perfectly natural. The details may have been somewhat problematic and indeed remain so to date, but the basic notion held that the kind of being we are, namely, human (and thus possessed of personal authority or sovereignty) has the right to private property as a basic principle of his or her social existence.

ONE ROLE OF PRIVATE PROPERTY IN SOCIETY

Property rights may not have been explicitly identified as such in ancient times, although the Old Testament ban on stealing is not far from the doctrine as understood later by Locke and other classical liberals. Moreover, there have been strong philosophical intimations of it in, for example, the work of Aristotle. In his *Politics*, Aristotle addresses the question of the soundness of Plato's communism in the *Republic*. Plato held that at least within the ruling class of a political community, there may not be any private property and indeed privacy at all. Aristotle's objection goes as follows:

> That all persons call the same thing mine in the sense in which each does so may be a fine thing, but it is impracticable; or if the words are taken in the other sense, such a unity in no way conduces to harmony. And there is another objection to the proposal. For that which is common to the greatest number has the least care bestowed upon it. Every one thinks chiefly of his own, hardly at all of the common interest; and only when he is himself concerned as an individual. For besides other considerations, everybody is more inclined to neglect the duty which he expects another to fulfill; as in families many attendants are often less useful than a few. (*Politics*, 1261b34)

In short, communal ownership leads to reduction of responsibility and a corresponding lack of care for and attentive involvement with whatever is owned. Although Aristotle made this observation nearly twenty-five hundred years ago, its truth is evident today as we consider the condition of, say, public beaches or bathrooms or roadsides. On a U.S. public beach, where the tradition of public propriety is weak, litter flourishes.[3] This does not mean that people are evil. Some simply don't care and drop their trash where it's most convenient. Others may find themselves short of time and leave their trash scattered, without returning to clean it up, perhaps thinking, somewhat vaguely, that the mess will get cleaned up. At their home, this is likely to be quite different—if one is late and rushes off, the trash is there to be cleaned up on return. At a public place the attitude seems to be "It will get cleaned up somehow, by someone, at some time." So the issue isn't that people are generally lazy or careless, though they sometimes are. It is more of a systematic problem: People are unable to incorporate the significance of managing the public property within the scale of their values. It is difficult to assess what value it is to oneself that some public sphere receives one's care, whereas it is not a problem to place the significance of the management of one's private sphere within one's hierarchy of values.

More simply, each of us knows how important or not it is for oneself to keep one's backyard clean, so one will take care of it commensurate with that, but it is not possible for an individual to know how important it is for the community or society or for humanity at large that one keep the air or river or lake clean and to what degree. This is because values cannot be separated from those who are to benefit by them. The community is composed of individuals with a highly varied set of values, which depend not on the universal fact of what they are but on the more particular facts of who they are, what subgroups of human beings they belong to, and so on. There is no concrete universal com-

---

3. Europeans, in contrast, are more used to adhering to public discipline and so public order and neatness tend to be intact in most European communities. Yet, arguably, there is a price, namely, overall economic weakness, lack of private initiative, which may account for why the United States has been such an active provider of economic assistance throughout Europe and the world.

munity that might benefit, only individuals and the diverse groups to which they belong, not all of which share the same values. Where ownership is divorced from usage, control, or economic impact, care is nearly impossible to bestow.

CAN WE DO WITHOUT PRIVATE PROPERTY?

Some propose that all this can be avoided in a society in which public service is inculcated at an early age. It is, they might argue, a matter of education and training toward common values, not so much a fact of human nature or a basic feature of human psychology. However this may be, a program to educate (some would say indoctrinate) children toward an inclination to public service may come at the costly price of precluding other important alternatives as well as the misallocation of resources. The reformation of human nature is, in fact, the goal of some radical critics of the business culture of capitalism. They argue that human nature itself needs to be redirected so that the spirit of service, not profit, will motivate people. This view faces several challenges. First, service tends to be a weak motivator for long-range, complex objectives; second, service presupposes knowledge of what other persons would benefit from most, but such knowledge is less readily available than knowledge of what benefits oneself; and third, efforts to redirect the human spirit tend to be subverted to personal ends, which are then pursued without the constraints of individual rights, resulting in harm to others. This is clearly and dramatically exemplified in the major collectivist states of human history.

Aristotle's insightful observation, taking only a few lines in the *Politics,* was developed into a major thesis in the twentieth century by Garrett Hardin, in a previously mentioned essay. In short,

Hardin argues that common ownership leads to tragedy.[4] His example is a grazing area used by private citizens, owners of cattle. This area, belonging to everybody, is more likely to be exploited and abused than if it were privately owned because no one knows the limits of his or her authority and responsibility and will thus tend to use more than would be prudent relative to the general interest. And if not, all that it would take to bring the "commons" to ruins would be one or two participants who, even if they knew the proper limits, would ignore them thoughtlessly. To prevent this, strict regulations, backed by threat of serious sanctions, and accompanied by vigorous surveillance and enforcement, would be required.

Both Aristotle's and Hardin's theses point out a practical or utilitarian feature about what property rights do for human beings in societies. These rights place a limitation on what people may do and also on what may be done to them, producing an overall benefit. In other words, if one's predominant social concern were to maximize the net benefit for the most people, a policy issuing from respect for property rights would most likely satisfy that concern. Just as one's own backyard limits what one may do, thus confining one's good or bad activities, there is everywhere a practical use for the idea of private property rights. Private property rights provide the proper limits against those who would fail to act responsibly, while also promoting public welfare resulting from those who do act responsibly while exercising their rights.

It would appear, then, that avoiding the "tragedy of the commons" is at the very least a practical necessity for human social life. If human beings were omniscient and always acted from benevolent motives, perhaps there would be no such tragedy, for

4. Garrett Hardin, "The Tragedy of the Commons," *Science*, no. 162 (December 13, 1968).

we would know what ought to be done within the commune and we would be moved to do so. But we are in fact subject to error, to mistakes, to be motivated by less than moral drives, so it is vital to confine these mistakes within a sphere identifiable with the agent. If something is mine and I make a mistake with respect to that possession, then I should be the one who suffers the consequences of my mistake and so too with everyone else and his or her possessions. If we voluntarily pool our resources, as in a corporation, club, or family, then mistakes will overlap, but no one will be justified in complaining about it since we have freely chosen, consented, to enter that "community" or group.

BEYOND THE SOCIAL TO THE MORAL VALUE OF PRIVATE PROPERTY

Over and above practical benefits, private property rights can be shown to have significant moral implications. This is evident in the social world, where we live in the vicinity of strangers, other people with whom we often choose to interact even when they are not our intimates. Consider, by way of contrast, living alone on a desert island. Here, property rights would be of no significance, for no one could threaten one's authority over one's actions or one's relationship to the natural world. But if there is somebody else, as, for example, when Robinson Crusoe encounters Friday, both have the choice to do good or bad, and each may have an impact on the other. Under these conditions, the two must decide when they want to cooperate and when they do not.

If people are to act morally, everyone needs to know one's scope of personal authority and responsibility. One needs to know that some valued item, skill, or money itself is in one's jurisdiction to use before one can be charitable or generous to other people. Short of such knowledge, one could hardly know whether it would be courageous or foolhardy to protect something, whether it would be generous or reckless to share it, and so on.

In other words, private property rights are the social precondition of the possibility of a personally guided moral life. If one wants to be generous to the starving human beings in the Sudan but has nothing of one's own, generosity will be impossible. There is, in effect, a necessary connection between a practical moral code or set of guiding moral principles and the institution of private property rights if a moral code is to include such virtues as generosity, courage, honesty, prudence, and such as they relate to limited resources and other things of value to human beings.

John Locke, perhaps the most prominent philosopher to defend private property rights, was partially aware of their moral significance. He drew a connection between acting freely and responsibly, as moral agents, and having the right to private property. He defended the institution of the right to private property as well as the way that property might be assigned.

There are two issues here. The first is whether this system of private property rights is a morally necessary system. We have thus far suggested that it is or, at least, that it is necessary for a robust system that would allow for the exercise of certain virtues. Without knowing what in the world is one's own and what belongs to others, the practical moral decisions one makes will get hopelessly confused. A tragedy of the commons of a moral sort, not just practical, will take place.

Karl Marx emphasized the destructive possibilities entailed by the right to private property. He observed, one-sidedly but accurately, that if one has acquired private property and thus authority over that property, this implies that no one may interfere in how one uses what one owns, provided one does not encroach on other people's rights in the process. This means, of course, that one is thus free to misuse one's property, but it also means that it is possible to use it prudently, productively, wisely, charitably, and so on. Indeed, as Aristotle suggests, the right to private property may very well encourage just that.

PROBLEMS WITH ASSIGNING
PRIVATE PROPERTY

Having said that these rights are a necessary condition for the personal moral life of human beings does not yet solve the second issue, namely, how property rights may be assigned over various valued items, including one's skills. Some people suggest that such an assignment is impossible. It can be argued, for instance, that property rights must be compatible; that is, each person's right to private property must be compatible with every other person's similar right.[5] A system of incompatible rights, being inconsistent, is thus a flawed system and would lead to internal conflict. We need here to distinguish between conflicting rights and conflicting claims, for, although it is true that a system of private rights must be compatible, there could nonetheless be conflicting *claims* to rights (to something). After all, if people have free will they are able to either exercise their property rights or violate those of others. So just because rights may be *in principle* compatible does not mean that people will not violate each others' rights. However, if such rights are not compatible and no harmonious assignment of them can be obtained, there would be no way to avoid violating other people's rights. Such a system would be impossible to implement.

5. We use the term *compatible* here as a rough synonym for the more precise technical term *compossible*, which means mutually possible. For an extended discussion of this concept, see Hillel Steiner, *An Essay on Rights* (Oxford, England: Blackwell, 1994). See also David L. Norton, *Personal Destinies: A Philosophy of Ethical Individualism* (Princeton, N.J.: Princeton University Press, 1976).

A system that aims to protect both "negative" and "positive" property rights is on a collision course with itself. If persons have a right to be free of interference as well as to be provided with what they need, conflict is inevitable. For example, if persons have a positive right to (be provided with) health care, and the doctor has a "negative" right (of noninterference with respect) to his or her skills, occasions will certainly arise where these rights will conflict. Just to the extent that the doctor must acknowledge everyone's (positive) right to her or his skills, the doctor's (negative) right is compromised. Thus, should the doctor wish to help a friend or simply to relax rather than work, another's right to medical help would result in a conflict of rights. The doctor cannot both exercise his or her right to noninterference and, at the same time, honor the other's right to medical assistance. These are not compatible rights.

In contrast, "negative" rights are compatible. If both the doctor and the patient have a right to their property—the patient to her or his money and the doctor to his or her time and skills— the exercise of these rights need never clash.[6] The patient will be the one to decide how and when to spend her or his money, the doctor will be the one to decide how and when to spend his or her time and skills. They can agree to come to terms, to negotiate, or to pursue another course of action to attain their goals. If this situation is protected from disturbance, neither party will be required to sacrifice what belongs to him to serve someone else. Another objective may not be realized (e.g., the illness may re-

---

6. This is not to say that there can be no emergency circumstances, rare as they may be, in which rights cannot be respected and need to be disregarded. For more on this, see Tibor R. Machan, "Prima Facie v. Natural (Human) Rights," *Journal of Value Inquiry* 10, no. 1 (1976): 119–31. In the kind of situation so well depicted in Hitchcock's famous movie *Lifeboat* and faced by members of the Donner Party, rights are impossible to consider since politics has been rendered impossible.

main untreated), but that is an entirely different matter. No one is entitled to the involuntary servitude of another person, even if that's the only way to obtain a valuable service. It may turn out that, in some situations, the doctor ought, morally, to attend to someone, but not because persons have a general "positive" right that she or he do so. It may be the doctor's professional obligation, or compassion, pity, or charity may call on the doctor to assist.

Another attack on private property rights is the argument by Marx that such rights are necessary only for bourgeois society, not because an institution of private property rights would be just but because it would increase material production. This would serve the historically important purpose of supplying society with ample goods that, under socialism, would be distributed in an equitable and sensible way.

Yet another argument against property rights, advanced by Pierre Joseph Proudhon, the prominent French anarchist, is that all property is theft: No one knows whether what is currently assigned to someone is in reality his or hers since it was probably stolen or acquired by conquest several times over throughout history. Thus, so this argument goes, by the time it gets down to the present generation, ownership is so corrupt and unclean that any claim to private property rights is insupportable. (A curious feature of this view is that it unwittingly implies the wrongfulness of theft since, if simple possession were sufficient warrant for ownership, past ownership would be irrelevant; if theft is indeed unjustified, then simple possession cannot be a warrant for ownership! It seems to follow from this that any claim to undermine the institution of private property rights by appeal to historical theft or conquest begs the question.)

Clearly, if we wish to defend the institution of private property rights and its concomitant political economy (capitalism), we need more than a practical defense. We need a principled, morally convincing case that shows this system to be right and just, not simply useful.[7] It is now necessary to outline the case showing that private property rights is a just institution and that particular ownership can also be assigned justly. Even if most people in a society favoring private property were to fare well, there remains the question of how individuals in such a society are treated. For example, in *The End of Laissez Faire* (1926), John Maynard Keynes likens a capitalist system to the heartless, untamed wilderness, in which the strong survive but those without advantages are doomed. According to Keynes, people who are helpless are callously left abandoned. Although some charity or philanthropy may exist, the capitalist system itself lacks the compassion, kindness, or generosity to help the millions of abandoned, needy people.

Keynes, and his many followers, accordingly advocated the interventionist welfare state to counter the social evils of capitalism. He believed that some intervention, some regulation, some redistribution of wealth are moral imperatives. Even John Stuart Mill, the English utilitarian political economist and philosopher who advocated the market system, had misgivings about capitalism. He maintained that pure capitalism should prevail at the production stage but that some statism is necessary at the distribution stage to help the unfortunate.

Given such concerns, it is evident that in order to defend the system of consistent, uncompromised private property rights, one must offer more than the practical argument that in the long run

7. What is useful for one thing may not be for another, so if property rights are useful for purposes of, say, improving productivity, efficiency, and prosperity, the question may always be raised further: But are those the goals we ought to pursue, encourage, in a society? This is why arguments establishing the instrumental, pragmatic, or practical value (i.e., efficiency) of the right to private property will never suffice to settle the matter of whether it is a just institution.

we are all better off in a system that provides such wealth as does capitalism. One must provide a principled, moral defense. A system that is truly just must in general be right for any human being. Everyone, on reflection, should be able to appreciate that rights, dignity, justice, and fair play are honored by this system. Absent a moral defense of capitalism, thoughtful and unbiased persons are likely to find it wanting and will then fail to provide the support that it requires to survive.

Furthermore, without a sound moral defense of private property rights, the system will be ever vulnerable to significant legal erosion, despite its efficiency and productive potential. In the legal process, judges tend to move the law in the direction of moral convictions since they must often make discretionary judgments that rest on morality. If people know well enough that some assignments are unjust and the law fails to take notice, the system of law will lack moral force.

A case in point is environmental law. In contrast with criminal law, matters of conservation, such as protection of endangered species and wetlands and the provisions of the prosecution carrying the burden of proof and bans on prior restraint, are not upheld. In general, regulatory law treats individuals, companies, and their right to property along lines introduced in a dissenting opinion of U. S. Supreme Court justice Oliver Wendell Holmes. In his *Lochner vs. New York* dissent, Holmes argued that, for a government action to be held invalid, "a rational and fair man necessarily would admit that the statute proposed would infringe fundamental principles as they have been understood by the tradition of our people and our law."[8] This requirement is nearly

---

8. Quoted in William Letwin, "Economic Due Process in the American Constitution and the Rule of Law," in R. L. Cunningham, ed., *Liberty and the Rule of Law: Essays in Honor of F. A. Hayek* (College Station: Texas A&M University Press, 1979), pp. 53–54.

impossible to satisfy. If it were applied to, say, efforts to undermine the principles of the First Amendment, there would be little left of freedom of speech in America. However, the real threat is in the modus operandi of nearly all cases where legislatures and regulatory agencies challenge people's private property. The mere metaphysical possibility of something affecting a species of animal or the condition of wetlands can serve as justification for overriding the private property rights of citizens. One reason for this is the lack of a clear, well-enunciated, and propounded defense of such rights.

It is also arguable that most people desire to be on the side of morality, no doubt a source of widespread hypocrisy. So their loyalty to a system lacking this alliance is likely to be weaker than if they are confident in the moral justness of the legal system.

Finally, there is the concern that members of society be treated decently and justly. Lacking a serious attempt to realize such treatment, the authority of the law will likely suffer. What reason would people have not to steal or (its political equivalent) vote themselves portions of other people's money, if the only objection to stealing is mere economic expediency?[9]

Considered from a purely utilitarian point of view, where individual well-being is subservient to the collective well-being, it is irrelevant whether private property rights are assigned to one or another, so long as they are privately assigned. Property may be given to one we now regard a thief or to one from whom the thief stole, and overall *social* gain or loss would be the same, at least for the time being. This is one of the insights of the late Nobel laureate Ronald Coase, a major contributor to the Law

9. For arguments defending the general system of free market capitalism against those who claim that it would foster poverty and neglect for the helpless and hapless, see Tibor R. Machan, "The Nonexistence of Basic Welfare Rights," in Lawrence M. Hinman, ed., *Contemporary Moral Issues* (Upper Saddle River, N.J.: Prentice Hall, 1996), 387–97.

and Economics School of analyses of community affairs. His famous "Coase theorem" establishes that, regardless of how property rights are assigned at a given moment, the social consequences are unchanged. All that is important is that *some assignment* of property rights occurs.[10]

Surely this perspective is limited, for it overlooks the moral dimension of the assignment of property rights. This invites the question "Is there a method for correctly assigning property rights?' The moral reputation of business and commerce in general depends in some measure on whether ownership itself is morally just since trade, the activity of commerce and business, presupposes that one cannot trade in what one does not own.

FROM MIXING LABOR TO
REWARDING GOOD JUDGMENT

John Locke advanced the theory that, when one mixes one's labor with nature, one gains ownership of that part of nature with which the labor is mixed. Thus, for example, if I gather wood from the forest for a fire, or for materials to build a shelter, I have a "natural right" to what I have gathered inasmuch as I have "mixed my labor" with it and to that extent put some of myself

---

10. Ronald Coase, "The Problem of Social Cost," *Journal of Law and Economics* 3 (1960): 1–44. The utilitarian will concern himself morally only with social cost so that injustices, in particular assignments of property, are morally irrelevant. Coase goes on to show that, from the point of view of the overall cost to society, initial assignments of property are irrelevant. In his example, it makes no difference whether the farmer or the railroad is assigned ownership of the land adjacent to the track so far as benefits and costs to society are concerned. The important thing is to make some kind of property assignation. It is of course quite clear that the farmer, who has worked the land for years, will find it unjust to have it assigned by some court to the railroad, however irrelevant this may be to the welfare of society as a whole (whatever that means anyway).

into it. Since I have a self-evident right to my own body, including my labor, that part of nature that includes myself (i.e., my labor) is also mine. Although Locke held that nature is initially a gift from God to all of us, he argued that, once we individually mix our labor with some portion of it, it becomes ours alone.

This idea, though perhaps commonsensically compelling when limited to simple examples of physical labor such as gathering wood, has not carried sufficiently wide conviction, mainly because the idea of "mixing labor with nature" is too vague. Does discovering an island count as an act of labor at all, never mind "mixing" one's labor? Does exploring the island? Fencing it in? Does identifying (discovering) a scientific truth count as mixing labor with nature? What about inventing? Or trade—should the act of coming to an agreement count as mixing one's labor with something of value? Challenging examples to Locke's principle abound.[11]

A revised Lockean notion has been advanced in current libertarian thought by way of a theory of entrepreneurship, an idea advanced at about the same time by philosopher James Sadowsky of Fordham University and economist Israel Kirzner of New York University.[12] The novelist-philosopher Ayn Rand, perhaps the modern era's most fervent advocate of capitalism based on a theory of the unalienable individual right to life, liberty, and property, also emphasized the moral role of individual judgment and productivity.[13]

11. George Mavrodes, "Property," in Samuel I. Blumenfeld, ed., *Property in a Humane Economy* (LaSalle, Ill.: Open Court, 1974).

12. James Sadowsky, "Private Property and Collective Ownership," in Tibor R. Machan, ed., *The Libertarian Alternative* (Chicago: Nelson-Hall, 1974), pp. 119–33, and Israel Kirzner, "Producer, Entrepreneur, and the Right to Property," *Reason Papers*, no. 1 (1974): 1–17. See also Israel Kirzner, *Competition and Entrepreneurship* (Chicago: University of Chicago Press, 1973).

13. Ayn Rand, "The Objectivist Ethics," in *The Virtue of Selfishness: A*

According to the entrepreneurial model, it is *judgment* that fixes something as possessing (potential) value (to oneself or others), and thus the making of this judgment and acting on it are what earns oneself the status of a property holder. The rational process of forming a judgment is neither automatic nor passive; neither does the process involve more than minimal overt physical effort, but it is an *act of labor* nonetheless. What gives the judgment its moral significance is that it is a freely made, initiated choice involving the unique human capacity to reason things out, applied to some aspect of reality and its relationship to one's purposes and life goals. One exerts the effort to choose to identify something as having potential or actual value. This imparts to it a practical dimension, something to guide one's actions in life. Whether one is correct or not in any given instance remains to be seen, but in either case the judgment brings the item under one's jurisdiction on something like a "first-come, first-served" basis.

For example, assume that George identifies some portion of unowned land as of potential value. Having made this judgment, George now has rightful jurisdiction over the property, so that others may not (rightfully) prevent him from exploring it for oil, minerals or using it as a museum or private home. His judgment may have been in error—the land may turn out to be unproductive or otherwise unsuitable for his purposes. But, by his having first made and acted on the decision to select the land, he has appropriated it.

On this model, then, the appropriation of items in nature has

---

New Concept of Egoism (New York: New American Library, 1961). Rand identifies rationality as the highest of human virtues, given that human nature amounts to being a rational animal and the excellence of any individual human being would be to manifest as fully as possible the choice to think and act rationally. This view is similar to the Aristotelian idea that practical reason or right thinking, prudence, is a vital virtue for human beings. See Douglas J. Den Uyl, *The Virtue of Prudence* (New York: Peter Lang Publishers, 1991).

moral significance because it exhibits an effort of prudence, of taking proper care of oneself and those for whom one is responsible. George's attempt to exercise the virtue of prudence by his judgment and subsequent use of what he has chosen to appropriate is potentially morally meritorious. Under this description, the act of appropriation is a *moral* act. Apart from actual outcomes, George's exercise of his judgment here is of prima facie value as an expression of his prudence, industry, good sense, practical savvy. All this being so, to live as a moral agent, as one responsible for oneself and perhaps others, George must be free to make such attempts without intrusion by others.

Critics would see such acts not as morally worthy but as acquisitive or possessive, implicitly deeming as morally insignificant a person's attempt to benefit himself or herself or one's loved ones.[14] Without supporting argument, the critics implicitly reject the idea that advancing one's own well-being, aiming for one's own prosperity, is something morally negligible or demeaning.

The case just made in support of private property rights is merely the beginning of the development of an elaborate legal system of private property rights. In complex social contexts such as industrial society, property acquisition occurs via thousands of diverse acts of discovery, investment, saving, buying and selling, with willing participants who embark on the same general approach to life. Nor is anyone coerced into one particular approach, which accounts for what Harvard University philosopher Robert Nozick made note of in his defense of capitalism: the system's hospitality to diversely conceived utopias, to experiments with great varieties of human conceptions as to the good

---

14. Consider the disdain in which property acquisition is held by such political theorists as C. B. Macpherson, for example, in his *The Political Theory of Possessive Individualism: Hobbes and Locke* (Oxford: Clarendon Press, 1962).

social life.[15] This is evident in all the experimental communities, churches, artistic colonies and economic, educational, and scientific organizations that abound in what has come to be perhaps the largest, most closely capitalist, private property–respecting society in human history.

APPLIED RIGHTS THEORY

Theoretical defenses of the system of private property rights do not begin to answer all the questions concerning the best application of that system with regard to the multitude of complex problems involving acquisition and use. Although the 1980s ushered in the global movement toward privatization, including Eastern Europe's substantial rejection of the planned economic system, we are far from having full confidence in the concept of private property rights to serve as a foundation for a sound socioeconomic system. As we have seen, this lack of faith is not due essentially to problems inherent in the system of private property. Rather, resistance comes from the philosophical climate and attitude that has surrounded those who are perhaps the most visible beneficiaries of private property, namely, commercial agents, people in business, and entrepreneurs. Although countless others are just as much beneficiaries, this is less obvious. Consequently, capitalism is condemned roundly for a lack of fairness and for permitting great inequities of wealth, as if these would not arise or would be more effectively addressed by another system! It is the simple failure to consider the alternatives to capitalism, coupled with an ignorance of its widespread benefits, that nurtures the anticapitalist prejudice.

Defenders thus argue that the capitalist system has proven itself

---

15. Robert Nozick, *Anarchy, State, and Utopia* (New York: Basic Books, 1974).

in comparison to all other alternatives. Furthermore, when problems do arise within this system, the courts adjudicating the difficulties can arrive at appropriate solutions concerning particular applications of the right to private property in everything from radio signals to frozen embryos and from the air mass to bodies of water. Without elaborate legal and technical discussions, which would be prevented within alternative models, the great potential of the system of private property will remain unexploited—for example, with respect to environmental and ecological concerns.

Thus, there appear to be two candidates for the philosophical foundations of the system of private property rights. One, that the system is necessary for the provision of "moral space"; two, that it makes the realization of prudent conduct possible vis-à-vis our natural and social world (*natural* in the case of initial appropriation, and *social* in the case of voluntary trade). Unless these are sound, the system of private property rights is eventually likely to be defeated as a political-economic model for the modern world.

NATIONAL DEBT AND THE
TRAGEDY OF THE COMMONS

We can now address a public policy result of the gradual erosion of the role of private property in our legal system. This consequence has seldom been noted and is different from the more obvious problems identified by economists such as Ludwig von Mises and F. A. Hayek. Both von Mises and Hayek have noted throughout their scholarly works that without private property rights the price system is corrupted, leading to the development of widespread economic inefficiency in the community.

As we observed earlier, Aristotle demonstrated the social value of the right to private property when he said that "that which is common to the greatest number has the least care bestowed upon it. Everyone thinks chiefly of his own, hardly at all of the common interest; and only when he is himself concerned as an individual. For besides other considerations, everybody is more inclined to neglect the duty which he expects another to fulfill; as in families many attendants are often less useful than a few."

The principle here has been applied successfully to environmental problems, and many scholars have concluded that, without extensive privatization of public properties such as lakes, rivers, beaches, forests, and even the air mass, environmental problems will remain largely unsolved. It seems to be generally agreed that there are inherent problems in common ownership but less apparent, evidently, that what is required to solve the problems is to transfer common ownership into private ownership. The political will to effect the solution is lagging far behind the analysis that identified the solution. Nevertheless, in this area at least, the identification has been made.

What has not been widely noticed is that a tragedy of the commons exists in our national treasury. We have what by law amounts to a common pool of resources from which members of the political community will try to extract as much as possible to serve their purposes. Whether it's for artistic, educational, scientific, agricultural, athletic, medical, or general moral and social progress, the national treasury is the trough for all citizens in a democratic society. Of course, everyone has noble reasons to access it, and their goals are usually sufficiently thought out so as to inspire confidence in their plans. All they need to further their goals is support from the treasury, so they devote great energy, will, and ingenuity to extracting from the commons whatever they can for their purposes.

Unfortunately, as both Aristotle and Hardin knew, the commons are fated to be exploited without regard to standards or limits: "That which is common to the greatest number has the least care bestowed upon it." This explains, at least in part, the gradual depletion of the treasuries of most Western democracies. Japan, Germany, Great Britain, and the United States are all experiencing this, as are numerous other societies that open their treasuries to the public for uses that are essentially private.[16] How can we view education, scientific research, the building of athletic parks, upkeep of beaches and forests, and so forth other than as the pursuit of special private goals by way of a commons, the public treasury?

Some might claim that all these goals involve a pubic dimension, a public benefit. Indeed—so does nearly every private purpose, including the widely decried phenomenon of industrial activity, which produces the negative public side effect of pollution and the depletion of a quality environment. Private enterprises can certainly have public benefits, but their goal is to serve the objectives of private individuals. When the public treasury is tapped for, say, AIDS research, the primary beneficiaries of success would be those with AIDS, not the general public; when theater groups gain support from the National Endowment for the Arts, the primary beneficiaries are those working in theater; when milk producers gain a federal subsidy by price regulation or by being compensated for withholding production, the dairy farmers are the first to gain, not some wider public.

So we find, one after the other, to the thousands, "public" projects that in reality are supporting private goals, first and foremost. One need only observe who lobbies for the money. But since the "treasure chest" is public property, it is impossible to rationally allocate the wealth consistent with proper budgetary constraints. Such constraints arise from considering the implicit limits on spending that are determined by the wealth of the in-

---

16. For the details on this point, see Tibor R. Machan, *Private Rights and Public Illusions* (New Brunswick, N.J.: Transaction Books, 1995).

dividuals who comprise the society, as well as their creditworthiness. Without reference to specific individuals or companies
as such, no limits and thus no clear constraints can be identified.
Instead, politicians spend to the extent that they can borrow and
print money, using only anticipated funds; or they reduce the
value of existing moneys, funding requests with hardly any restraint other than public opinion. This tendency is fueled by the
urgency of various groups of constituents, who express their
urgent desires in the ballot box. The inevitable result is the tragedy of the commons, as the public treasury gets looted

Without structural remedies, there is no end in sight to this
process.[17] Only when the country loses its creditworthiness in the
world community will this near Ponzi scheme come to a halt. The
country will then have to declare bankruptcy, leaving those citizens who had nothing to do with the tragedy—our children and
grandchildren—holding the empty bag. Such is the final end of
treating with cavalier disdain people's right to private property
and individuals' efforts to enrich themselves. When intellectuals
commonly pit human rights against property rights, as though
the right to what one owns is not a human right, we are increasingly impoverished, not just individually but as a society and
government as well.

According to Bernard Mandeville and others, "private vices
[make] publick benefits." Here is economic insight but moral
ignorance: Indeed, if we denigrate the pursuit of prosperity, we
will produce general misery for everyone; what these political
economists failed to realize is that *the striving for personal prosperity is not a vice but an aspect of the virtue of prudence.* It is

---

17. It is to this problem that many political economists have been addressing
themselves with such possible measures as a balanced budget amendment. See
James M. Buchanan, "Boundaries of Social Contract," *Reason Papers*, no. 2
(1975): 15–28.

private prudence, not vice, that leads to public benefit, so we ought not demean that which enables us to obtain personal prosperity.

An additional fallacy common to social philosophizing is the view that what really matters as we consider public affairs is the general good, a rather vague idea of collective utilitarianism whereby the "greatest happiness or good or well-being of the greatest number" is the central goal of politics. It is not to our purpose to enter that debate here. Suffice it to say that such remnants of tribalism draw heavily on an initial discrediting of the worthiness of individual human lives.[18]

18. For an extensive exploration of these matters, see Machan, *Private Rights and Public Illusions*. This chapter is a substantially revised version of a previously published essay, "The Right to Private Property," *Critical Review* 6 (1992): 81–90.

CHAPTER EIGHT

The Moral Status
of Entrepreneurship

Make your explanations as simple as things are ... and no simpler.
—Albert Einstein

ENTREPRENEURSHIP AND CAPITALISM

It is crucial to classical liberal political economic analysis that the moral status of entrepreneurship be established. Unless it can be shown that the entrepreneur is engaging in a morally worthy activity, one that merits praise when performed competently, thoughtfully, professionally, not only the status of the entrepreneur in the process of the market but the market itself will be open to serious moral criticism. At best, the market would be hospitable to morally indifferent kinds of behavior; at worst, it would encourage moral callousness and discourage the pursuit of morally significant objectives such as order, self-restraint, artistic excellence, and family values. A system with such a fundamental weakness cannot long compete with alternative systems that are morally grounded. Indeed, it seems evident that much of the prejudice against business and commerce that we discussed earlier stems from the belief that at bottom the economic life is without redeeming moral value—at best, it is a necessary evil of an imperfect world. In a perfect world, the hereafter, perhaps, there would be no need for business, commerce, or economics.

Everything will be provided. And so, against this view, we need to establish that there is something fundamentally right, good, morally worthy in efforts to prosper in this life. It is possible to do so by considering the role of the entrepreneur, the "hero" of commerce.

Entrepreneurship, the "getting up" of the wherewithal to prosper, is vital to capitalism; it is the engine and the energy of the system. As Israel Kirzner observes, "Entrepreneurs . . . we perceive as becoming aware (with no resources of their own at all) of changed patterns of resource availability, of technological possibilities, and of possibilities for new products that will be attractive to consumers." He adds that "flesh and blood resource owners are, of course, also to some extent their own entrepreneurs (just as flesh and blood entrepreneurs are likely to be owners of some factor services themselves)."[1]

Those who arrange the various factors of production so as to aim at a successful business enterprise are the mainspring of capitalism. Ownership, though a necessary condition for the system, is not sufficient for it to be productive. Those who own their labor/time, and the capital that previous successful use of such labor/time has created, are not necessarily going to continue with the process. Why?

Put simply, human beings have free will. This means that they have a choice whether to do anything at all, as well as what to do, with the capital at their disposal, even under ideal political-economic conditions. Even in the context of a hospitable legal environment, with free trade in goods and services, freedom of

---

1. Israel Kirzner, "Producer, Entrepreneur, and the Right to Property," *Reason Papers*, no. 1 (1974): 1–17. It should be noted that not only lone individuals but entire companies can be entrepreneurs. For more on this, see Edward B. Roberts and Ian C. Yates, "Large Company Efforts to Invest Successfully in Small Firms," *Journal of Private Enterprise* 10, no. 2 (spring 1995): 47–80.

contract and association, and the freedom to market and advertise what one has for sale, prosperity requires the entrepreneur, one who is willing to get things started, to move things forward. This is *the* crucial ignition key and motor of successful commerce.

FREEDOM AND ENTREPRENEURSHIP

It is an illusion to believe that prosperity requires only an hospitable environment, like seeds that require only fertile soil. In the freest of societies many potential market agents can be lazy, uninspired, alternatively engaged, or otherwise not moved to entrepreneurial action. Freedom means precisely that: One has a genuine choice whether or not to be productive. So it is not enough to show that human beings are free under capitalism, unless the uses to which such a system puts human effort can themselves be morally worthwhile. For example, in the U.S. system of constitutional republicanism, the freedom of the press is relatively secure, mainly because of the generally agreed-on *value* of such a freedom to a democratic society. But unless this value is perceived in the bulk of the journalism read by the public, the full merits of the system have not been demonstrated and the freedom is at risk. Thus, if the freedom of the press yielded little of value, which many believe is the case today, such freedom would come under serious moral suspicion. And so the questions, why should one be productive, why should entrepreneurship be practiced, what is good about it?

One possible answer is that entrepreneurship is the gateway to a decent chance for wealth. One can certainly agree that producing is more honorable than stealing. But what if quietism is offered as an alternative, that is, the form of religious mysticism that involves complete extinction of the human will, drawing away from worldly things? or another alternative, asceticism, the religious ideal that one can reach a higher spiritual state by self-discipline and self-denial? These traditionally and widely honored viewpoints are opposed to the seeking of wealth. How can capitalism, the system that is most hospitable to entrepreneurship, be defended against such powerful challenges?

To be blunt, the most serious challenges to capitalism come from those who hold that making entrepreneurial effort possible, by protecting the rights to private property and the pursuit of happiness here on earth, open the door to the corruption of human life. In other words, the greatest challenge to capitalism is the view that this system tends to corrupt by permitting the commercialization of human relationships, making us self-interested economic agents, instead of the altruistic members of society that we ought to be. It is hardly sufficient to reply that capitalism makes it possible for people to attain a better life here on earth, for that begs the question of the challenge: Why should we strive for such a life in the first place?

ENTREPRENEURSHIP FOR WHAT?

Entrepreneurs explicitly and unabashedly pursue the goal of enrichment. Some are generous, if not altogether altruistic, with the wealth they attain, though most attain wealth by providing other people with goods and services that promote flourishing here on earth. A typical contemporary shopping mall, department store, car lot, discount warehouse, or industrial exhibit all seek to demonstrate to potential buyers that the goods and services provided by the entrepreneur will make life better, more comfortable, safer, more enjoyable, even more thrilling, than it would be otherwise. So, what can be said in defense of a profession that is dedicated to the widespread enhancement of this life?

THE DRIVEN ENTREPRENEUR

The *homo economicus* answer is that we are all necessarily involved in self-interested pursuits. As Milton Friedman so succinctly expressed it:

> Every individual serves his own private interest. . . . The great Saints of history have served their "private interest" just as the most money grubbing miser has served his interest. The *private interest* is whatever it is that drives an individual.[2]

The view that we are all relentless utility maximizers is best laid out by the late George Stigler:

> Man is eternally a utility-maximizer—in his home, in his office (be it public or private), in his church, in his scientific work—in short, everywhere. (Lecture ll, Tanner Lectures, Harvard University, April 1980)[3]

The Austrian position is remarkably similar. Ludwig von Mises states:

> Human action is necessarily always rational. . . . When applied to the ultimate ends of action, the terms rational and irrational are inappropriate and meaningless. The ultimate end of action is always the satisfaction of some desires of the acting man. . . . No man is qualified to declare what would make another man happier or less discontented.[4]

2. Milton Friedman, "The Line We Dare Not Cross," *Encounter*, November, 1976, p. 11
3. Quoted in Richard McKenzie, *The Limits of Economic Science* (Boston: Kluwer-Nijhoff, 1983), p. 6.
4. Ludwig von Mises, *Human Action* (New Haven, Conn.: Yale University Press, 1949), p. 19.

The logic is unassailable: Certainly, if one cannot refrain from satisfying one's desires, then one must pursue them, and such pursuits can hardly be evaluated as more or less rational since they are not chosen. On this view, all self-interested action reduces to an automatic urge, something that all of us have but that is translated into diverse pursuits, either entrepreneurial, spiritual, benevolent, cruel, miserly, or generous. In the end, each of us does what we have to do, which is to play out our "private interests" in various ways.

This position supposedly secures for capitalism a kind of scientific legitimacy, not unlike that which dialectical materialism tried to secure for socialism: empirical, historical validity. As a matter of our "selfish genes," to quote the title of Richard Dawkins's book that is popular with neoclassical economists, we are driven to do what we do, as a simple fact of our nature. Accordingly, the entrepreneur is one of the many puppets pulled by the strings of our genetic inheritance, just as are the great saints of history or anyone else. Who can blame the entrepreneur? Why, no one, anymore than one can blame the lion for devouring the zebra or the criminal for committing his crime. *Que sera, sera.* On this, the *homo economicus* view, the conditions of the marketplace are natural and unavoidable, and thus beyond criticism. The idea that human life could be anything else is but an illusion, a stubborn holdover of prescientific thinking. The altruistic dream of a communistic, socialistic, or some such form of universal human community is hopelessly at odds with the biological imperatives that control life, but the marketplace is not. And so, it is argued, capitalism works because we are the kind of beings that we are, because of our nature as *homo economicus*. It follows from this, of course, that to lament the processes of the marketplace, including the energetic endeavors of the entrepreneur, is akin to lamenting the storm that spoiled our Sunday picnic.

THE FALLACY OF
HOMO ECONOMICUS

The account just described is faulty in that it oversimplifies by reducing all human actions to mere reactions, with the mistaken implication that the entrepreneur is essentially the same as the ne'er-do-well, the loafer, or the lazy bum since neither has a determinate effect on what happens. At a fundamental level the *homo economicus* view is also self-defeating. Its radical determinism undermines its own justification since, by its own tenets, those who hold it simply must, while those who do not cannot help but deny it. Neither side can be evaluated independently, objectively, based on sound analysis and good thinking.[5]

On this view all thinking is equally valid (or equally beyond logical assessment), for none of us can escape our biases and prejudices; we are simply doing what we must do, given the forces acting on us, like billiard balls that must obey the laws of physics. However, such a view disqualifies itself from the ranks of possibly true accounts since by its own premise, its truth can never be told or established. No theory can be correct that makes it impossible to determine whether it is correct. "Correct," "right," or "true" are properties of judgments or claims made by conscious beings who seek to understand things correctly rather than incorrectly, rightly rather than wrongly, truly rather than falsely, and who recognize themselves as capable of discovering the truth as well as making errors.

In response, it might be claimed that *homo economicus* is not part of such a deterministic system since, after all, he or she is out there making choices in the marketplace. Choices are the bedrock of economic activity.

---

5. For more on the problems with determinism, see Tibor R. Machan, *A Primer on Ethics* (Norman: University of Oklahoma Press, 1997).

This would be to equivocate on the term *choice*, at best, or to betray an ignorance of the concept, at worst. In truth, what *homo economicus* does is make *selections* based on the options available, and the desires that drive her or him. Such is the case with the bird that selects the materials with which to build a nest or the dog or cat that "chooses" to move from the hot sun into the shade. Given its instincts, the bird cannot help but move as it does to build a nest; given the hot sun, the dog is driven to the shade. Neither the bird nor the dog can be said to have *initiated* their actions, and so it is proper to describe them as having selected. But selections are not enough to account for the kind of behavior that characterizes *human* action generally, the *initiation* of which makes for responsible human action. In the marketplace, the home of *homo economicus*, nothing new or creative would ever arise except by accident or the happy coincidence of drives and resources. The system would soon come to a halt or end in chaos for lack of direction if human beings were simply making selections on the basis of their drives and the available resources. No one would recognize that there was a demand that could be filled, nor is there a natural human drive to fill demands. Success and failure in the marketplace would be a matter of sheer luck. Enter the entrepreneur, whose intelligence recognizes the opportunity created by a demand, and whose *initiative* provides direction in the marketplace and in large measure sets the stage for success or failure.

IS THE ENTREPRENEUR WORTHY?

No doubt the entrepreneur is a discoverer, an effective processor of information, a useful factor in the productive processes of capitalism. As Israel Kirzner has argued, "a sharp distinction must be drawn between means of production ordinarily conceived, and entrepreneurship," to start with because "entrepreneurship *cannot be purchased or hired by the entrepreneur.*"[6] Nevertheless, many who have tried to understand the market as a kind of productive system have treated the entrepreneur as a factor of production. As Kirzner notes, for Joseph Schumpeter, for example, "the means of production include *all* agents required to produce the product in the state of circular flow."[7] On this view the entrepreneur is but one part of a large machine that leads to wealth, not a decisive and potentially problematic element without which everything else would lie idle.

Indeed, a more humanistic conception not only of people in business but of all economic agency would recognize that to an extent we are all entrepreneurs, though some of us become professional at the task. Each of us decides whether, when, and how to make use of available resources and secure the authority to direct them by enlisting the support of others. These in turn are themselves making entrepreneurial decisions by trusting us with these resources, which would come to naught without this concerted mutual effort. And when such entrepreneurial efforts are thwarted by natural factors such as catastrophes or disease, or by criminals and bureaucrats, the productive process slows down, resulting in stagnation, shortages, and other losses.

If we view entrepreneurial activity as initiated by human beings and as something that might or might not be ignited by the human will (with support from other factors of production), the question can be raised: Is this a good thing? Should we be entrepreneurs at all? Such a question cannot arise within the *homo economicus* model, where human action is seen as driven, rather than freely chosen.

6. Kirzner, "Producer," p. 3.
7. Ibid.

OBSTACLES TO OUR QUESTION

The line of thought we have embarked on gains considerable resistance from perhaps the most persistent aspect of economic science, namely, scientism. This is the view that sound thinking requires that we follow methods of demonstration and forms of explanation and proof that have been found appropriate in the basic natural sciences.[8] The major tenets of what we are calling *scientism* were laid out by followers of the Vienna Circle, a group formed around the turn of the century made up of scientists, engineers, and philosophers who were disturbed by the direction philosophy had taken under the leadership of neo-Hegelian idealism. The Vienna Circle perceived philosophy to have turned vague and muddled and took it on itself to clear the muddied waters of philosophy. Thus, obscurantism invited reductionism.

For our purposes, the most important result of scientism was the demand by many economists that any understanding of market activity be put in terms conforming to the language of the natural sciences. The main natural science guiding the field of economics had been classical mechanics.[9] By the tenets of classical mechanics, every cause must be an efficient cause, an event antecedent to and productive of what needs to be explained.

It follows from this that the entrepreneur cannot have a distinctive, decisive role in economic life because his or her behavior is but one link in a chain of ongoing causation, with no room for personal, individual initiative. Neither is it possible to see anyone as deserving any of the fruits of her or his labor if everything in economic life is causally necessitated.

Even the instrumentalist defense—that certain behavior will

8. See Tom Sorell, *Scientism* (London: Routledge, 1991).

9. See John C. Moorehouse, "The Mechanistic Foundations of Economic Analysis," *Reason Papers*, no. 4 (1978): 49–67.

lead to more wealth in a society—does not focus either on the entrepreneur's rights or on what is deserved for good work but on the stimulus for continued entrepreneurial activity provided by the promise of greater profits. (In a sense, supply-side economics amounts to a loose version of this analysis—that by rewarding the producers or removing obstacles before them, the government stimulates production.)

FLAWS IN THE MECHANISTIC MODEL

Although grand in origin and initially wide in scope, classical mechanics has turned out to be a limited *physical* science. It is not the all-embracing metaphysics that many who followed the scientific revolution, especially Newton, had hoped it would be. It suffered from a number of serious paradoxes, including those that led modern physicists to replace it with the more comprehensive quantum physical view of the world. It also failed to explain much of what goes on in human life, including the marketplace. For example, classical mechanics does not make sense of entrepreneurial or intellectual failure and success and of the possibility of rationality concerning theoretical matters. Nor is classical mechanics or its sophisticated offspring, logical positivism, sufficiently comprehensive for purposes of understanding the nature of the universe, especially the uniquely complex and often subtle phenomena of human life.

Furthermore, more successful alternative views widen, rather than narrow, the range of possibilities concerning the kind of phenomena that can take place in nature. Some of these phenomena will be of the mechanical type, involving what certain scientists call *downward causation*, and some will reintroduce teleology or purposiveness, at least with respect to animals with brain capacity, those capable of thinking. This brings us to a crucial point.

THE ATTRACTION OF SCIENTISM

What the scientistic spirit abhors most is dualism, which divides the world into two irreconcilable, arbitrarily demarcated realms, along lines illustrated in the philosophy of Plato's Socrates and René Descartes and reinforced by Immanuel Kant. This view holds that reality consists of two realms, the natural and the spiritual, and never the twain shall meet. Dualism annoys the scientifically minded among us, especially social scientists such as economists, who desire that their discipline be received as respectable, worth studying, and productive of results worthy of attention in the world of practical affairs. Dualism puts out of scientific reach a significant portion of reality, namely, the "higher-order" activities of human beings, the source of which, dualists argue, is something spiritual, nonphysical, and thus beyond the scope of the empirical sciences. This Descartes called "spiritual substance" or soul, something that Kant elevated to the "noumenal" world inaccessible to science.

Given all this, if there is to be a scientific study of human beings (the social sciences), then human beings must be rendered in terms that account for all the other phenomena of nature, which are understood to be wholly subject to deterministic forces. Thus, dualism is avoided, at the cost of scientific reductionism, or what we have called scientism. The social sciences thus proceed by translating human activity into the language of drives and stimuli, desire-gratifications, chemical imbalances, genetic structures, cultural conditioning, and the like. But despite the language and the ingenious attempts to quantify human behavior, scientism fails, for its initial assumption—that human beings are wholly explainable in the same terms that science uses for explaining the rest of nature—is false. Thus, scientism precludes the understanding of precisely the kind of behavior that is unique to human beings, including behavior that manifests itself in the marketplace.

Scientism prevents us from making sense of such matters as entrepreneurship. The reason for this is that entrepreneurship assumes that human beings can begin to act on their own, that they have the capacity of initiating action, that they have a measure of basic freedom, in short, free will. It is this feature of human beings, combined with our unique intelligence, that separates our species from the other animals.

SCIENTISM IS BAD SCIENCE

Mechanistic science cannot make sense of this. Are we then faced with the dilemma of choosing between an obsolete scientism and an awkwardly divided dualism? This is a false dilemma. As Fraser Watts observes, "It would be wrong to think that a crudely materialistic view of the body is the only alternative to keeping a dualistic concept of the soul; that is to take one half of Descartes' two part conception of the human being without the other. It would be more helpful to return to the Aristotelian view of the soul that antedated Cartesian dualism."[10] The idea is familiar: Nature has evolved into a system with many levels of complexity, some fundamentally different from others. Human beings are certainly different from other, even the most highly developed, animals, and animals in general are different from plants, and so on, with gradations of complexity. There is, in short, a *hierarchy* in nature, with different capacities evident in line with where things belong on this hierarchy.

Human beings are able to form ideas, often original. Animals

10. Fraser Watts, "You're Nothing but a Pack of Neurons" *Journal of Consciousness Studies* 1 (1994): 279. See also Edward Pols, *Mind Regained* (Ithaca, N.Y.: Cornell University Press, 1998).

in general are capable of locomotion, moving along from place to place. Plants, animals, and human beings all require nourishment, while inert matter does not. From inorganic matter to vegetation to animal life, there is increasing complexity and additional capacities. With human beings, the capacity for self-determination or self-causation has evidently emerged in the universe. This idea, though ancient, has enormous explanatory power, enabling us to make sense of a great deal of what common sense readily admits, namely, personal responsibility, right and wrong conduct, good and bad ideas and arguments, criminal responsibility, artistic creativity, as well as the enormous diversity among cultures and individuals throughout history and across the globe.

If all this is right, why should it be so shocking that human beings move differently from the rest of nature by initiating their own significant behavior? It would not, but for the influence of scientism and classical mechanics.

Thus, scientism yields bad science. It rejects, out of hand and prejudicially, what needs to be recognized as an aspect of nature: the phenomenon of self-caused actions by human beings, creatures of nature capable of making original decisions and initiating actions. It is in this way that bad science precludes the possibility of entrepreneurship and severely handicaps the social sciences from advancing our understanding of ourselves. By reducing the complex and unique phenomena of human life to explanations in terms of efficient causation (the language of classical mechanics), scientism has dehumanized the human dimension.

THE CONSEQUENCES OF
HUMANIZING ECONOMICS

Adding the factor of initiation to our understanding of human behavior yields a richer view of reality. It also requires that we alter our expectations, for human beings, who can start things up, can also fail to do so. Thus it is that the humanization of the social sciences, and of economics in particular, brings forth a normative element, one that scientistic thinking attempts to avoid. When we come to economics, a realm of human activity, we must at certain points consider what happens in terms of standards of right and wrong. As Kirzner puts it, "In deciding to initiate the process of production, this human being has *created* the product."[11] Accordingly, the entrepreneur can be evaluated as having made discoveries, gathered information, and garnered capital support that lead to successful enterprise or as having failed to do so, with more or less success.

ENTREPRENEURSHIP: IS IT MORAL?

What place is there for morality in a social science that needs to remain rigorous and scientific? First, and most fundamentally, we need to understand that morality arises from a basic question that all human beings ask, either explicitly or implicitly: "How should I conduct myself?" (As we have already seen, this can be phrased in several ways, including "What standards should guide how I conduct myself?" and "What ought I to do?" and "What is praiseworthy, proper conduct?") This question arises for human beings because we lack instincts, and because a vast portion of our conduct is not predetermined by prior events or genetic structures, even when these form limiting conditions on what we can do.

There is normally an array of alternatives available to people, from which they will select what to do. Because the selection of an alternative is itself something *they* do and is not determined for them, human beings need to decide which of the alternatives

11. Kirzner, "Producer," p. 10.

ought to be taken. Although not every choice that human beings make is of a moral order, at the most basic level it is morality that identifies the right choice.

The one area of genuine, undetermined choice for all normal human beings is the choice to activate their rational thinking, their specific type of awareness. We have to *choose* to think, to use our intelligence, to pay attention. Thinking is not automatic; it must be willed to be initiated and is thus volitional. This is what is meant by *free will* and is where human beings possess their basic freedom. In the words of Emerson, "Intellect annuls Fate. So far as a man thinks, he is free. . . . The revelation of Thought takes man out of servitude into freedom" (Ralph Waldo Emerson, "Fate"). This makes clear enough sense, though it would be far too ambitious and beyond our purposes to attempt to establish it here as fact.[12] What Emerson's observation underscores is that the area of human activity that defies explanation in terms of antecedent causes is the formation of ideas. It is just this area that includes theorizing, judgment, planning, decision making, and the entire range of rationality. It is here that some of us go right, others wrong; it is here where human responsibility lies, whether in ethics, law, or intellectual and scientific performance. We are held responsible for our judgments, first and foremost, since our actions are *actions*, as distinct from mere behaviors, precisely by virtue of their being guided by judgments. This is also why we can and ought to properly call them *our* actions.

At this point a difficulty arises, disturbing for those who wish to subsume human behavior under natural laws. Unlike other things in the world, human lawfulness—logical, ethical, or legal—is voluntary. It cannot be *scientifically* predicted that some-

12. For such an effort, see Tibor R. Machan, "Applied Ethics and Free Will," *Journal of Applied Philosophy* 10 (1993): 59–72.

one will indeed think whether she or he will initiate and sustain this mental effort. It is up to the individual. As Lester Hunt notes,

> The sort of thinking that is involved . . . is capable of producing infinitely many different outcomes concerning a single issue. The rationality of the outcome is the fact that, in a certain way, it is appropriate to a total ensemble of factors, each one of which admits of indefinitely many different degrees.[13]

Admittedly, much of our thinking is predictable but only because we are known to have got it going, as it were. That is, once a person starts on a task, such as embarking on a research project, seeking to live successfully, or abiding by the laws of the community, it is a safe bet, often enough, that he or she will carry on with it. That, after all, is a reasonable expectation of one who has made a commitment of one sort or another. And, for various reasons, human beings generally follow through, though nothing but their own commitment and effort causes them to do so. It is always possible to be surprised by our fellows, who may suddenly abandon their efforts to think, judge, reflect, or theorize successfully—we are, after all, human, neither machines, wholly and predictably subject to the laws of physics, nor merely animals, wholly and predictably responding to stimuli. But we can usually anticipate that many of us will carry forth as we have set out to do, which is what it means to take up the task of living a human life, of living as a human being. The moral element in human life does not yield natural laws of the sort that provide reliable scientific predictions, although neither is it the case that we are without reasonable anticipation as to how someone will carry on.

13. Lester H. Hunt, "An Argument against a Legal Duty to Rescue," *Journal of Social Philosophy* 36 (1994): 22.

THE MORALITY OF PRUDENCE

Living a human life is much like a project, something that can be done poorly, moderately well, or admirably, and success in living, in being a person, is largely a matter of the choices we make and the thoughtful care that we bring to our decisions. Morality generally is concerned with how this is done. Thus, Socrates said of ethics when asked, "It is no small matter, but, how should I live my life?"

Prudence is the virtue of applying oneself rationally to the business of living. Aristotle called it *phronesis*, or practical reason. It has also been understood as the concerted effort to do well at living, to flourish, to make the most of one's opportunities, to live carefully, economically. It is possible to understand prudence in different ways, depending on what we understand as the self. That is, whether we take ourselves to be primarily earthly creatures, spiritual substances aiming for an afterlife, or whatever. But it seems most reasonable to understand that, for all we know, we are part of nature with a life to live dependent on our biological attributes and capacities. This much, at least, seems evident.

Accordingly, prudence is the virtue that guides one toward living a good *life*, and a significant aspect of such a life concerns securing for oneself the benefits that economic success provides. For the most part we have to *think* our way through life, and to do so well is to exercise prudence.

Entrepreneurial conduct is specialization in prudence. It can be good or bad, as can nearly all human conduct, for one can overstep the limits of any of the virtues. A good human life involves the integration of all the virtues, a balance among them, so that one is not, for example, generous *to a fault*. If prudence is itself a genuine human virtue, then entrepreneurship is something morally worthy.

As we have noted earlier in this work, some philosophies and religions consider prudence to be worthless because it leads to worldly riches, material acquisition, and the satisfaction of earthly desires. There are some themes in Christianity, as we have seen, that have been interpreted as antienterprise, as when Jesus chased the money changers from the temple, saying, "It is written, *My house shall be called a house of prayer*; but you have made it a den of thieves." This strongly suggests that selling, buying, and changing money amount to theft. Certainly this sentiment is widespread in many cultures, including Western civilization, as the earlier sections of this book make clear.

We have been arguing for entrepreneurship as a morally worthy activity, just as it has already been deemed a proper subject of scientific study. In essence, what makes entrepreneurship a moral endeavor is its link to prudence, a bona fide human virtue. It is, in fact, the first of the cardinal virtues, so recognized as far back as Aristotle.

ENTREPRENEURSHIP AND POLITICS

Given the moral status of entrepreneurship, we can now consider why it ought to be rewarded and why a just human community must welcome it as one of its valued institutions.

The free society makes it possible for morality to flourish. The behavior of unfree persons cannot properly be called *actions* since that behavior is legally forced, not the product of free choice. The protection of and respect for rights in a free society amounts to the protection of the moral nature of human life in a community. Unless one's actions violate others' rights, thus preventing them from enjoying their sphere of personal authority, no force may be imposed on that person by others. By guaranteeing rights, the free society provides the moral space within which its members may make uncoerced choices, which is the sine qua non of human agency. As Ayn Rand puts it,

"Rights" are a moral concept—the concept that provides a logical transition from the principles guiding an individual's actions to the principles guiding his relationship with others—the concept that preserves and protects individual morality in a social context—the link between the moral code of a man and the legal code of a society, between ethics and politics. *Individual rights are the means of subordinating society to moral law.*[14]

In a just human community, prudence is the engine, so to speak, of production. It is the specific virtue whose practice nurtures the values that sustain one's life and help it to flourish. Within the framework of our economic lives, prudence takes the form of entrepreneurship.

Because of this, only a system of laissez-faire economics can do proper justice to our moral nature, for in such a system entrepreneurs are free to create and to reap the benefits that others deem appropriate to bestow on them for their contribution. The entrepreneur seeks to create wealth in innumerable ways, and if she or he is authentic—does not resort to theft, cheating, coercion, or other vicious means to attain his or her ends—the wealth, goods, services, and other benefits that result will be the product of his or her virtuous conduct. What the entrepreneur gains from these efforts should remain under personal jurisdiction. The government that taxes away the gains of entrepreneurial effort undermines the moral nature of human community life, just as does the government that transfers wealth from successful entrepreneurs to failed ones, so too with taxing away the earnings of novelists or other artists and redistributing it. No social contract can authorize such state action since a contract that bears on third parties who are not signers is fraudulent and morally empty.

---

14. Ayn Rand, "Value and Rights," in John Hospers, ed., *Readings in Introductory Philosophical Analysis* (New York: Prentice Hall, 1968), p. 382.

PRUDENCE AND PROPERTY RIGHTS

We must now consider the influence of morality on the development of law. In a free society there will occasionally arise hard cases where legislators and judges must decide whether to protect certain rights over others. Rights develop hierarchically, beginning with the right to life, then liberty, property, and more specialized rights that follow. One cannot overstate the importance of the ranking of these rights.

No one doubts that the general intellectual climate has been disdainful of private property rights, a crucial framework for entrepreneurship. This stems from the intellectual community's demeaning view of the efforts of individuals to enrich themselves. From the time of the ethical writings of Immanuel Kant, prudence has been consigned to a morally minimal role in human life. Kant shared the Enlightenment view that self-interested conduct was very nearly automatic, a drive to do right by ourselves, to be prudent. So he excluded this from his enormously influential moral philosophy, one that stresses, above all, disinterestedness as the mark of moral behavior. As we have noted, the pursuit of earthly enrichment had been widely denigrated even from antiquity, but Kant's influence as a towering intellectual has been great.

From the ethical viewpoint of Kant and many neo-Kantians, entrepreneurship cannot be morally praiseworthy since the entrepreneur cannot be seen as acting disinterestedly, without concern for his or her goals, particularly the goal of economic profit. Kantian ethics is purely formal, with reason sharply severed from feeling, desire, concern, ambition, or spirit, the lifeblood of anyone setting out to prosper in life. Small wonder that prudence gets excised from Kant's list of virtues.

Even apart from the Kantian influence are the equally urgent efforts of some to demonstrate that individualism is a myth. Entrepreneurship without individualism is wishful thinking. Unless an individual has the capacity to act on her or his own, entrepreneurship is impossible. Socialists have been eager to show that the individual is a myth, that we are all species-beings, mere parts of a large organism, which is society or humanity. Even after the demise of socialism's reputation there have been other collectivist doctrines, such as communitarianism, that would subsume the individual within some other social whole such as the tribe, the ethnic, racial, or cultural group. These doctrines also assert the ethical priority of other people's interests, or that of the group, before one's own. Their legal influence, especially in hard cases where some ambiguity remains, can work against the idea of private property rights and entrepreneurial liberty.

One result of this is that whenever conflicting claims of rights violation come to light, say, between the rights to property of landowners and the rights of cultural groups, or so-called rights to life of birds or fish or other wildlife, there has been a public and even judicial inclination to dismiss the former as simply lacking moral merit. Despite a constitutional tradition of some attention to private property rights and of opposition to "takings," in the present moral climate the claims supporting property owners will likely fall on deaf ears.[15] The clarion call seems to be something like this: "All they want is wealth, and there is nothing moral about that, is there? Environmentalists, in contrast, are moral people, they care for living creatures, so their claims must be given higher priority."

Unless the ethical status of property rights is reaffirmed, and unless it is acknowledged that those who exercise their private property rights in entrepreneurial ways have a moral purpose

15. *Takings* refers to government confiscation of private property for purposes of facilitating some public objective. It is the Fifth Amendment of the U.S. Constitution that construes such taking in need of fair compensation, thus punctuating the seriousness with which the Founders viewed the right to private property.

and are not simply greedy, the chances of entrepreneurship gaining headway in public policy determination will be minimal. Even more fundamentally, until it is more widely understood that human nature is not, as Marx claimed, the "true collectivity of man" but is instead essentially a matter of each person's individuality, the case for public policy supportive of entrepreneurship will continue to falter.

LAST WORDS ON ENTREPRENEURSHIP

Admittedly, this has been far from a comprehensive treatment of entrepreneurship. Our purpose was to make clear and to support, with a reasonable array of arguments, the view that the entrepreneur is doing honorable work, that this is compatible with a naturalistic and scientific view of the world, and that the inherently moral nature of entrepreneurship requires a free, capitalist political economy.

The case for a free society rests on numerous considerations, but the critics of this system are especially keen on finding fault with how the various lines of support cohere. If the scientific approach is not consistent with the moral or political perspective, this will be noted. For example, neoclassical economists tend to preclude normative or moral considerations from their discussion of the market processes. Others of a more political bent argue that the market encourages moral responsibility. Still others claim that they are able to predict that under market conditions greater productivity and wealth will be achieved in a society. And others yet hold that markets are unique in resisting predictions of how resources will be utilized.

It is likely impossible to demonstrate the moral role of private property rights within the framework of a purely positivist economic analysis since property rights engender certain inequalities between those who act prudently and those who do not. Why should the former be able to keep what they obtained if they do not deserve it, if there is nothing morally worthy about their entrepreneurial conduct?

We have argued here that the purely positivist approach to market analysis is mistaken because of its metaphysical assumption that human beings cannot help what they do, nor in this framework is there any meaningful way to determine if what they do is right or wrong. We submit that a richer, more comprehensive view is in order, one more commensurate with the actual complexity of human life but simple enough for the common understanding. On this view human beings are seen as capable of making significant decisions, of taking the initiative to implement them, and of differing in the quality of how they do this. Humans' behavior is predictable only in broad, statistical terms, based on what we know about their habits of mind and action, not on knowledge of causal factors that will determine what they do. We have also argued that one moral feature of human conduct is the effort to further one's economic well-being, which amounts to practicing the virtue of prudence. Entrepreneurs make a specialty of this, for which they are rewarded by others with profits, and deservedly so.

A society of just human relationships must be consistently and constantly hospitable to entrepreneurship, for without it, a significant moral dimension of human life would be impaired. As support for entrepreneurship diminishes, public policy and law will yield to more widely accepted moral sentiments such as the environmentalists' call for greater and greater state power to regiment society. With this will come the shrinking of the moral space within which persons are free to make choices. Taken to its logical extreme, human beings would become precisely the kind of dehumanized, wholly predictable organisms that the view we have been arguing against assumes that they already are.

CHAPTER NINE

Dualism Disputed

REPLACING DUALISM

We suggested earlier that a major obstacle to a general acceptance of commerce and business as a noble enterprise is the widespread conception of human nature in dualistic and idealistic terms. That is, much of our culture takes it as fact that each person has two selves, the higher and the lower. The higher self is seen as deserving honor, while the lower is the source of evil, sin, corruption, and vice. With the former lies salvation, while the latter leads to eternal damnation and thus ought to be forgone. In the words of Jesus (Mark 8:34–35): "Whosoever will come after me, let him deny himself, and take up his cross. For whosoever will save his life shall lose it; but whosoever shall lose his life for my sake and the gospel's, the same shall save it." And in the light of such dualism, we are asked, immediately following: "For what shall it profit a man, if he shall gain the whole world and lose his own soul?" The implicit premise is that the soul belongs outside this world, that one cannot save one's soul without giving up this world: The world and the soul are at odds.

From Plato to Christianity and other religions, to the more secular views of such prominent writers as Herman Hesse, this has been a favored view, no doubt partly because it accords well with our initial and somewhat primitive conceptions of ourselves. We have already noted the clear exclamation of Saint Augustine: "How great, my God, is this force of memory, how exceedingly great! It is like a vast and boundless subterrranean shrine. . . . Yet this is a faculty of my mind and belongs to my nature; nor can I myself grasp all that I am. Therefore the mind is not large enough to contain itself. But where can that uncontained part of it be?"[1] As evidenced in this passage, when confronted with awe and wonder, inspiration and grandeur, there seems to be a tendency among certain types of thinkers, perhaps even temperaments, to place the source and origin of such wonder in a special realm beyond this world. It is as though the natural world were inadequate, somehow deficient. Thus, another world, a better world, is posited, wherein the highest of our yearnings and deepest of our intimations have a home, unsullied by the limitations and imperfections of this world. So it is that dualism has such enduring force, for it is born of something grand that we find within ourselves.

Without denying the force of awe and wonder, we must ask, is dualism correct? Is reality and our experience of it such that a division of reality and ourselves into two realms is necessary? We have suggested earlier that it is not and have offered some preliminary grounds for this answer. We should now explore this further.[2]

---

1. Augustine, *Confessions*, lib. X, chap. 17. 8ff.
2. In the following passages we will be drawing on the extensive works of Mary Midgley and Susanne K. Langer, as well as John R. Searle, and on the broader philosophical ideas of Ayn Rand, as we sketch, necessarily briefly, a nonreductionist naturalism, a view that although human life is at the pinnacle of what we know of nature, it is entirely at home in the natural realm, albeit characterized by some extraordinary attributes and capacities. See, for example, Mary Midgley, *The Ethical Primate* (London: Routledge, 1994); Susanne K. Langer, *Mind: An Essay on Human Feeling*, vols. 1 and 2 (Baltimore, Md.:

The widespread and long-lived acceptance of a mistaken understanding of the world suggests that some measure of truth is being served. In such a case we will not, perhaps ought not, abandon it lightly, for the insight or conviction has withstood some tests of time and experience. A wholesale rejection thus seems more foolhardy than to live with it despite its inadequacies. The better part of wisdom appears, at times, to be acquiescence.

Such is the case with dualism, a view that is tempting for its promise of not only an answer to our yearnings for fulfillment but a consolation in the face of perceived dangers of a secular existence. Consider much of what is taught in many dualistic religions and philosophies, including, at times, the occult. For example, in their insistence on a moral dimension of human life, given the widespread secular amoralism evident in the social sciences (especially economics, the discipline that studies commerce and business), many religions from Christian to Muslim understandably capture the allegiance of millions *in large measure because there is something perfectly right about it*. That which is right in this case is comingled with a good deal that is questionable and perhaps outright impossible, but few people have the luxury or inclination to examine such broad viewpoints in detail. Thus, most people remain relatively faithful to the familiar.[3] This economization has managed to preserve much

---

John Hopkins University Press, 1967/1972); John R. Searle, *The Rediscovery of the Mind* (Cambridge, Mass.: MIT Press, 1992); Edward Pols, *Mind Regained* (Ithaca, N.Y.: Cornell University Press, 1998); and Ayn Rand, *Philosophy: Who Needs It?* (New York: New American Library, 1982). Another, more recent, effort to establish the scientific credibility of the nonreductive approach in biology is Steven Rose, *Lifelines, Biology beyond Determinism* (London: Oxford University Press, 1998). See also Machan, *The Pseudo-Science of B. F. Skinner*.

3. Even in the natural sciences we witness this phenomenon often enough (e.g., the persistence of Johann Becher's phlogiston and, later, of the ether theories).

thinking that, when attended to carefully and objectively, can be shown to be flawed. Not only is this so in the particular case just mentioned, but it applies as well more generally to the widely embraced dualism, the underlying philosophical and theological underpinnings of which may well be wrong.

What truth is preserved in the dualist position? That human beings are unique for having minds and that having minds gives rise to a novel dimension of reality, namely, self-responsibility, creativity, and the possibility of moral good and evil. This insight, captured dramatically in the story of Adam and Eve, is compelling for its being nearly self-evident: Every step we take in life manifests this truth about us, as does every decision we make, even as we contemplate the issue itself. But does this insight necessitate dualism? Must we embrace dualism in order to preserve morality? It seems not.

ONE WORLD, WITH GREAT DIVERSITY

A simpler, more consistent, and paradox-free alternative is the view that, although reality is governed in essence by some basic principles, it also allows for an indeterminate variety of beings, including ones with minds. Such beings are not separate from or in conflict with reality, but, because of their unique nature, they must adjust to reality to find their way about by the use of their minds. What makes human beings unique is that they have minds that do not function automatically or instinctively; they can thus make mistakes.

This "monistic" account of reality holds that reality is one system governed by certain basic principles that ensure order, cohesion, and consistency. None of the beings in such a system of beings is at fundamental odds with any other. The type and kind of things in nature can vary indefinitely, ranging from subatomic particles to supernovas, from amoebas to human beings. This amounts to the pluralism of reality.

At some level we all recognize this. For example, in the sciences, law, and other disciplines where we demand rigorous thinking, no contradictions are admissible because reality is an integrated system of entities, beings, and relations, not in conflict with itself. Were reality to admit of contradictions, we would be foolish to insist otherwise. Even the currently fashionable chaos theory avoids attributing basic contradictions to reality, holding only that things happen unexpectedly, and that not everything can be predicted. This does not conflict with the basic fact that reality is one consistent system of beings with innumerable features, elements, and types.

In turn, we recognize ourselves as beings with minds, and this knowledge at times leads us astray since minds are not experienced in the way that we experience other things such as rocks, liquids, stars, and the vast array of natural phenomena. We know ourselves as thinkers, dreamers, imaginative beings; we know ourselves in a way that we know nothing else, introspectively. It is immediately and intuitively apparent to ourselves that we are conscious entities. As Heraclitus put it, "You would not find out the boundaries of the soul though you traveled every road, so deep is its logos."[4] Consciousness is the enduring and inherent feature of human experience as such. It is the "given" of experience and is so undeniable that room must be made for it in the world.[5] This seems to be perhaps just what the dualist is saying;

4. Heraclitus (DK22 B45).

5. In the history of philosophy the basic fact of consciousness in human life has been defended by many. Among the best is Ayn Rand's, whose argument is that consciousness is axiomatic, that is, any effort to do without it presupposes it, including any attempt to deny its reality. See Ayn Rand, *Introduction to Objectivist Epistemology*, 2d ed. (New York: New American Library, 1989).

there are two realities, the material and the intangible, spiritual, or mental. But we can make sense of the undeniable experience of our mental lives without embracing a paradoxical, internally conflicted view such as dualism, as tempting as that view may be at first sight.

A better alternative is the view that though we are mental beings, we are also very much a part of the natural world, containing within our makeup every element of nature, none of which is to be demeaned. Nature allows for all manner of beings. To begin with, there are no purely material things at all. Whatever there is takes some specific *form*. Although we can speak of primordial matter, no such matter that is not of some specific kind has ever existed. The idea of matter in itself, or formless matter, is a kind of analytic postulate, akin to an absolute vacuum, totally frictionless motion, or absolute zero temperature. These ideas serve as devices by which to evaluate or measure actual things. This is true as well of the formal systems of logic and mathematics, whose provisions are applicable as mental devices but for which there are no corresponding entities in fact. There is no such being as matter pure and simple, without form, anymore than there is such a thing as infinity.

What there is in reality amounts to all kinds of beings, from the very simple, such as pebbles, to the more complex, such as birds or fish. And on the continuum from simple to complex, there is a corresponding increase in the complexity of explanation and analysis necessary for our understanding. Human beings are evidently the most complicated of known beings, with the widest range of potentialities, capabilities, and faculties, for good as well as ill.

Nature appears to be hospitable to a great variety of beings

See also Tibor R. Machan, "Evidence of Necessary Existence, *Objectivity* 1 (1992): 31–62, and Pols, *Mind Regained*.

with greater and lesser complexity. Among these, human beings are known to be the most developed, with the distinctive faculty of higher, conceptual consciousness, the mind or spirit that we find undeniable about ourselves.[6]

DOUBTING SUPERNATURALISM

Although perhaps initially tempting, there is no need to take this mind and spirit outside the natural order of things. There is no clear and evident reason why the kind of intricate, complicated, awesome being that human beings are cannot be placed within the natural order of things.

Nothing rules out the possibility of minds being part of nature. Indeed, simpler versions of minds have always been included in nature. Cats, dogs, chickens, and other animals have forms of consciousness that are thought to be quite natural. Ours is a higher, more developed version of theirs, to be sure, but every bit worth the wonder and amazement that we experience at contemplating it in the works of great minds or even our own, as when Augustine invites us to ponder the wonder of human memory. No doubt the devious and vicious minds of the Marquis de Sade, Hitler, Stalin, and others are no less puzzling and baffling to most of us. But what do we gain in understanding by placing the human mind outside the natural world? Nothing at all. Such a displacement has brought as little enlightenment as it has produced great confusion, division, and suffering.

It is not the intent of this work to bash religion—there is

6. An exceptionally clear statement of this position may be found in Searle, *The Rediscovery of the Mind*. See also Midgley, *The Ethical Primate*.

enough bashing going on. The goal here is to clarify, develop, demonstrate, and praise. Religion has been valuable in certain ways, as Hegel and others have thought, such as by making a fascinating and complex philosophical and scientific story of vital importance simple enough to grasp by the common human understanding without our having to become full-time researchers. But when taken literally, most religions have required faith in place of reason. Faith, in turn, leads to trouble in the end because it amounts to belief unchecked by facts, evidence, argument, or even common sense.[7]

For all its prominence in human life, faith amounts to believing the unbelievable. It comes to believing what reason cannot tolerate when taken literally, requiring the believer to suspend belief in other things for which he or she has actual evidence. Thus, to believe that Jesus rose from the dead requires believing that he was God. Belief in a personal—wanting, willing, angry, or just—God, in turn, requires believing that without a biological nature it is possible for there to exist powers and functions that make sense only in the context of the existence of a biological entity.[8]

The human mind is so flexible and imaginative that it is able to entertain beliefs absent the moorings of reason or experience. In a way, faith is *serious* and *seriously recommended* fantasy. As

7. Faith is not the same as trust, although for millions of faithful it does amount at first to trusting, probably always misguidedly, those who claim to have the special facility to communicate with the supernatural realm. Faith, for those who proclaim it honestly, is a belief in what is quite explicitly contrary to fact and reason because it is only by being difficult in that way that faith can be regarded an extraordinary achievement. An excellent discussion is offered by Anthony Kenney, *What Is Faith?* (London: Oxford University Press, 1992).

8. Here we are confining this to a brief discussion of a personalized conception of divinity. In the Aristotelian tradition, as well as that of Spinozism, there exists a conception of divinity that lacks this strong tinge of anthropomorphism. Belief in God can thus rest on faith as well as the reasonable conviction that there exists some kind of necessary being.

such it can be satisfactory and in certain cases more valuable than what passes for information and understanding if these latter are badly formed and confused. But faith is not the highest form of understanding and certainly would not trump all others in some of the most important dimensions of human life.

Ironically, many praise religious faith precisely because it addresses the supernatural, the mysterious, the miraculous. Without this, religious faith would hardly be an accomplishment. The religious skeptic will make little headway with the believer because the crowning glory of religion is deemed to rest on the unique provision of faith, something lacking in the agnostic or atheist, but which the believer has taken as the precious gift of God's grace.[9]

We should note here that, for our purposes it isn't necessary to deny religion. Perhaps there is a religious dimension to reality. It may mean that we ought all be open to the unheard of, the unexpected, the yet to be discovered. And, given the vastness of the universe, and all that is possible, reason counsels an open mind. But the *extranatural* cannot be affirmed or made evident and reasonable. As human beings we must remain bound to nature, the only escape from which is properly called fantasy.

All this is to say that the standard version of the dualist view is unreasonable. And since this is so, the grounding of the central philosophical background behind business bashing is hopeless since it is divorced from reason, logic, science, and common sense,

9. For an extremely sympathetic, understanding, yet skeptical view of religion, see Karen Armstrong, *A History of God: The 4,000 Year Quest of Judaism, Christianity and Islam* (New York: Ballantine Books, 1994) and George Walsh, *The Role of Religion in History* (New Brunswick, N.J.: Transaction Publishers, 1998). Our own position on this issue is simply that whatever truth religion embodies needs to be squared with all other truths and must make reference to reality, not something supposedly outside it. We do not claim that all truths must be established by the means of the physical sciences, only that some way consistent with those means, not in contradiction to them, must be used for that purpose.

taking refuge in the mysterious and the miraculous. In the telling words of Martin Luther, the great Protestant reformer, "Faith has this quality, that it wrings the neck of reason." Such is the presumed power of faith among the faithful.

Admittedly, the "faith versus reason" issue, and its myriad related concerns, has been explored and debated in many forums and philosophies, and we are not in a position to dispose of all that here. Suffice it to say that, after surveying the writings of all the great thinkers, nothing seems more evident than that nature is extremely diverse and prolific, perhaps, to paraphrase the bard, more so than has been dreamed of in our philosophies.

For all its uniqueness and seemingly transcendent character, the human form of life is no less part of nature than other natural forms. We are, it appears, the remarkable unfolding of natural processes, resulting in nature becoming aware of itself. This may account for the seemingly transcendent nature of our being, this very special form of consciousness. Without in the least being diminished of value and wonder, the mind and spirit of the human being belongs as much to earth as the howl of the wolf, the flight of the bird, or the changing of the seasons.

THE ONTOLOGY OF COMMERCIAL HUMANITY

Whereas the troubled metaphysics of dualism leads to the disparagement of commerce, the metaphysics of monistic pluralism, with nature sufficiently robust and dynamic to include the likes of human consciousness, uplifts commerce. This is so because, given that human beings are a part of nature, our natural flourishing, which includes deriving pleasure from creating and producing, as well as other joys, is hardly a liability to be shunned. As Aristotle observed, human beings delight in the exercise of their natural faculties, and what is more natural for human beings, the rational animals, than to use intelligence to make their way through life?

In describing the British tradition of individualist social and political thinking, Shirley Letwin captures this basic feature of humanness.

Human beings are not divided between reason and passion. They are completely rational. Everything they do is permeated by their rationality because reason is not a power to discover indisputable arguments and universal patterns. Its essence is the power to choose what to see, feel, think, and do. In other words, reason is a faculty that enables human beings to interpret and respond to experience as they will. In this view, emotions are no less rational than mathematical calculations, because what causes fear or any other emotion and how people respond to it depends on how they interpret what they experience. And every interpretation is a rational activity.

Given this view of reason, the variety and uncertainty in the human world cease to be sinister products of irrational forces. On the contrary, the variety and uncertainty are attributed to the fertility of rational activity. For here reason is a creative power, which enables each person to choose differently from others, indeed even from what he himself did yesterday.[10]

Within such an individualist view, the desire for diverse measures and kinds of pleasure, comfort, delight, tastes, and enjoyments of countless sorts is to be sought and cultivated. If it is part of human nature to desire pleasure, to value enjoyment, and take

10. Letwin, *The Autonomy of Thatcherism*, p. 340. It is notable that Marx, for example, who was in many ways a modern universalist, found the marketplace anarchic and wanted to replace its penchant for diversity and uncertainty with the plan, with order. For Marx the beauty of socialism and communism is that in such communities order will prevail and reason will rule the desires and passions of people so they will not indulge these in their varied, chaotic ways.

delight in the possession of things beautiful, then being successful at securing these benefits is something quite becoming of a human being, an achievement, a demonstration of excellence deserving of praise.

A good human life, then, not only includes the so-called higher pleasures derived from literature, drama, music, and theoretical contemplation but consists as well of worldly delights—a sumptuous meal, the feel and look of quality attire, the comfort and convenience of spacious quarters, the release of spirit in play and leisure activities. In other words, living well in terms of the simpler aspects of life, though perhaps not as worthy as the elevated aspects, is nonetheless also a worthy goal. There may be a hierarchy of value from the used car salesperson to the heart surgeon, but everyone on that continuum has some measure of value in serving our pursuit of happiness; each is responding to some human need, interest, or desire. W. Somerset Maugham captured this insight precisely when he observed that

> Looking for the special function of man, Aristotle decided that since man shares growth with the plants and perception with the beasts, and alone has a rational element, his function is the activity of the soul. From this he concluded, not as you would have thought sensible, that he should pursue only that which is especial to him. Philosophers and moralists have looked at the body with misgivings. They have pointed out that its satisfactions are brief. But a pleasure is nonetheless a pleasure because it does not please forever.[11]

Admittedly, not every pleasure is as good as any other value that a person might attain in life, but neither are pleasures, in themselves, unworthy. And so, a good human life ought not be

---

11. W. Somerset Maugham, *The Summing Up* (New York: Penguin Books, 1963), pp. 35–36.

in fundamental conflict, with the person split into two warring selves. Rather, human good should be defined in terms of how well the whole person is served by one's judgment, choices, and actions. Accordingly, there can be nothing inherently immoral about commerce and the profession of business, for these are in the service of living a prudent life by providing economic well-being and satisfaction here on earth. Looked at in this light, commerce and business are among the great benefactors of mankind, far from deserving the disdain or indifference they have met throughout most of human history.

CHAPTER TEN

Prudence,
the Living Virtue

She'd been taught never to talk of money. It was rude, even shocking. Yet one had to, to live.

—Olivia Goldsmith, *The Bestseller*

WHY ANTIBUSINESS IS
MORALLY MISGUIDED

In a tidy nutshell, the antibusiness viewpoint misunderstands human nature. This is the source of the widespread, and often vicious, moral contempt for commercial and business endeavors that has been the focus of this book. Certainly, there are exceptions, which we have noted in this work, but in the main there is little in the Western intellectual tradition, let alone those of other cultures, that serves to balance this negative attitude. Commerce and business are roundly demeaned. The few exceptions, such as Daniel Defoe, and Ayn Rand, are marginalized.

The underlying philosophical culprit is the influential but basically mistaken doctrine of the dual nature of human beings.[1] In theological terms, to be human is to be part natural and part otherworldly. In secular terms, the self is driven partly by appe-

---

1. A recent contribution to the defense of dualism is Roy Mitchell, *The Exile of the Soul: The Case for Two Souls in the Constitution of Every Man* (Buffalo, N.Y.: Prometheus Books, 1983). This work contains an extensive collection of quotations from all ages and regions of the globe explicating the dualist outlook.

tites and instincts, and partly by ideals and principles of reason.[2] In some versions of this, reason can overcome the emotions and appetites; in others, reason is doomed to succumb.[3] In either case, the thesis implies that human beings are in a perpetual internal conflict between their noble and their base selves.

This is the origin of that now familiar lamentation about the materialism of Western societies, whose people fail to heed their spiritual or intellectual nature. Both Plato's and Aristotle's thinking is largely secular, though certainly neither is wholly free of supernatural elements, particularly Plato.

For Plato's Socrates the realm of being, the realm of the Forms, corresponds easily to the supernatural realm of many religions, which accounts, in part, for the influence of Platonic thinking on the early Christian church. Despite Aristotle's monistic metaphysics, his hypothesis of the unmoved mover, a sort of prime cause, does not exempt him wholly from the charge of supernaturalism. From both perspectives, the moral implication most often drawn from their metaphysics and conceptions of human nature is that we should live so as to realize our higher selves, that part of us which approaches the divine. For Plato, reason, the faculty that understands the nature of things, must rule the passions and the appetites; for Aristotle, the fully happy life, that

---

2. Sometimes there is a characterization in terms of three parts (e.g., in Plato's *Republic*). Yet even there the higher part of the soul is characterized by its contact with a higher realm of being, while the two subsidiary parts dwell in the more mundane visible realm.

3. In Christian theology there is an ongoing dispute, starting perhaps with Augustine's repudiation of the Manichaeists' radical mind-body dualism, concerning the precise nature of the duality of the world and human life in it. It is interesting that in this apparently intra-Christian dispute within Western culture we see, in fact, the signs of a universal concern with the problem of how to understand human life. Manichaeanism was brought to the West by Mani (ca. third century A.D.), influentially fusing Buddhism and Zoroastrianism with Christianity.

which is most fitting to our nature, is the life of pure contemplation, the state of human beings closest to divinity.

The basic profound insight about human nature captured by Plato and Aristotle can be put in simpler, nondualistic, natural terms, namely, that the best way to understand human beings is to see them as having a unique form of awareness, rational understanding, and as dependent on the use of this awareness to flourish in their lives. Contemporary neurology and psychophysics support this view with considerable detailed knowledge not available to the ancients.

UNDERSTANDABLE SELF-DELUSION

The major shortcoming of the ancient view is philosophical rather than technical. The ancients tended to think that only our distinctive feature, our capacity to reason, deserves care and concern. But why should we honor only our minds or spirits? Why not honor, as well, our bodies, our appetites and passions? These too are part of human nature and part of living an excellent human life. For all of their greatness, Plato and Aristotle seem to have confused what makes human beings excellent with what makes them distinctive. Now there may be an understandable measure of special pleading in this since, after all, Socrates, Plato, and Aristotle, being philosophers, were all specialists in matters of the intellect. Such imperialism is common among people who are peculiarly taken by the value of their specialty to human social life. But it doesn't follow from philosophy's importance to human life that living an excellent human life must involve being mainly philosophical. Human beings are constituted of many features that go into making them excel at being themselves.

Without doubt the mind is the proper instrument or faculty for grasping what is. Even when we discover that other, less direct or explicit, means of awareness are available to us, that discovery itself is understood and put to use by way of the conscious, intelligent mind. We certainly communicate much of what we want to share with others by means of explicit language, a principal instrument of our intelligent awareness.[4]

But none of this establishes that only our minds are worthy of concern, attention, and regard, as is often suggested by the ancients. When Plato's Socrates speaks in that manner, he is already convinced of that which makes things good or worthy, namely, their stability, permanence, timelessness—as with the clear usefulness of the geometric idea of the perfect circle, in contrast to more or less worthy approximations of circles drawn by human beings. For purposes of guiding us in measurement and design, such an idea makes good sense, but when this insight is extrapolated to serve as the most general notion of goodness, it is highly dubious. Admittedly, in evaluating things around us, we need to refer to something firm and stable, lest we be unable to make sense of things at all. Such is the threat of the Heraclitean claim that nothing is permanent and all is change. But the need for stable points of reference for purposes of understanding, evaluation, and communication does not mean that such a method is required for living successfully. It is a mistake to elevate into an ideal something that is merely a tool. To regard intellectual contemplation as the highest, indeed the only worthy, form of life, as did the Greeks, is to ignore that the mind is itself an aspect of life, not the whole of it. Such intellectualism amounts to a bias or prejudice, special pleading for a class of human beings, not a guide for living a successful human life. This is seen quite clearly in Plato's *Phaedo*, where Socrates, approaching death and think-

---

4. When some argue, as Desmond Morris did, that in fact we communicate a great deal nonverbally, that point itself, however, needs to be communicated verbally, in terms of complex ideas. Body language may be adequate for giving conscious and unconscious signals about sexual interests but it will not do for purposes of communicating a medical diagnosis or a political ideal.

ing about the search for truth and knowledge, makes the following telling observations:

> And when real philosophers consider all these things will they not . . . express in words something like the following? "Have we not found . . . that while we are in the body, and while the soul is infected with the evils of the body, our desire will not be satisfied? and our desire is of the truth. . . . I reckon that we make the nearest approach to knowledge when we have the least possible intercourse or communion with the body, and are not surfeited with the bodily nature."[5]

Because human nature is taken by many prominent writers and social observers to be divided into two parts, the spiritual and the corporeal, and because the spiritual is deemed to be nearer to God or of a higher order, whatever tends to serve the body is seen as lowly, even base. Thus, although some minimal supply of satisfaction for the body is deemed to be acceptable, going beyond what is necessary for sustenance is seen as greedy and avaricious and a sign of spiritual weakness. So it is that Socrates is depicted by Plato as indifferent not only to pleasure but to pain as well, for these are the most fundamental features of corporeal, sentient existence. And when reflecting on death, Socrates speaks of the body and of corporeal life generally as a curse to be joyfully lifted the moment the soul leaves the body.

REITERATING
PLURALISTIC NATURALISM

Although it is undeniable that philosophical contemplation proceeds best when free of distraction, a main source of which are physical desires and sensations, it does not follow from this that

---

5. Plato, "Phaedo," in *The Dialogues of Plato*, translated by Benjamin Jowett (Oxford, England: Oxford University Press, 1920).

we are thereby benefited by being free of the body altogether! Consider the logic of this intellectual prejudice by advancing the converse: Physical activity proceeds best when free of distraction, a main source of which are anxiety, fear, worry, and other mental disturbances. No doubt this is true, as any coach of an athletic activity will attest, but it hardly follows from this that the mind should be disparaged and that we would all benefit from being free of the mind altogether.

A more sensible view than this conflicted dualism is that human nature includes not just intellect but all aspects of being human that contribute to living life well. This idea emerges in Aristotle's philosophy, wherein the human individual is not separated into two substances. For Aristotle, soul is the living principle of the kind of being we are, not a separate organ. Thomas Aquinas had considerable difficulty with this idea, as he tried to reconcile the Roman Catholic Church's belief in the survivability of the soul beyond the death of the body with Aristotle's disbelief. Aristotle had held that the guide for judging right from wrong should be the distinctive element of our nature, our rationality or theoretical capacity. So he argued that ultimate value must be assigned to the life of contemplation, of intellectual exploration and under-standing. Not surprisingly, we find that the people most honored by Plato and Aristotle are the philosophers. This may be a some-what self-aggrandizing view, an early version of what might be called a professional vested interest. It is a view embellished and supported by its derivation from the proposition that the noble aspect of being human is the mind or the spirit.

PROFESSIONAL HIERARCHIES

It is likely true that some people's work is of supreme importance, while what others do is comparatively less significant. Common sense concurs in that understanding, as most of us comfortably and uncontroversially regard brain surgeons as doing more important work than, say, makers of pet rocks. It is not self-evidently mistaken to regard the profession of philosophy as special or of superior significance.

If the minds of human beings are of supreme significance in their lives, since it is with minds that we learn about and guide ourselves through the world, then the most abstract of all disciplines, involving the mind most resolutely and at its greatest level of effort, does warrant the highest regard.[6] This may seem arrogant and imperialistic, but in fact all that is involved in this view is that such a discipline requires the broadest level of abstraction and subsumes within its scope all the other intellectual disciplines. This is what gives philosophy its significance for everyone. Other disciplines, of course, often require extreme concentration, creative energy, and intelligence, but none has the scope of philosophy, which serves as the integrative discipline drawing on all the rest as it aims to provide an understanding of reality, of being as such, and our relationship to it.

In any case, whatever discipline does make the greatest contribution to our fullest understanding of our lives in this world would surely be of utmost importance to us. What else would it mean to prize a profession above all others than that it is of the greatest significance to human living?[7]

6. Philosophy is concerned with the most general account that is possible of reality and our relationship to it. Thus it must be comprehensive to the utmost degree, reliant on all other disciplines.

7. Those who deny that human life is more significant than the lives of other beings (e.g., some environmentalist and animal liberationists) will find this objectionable. For a discussion of such views, see Tibor R. Machan, "Environmentalism Humanized," *Public Affairs Quarterly* 7 (April 1993), and "Do Animals Have Rights?" *Public Affairs Quarterly* 5 (April 1991): 63–73. Essentially, the argument is that since animals, even at the level just below human beings on the evolutionary ladder, lack moral agency, they do not have any rights and they are not as important to us as we are ourselves. There is no other

What we learn from Plato and from his religious followers, for example in the Roman Catholic Church, is that the mind, above all other faculties, is uniquely suited for directing us through the challenges of living a complete and worthy human life. However, we are also taught that those embarking on mental or spiritual tasks are superior to the rest of mankind and ought to enjoy greater respect and even political power. This accounts, in large measure, for the special status of, for example, priests and nuns, as well as for the hierarchy exhibited in the structure of many Christian religious orders, as well as the widespread honor bestowed on intellectuals and theoreticians, such as professors, justices, and pure scientists.

Even granting that one profession might be more important than another does not imply that one practicing that profession is *morally* superior to others. On what does this depend?

MORE IMPORTANT IS NOT MORALLY BETTER

This takes us to the heart of our present concern, which requires that we touch on what morality is in the first place. As suggested earlier, morality arises because human beings are distinct in having to take initiative for living their lives and can do better or worse at that task. Unlike the rest of the animal world, human life, despite its complexity and variety, isn't guided by elaborate instincts. We need to take the initiative all on our own, make the choice to do what we do, and take responsibility for conducting or failing to conduct ourselves rightly or properly.

This is quite evident from simply considering what we do as we discuss our problems: Are we making sense, reasoning logi-

---

sense of importance, since whatever is important or valuable must be so to something or someone.

cally, keeping in focus, paying proper attention? Malpractice can be committed at any level of human life. There are standards for thinking properly, for using one's mental faculties. Even when one attempts to criticize that very idea, one invokes *criteria* and claims that those who fail to abide are doing something wrong. In other words, the normative dimension is inescapable, for it is inherent in the human condition. (This is why, as noted earlier, the purely materialistic, positivist flavor of the modern era offends many and why those offended often turn to ways of life that go to extremes in rejecting science.)

Simply noting all of this goes little distance in working out the standards by which to guide our lives, but it does address something fundamental. Even without the conceptualization of some otherworldly standard, we can see clearly enough that *some* standards of right and wrong are indispensable in our lives. For example, anyone who proceeds with the reading of this, or any other work, will quite naturally judge its merits based on some standard, however subjective, culturally bound, relative to time or place.

All this is no doubt evident from the history of our attitudes toward commerce and other human institutions. We value some and find others offensive, and when we want to learn why, we offer more or less well thought-out standards, criteria, or norms. Even the cynic or nihilist, who proclaims that standards are a myth, needs to apply standards that condemn hypocrisy and self-deception.[8]

So the question here is whether we have a persistent myth or some insight into reality, one often denied but nonetheless sound. It is arguable, as so many philosophers believe, that our nature is distinctive by virtue of our need for standards not automatically

8. Harry Newman, "Nihilism: Objections and Answers," *Claremont Review of Books*, fall 1985, pp. 26–27.

given in some form of genetic hard wiring. By embarking on our lives we invite the question, "How best do we do this?" or "How should I act, live, conduct myself?" This question makes sense, in turn, because we are free from forces that determine our course of conduct, and because it makes sense to distinguish generally between a life well lived and a life squandered or poorly managed.

If human beings are a kind of specific, definite being, then there may be good and bad and mediocre ways for them to carry on. However, since they are not given this information but must learn it on their own initiative, they will then have to take responsibility for how they act. The very phenomenon of business bashing, of holding commerce in contempt, suggests precisely this, that living so as to take commerce seriously, choosing a career in business, has been held to be morally suspect.

HUMAN NATURE IN FOCUS

There is more rocky terrain on our path to discovering standards of right and wrong that are more than mere prejudice. One of the most controversial spheres of philosophical as well as social scientific inquiries is the problem of whether a definite human nature exists. Plato, for example, seems to have thought that for everything that exists there is a form, an ideal, which particular things of a kind represent or approximate to various finite degrees. This includes human beings, for which there is the ideal of humanity, the definition of the concept of "human being" in which all human individuals participate and from which they obtain their identity. Aristotle thought that each human individual has within itself its essence, in virtue of which he or she is human. In more recent times no such confidence in the idea of a real and abiding human nature can be found. Thomas Hobbes, one of the founders of the modern view, seems to have thought that we ourselves construct the definition, based on our interests. David Hume appears to have believed that the idea of anything is but a generalization from past experiences. Existentialists, such as Sartre, in turn have argued that the idea of the essence or nature of being human is a pure fiction and that only particular individuals exist, who fashion out a nature or an essence by arbitrary choices. Furthermore, there is a good deal of such skepticism in the works of the pragmatists already mentioned, as well as in the views of deconstructionists, who hold that we are unable to specify a common standard for understanding the words we use, for example, in literature.

Despite the skepticism, we continue to proceed most often as if we could identify the nature of things. What is wanting seems to be a compelling explanation of what we are doing when we so proceed. One reason for this is that we require too much of our theories: We demand that all of them, in all areas of inquiry, be true forever and true beyond a conceivable doubt. This is clearly a hopeless requirement in all but a few cases, for we are finite, temporal beings who will not survive long enough to learn if our answers to questions will always be the best answers.

The most we can reasonably expect and hope for is to discover the most satisfactory answers to date in most areas of problem solving. This is surely within our power. To the question, "What is human nature?" a final, eternal answer should not be expected, nor is it necessary. To the extent that we appreciate this, we will be less likely to test theories against the impossible standard of an "ideal," *final* truth and find ourselves invariably coming up short. If, instead, we were to ask for the best answer or theory *thus far*, we would find that questions about human nature, the nature of government, justice, happiness, and so on may well be provided and may serve us well enough over a period of time. Ironically, the perfect turns out to be the enemy of the best!

When anything less than some absolute, final, timeless truth is offered in our quest for answers and solutions, the fear of relativism, subjectivism, or historicism has paralyzed us in our progress. This has become evident in our own time in the works of postmodern thinkers such as deconstructionists, radical pragmatists, and others who are essentially skeptical of our ability to know anything, to have any sound ideas about the world around us. There is enormous effort in the various intellectual disciplines to reach a sensible resolution of the struggle between the two extremes of absolutism and skepticism.[9]

The contextualist approach suggested in this work is complicated, and we will not develop it sufficiently here to judge its success. Yet in terms of what is envisioned, answers and solutions would not be arbitrary; they would have to accord with what we have learned from the past and would need alteration only for good reasons. In other words, we would have to be right beyond a "reasonable doubt," not beyond a "shadow of a doubt."

On such terms, we have ample reason to agree in large part with the ancient Greeks concerning what human nature is. Even such existentialists as Jean Paul Sartre, who say they reject essentialism, appear, in the end, to agree with the Greeks, for they too identify the most crucial aspect of human life as authenticity, the creative, original, expressive use of one's mind. In a famous illustration of this point, when Sartre condemns the waiter who cannot drop his poses, Sartre is complaining that such a person is not active in his conscious life but has become petrified, shut off from the natural human expression of creative freedom. But how does one remain creative and avoid the existential sin of having sold out, of acting in bad faith? By the active use of her

---

9. A good example of this struggle may be witnessed in Joyce Appleby, Lynn Hunt and Margaret Jacob, *Telling the Truth About History* (New York: W. W. Norton, 1994). The authors try very hard to reject the implications of relativism and historicism, ideas that make truth impossible, in the last analysis.

or his rational awareness, by the constant rejuvenation of the mind, and by the refusal to become a mere thing!

Consider some popular proposed answers to the question what is human nature: "Human beings are the laughing animals," Human beings are complex language users, "Human beings are toolmakers," and others. These definitions pick out one or another capacity that is, in fact, explained by our more basic capacity for abstraction and creative theoretical thought. We are, of course, more than this, but in the end this is how we differ from the rest of the animal world in the most general, comprehensive way discoverable thus far. Except for our rational capacity, there would be no questions, no competing answers, no theories of any kind, including theories that deny our nature as rational animals!

What of borderline cases and future possibilities? Some human beings are severely diminished, lacking even minimal rational capacity, while some animals, such as chimpanzees, seem capable of at least elementary abstraction.

Mentally deficient human beings are an exception to the rule and pose no more threat to our understanding of ourselves as rational animals than the occasional bird without wings, or any other biological anomaly within a species. As for the reasoning abilities of other animals, the evidence thus far suggests that their intelligence does not go beyond the perceptual, which explains why only human beings, whose intelligence is also conceptual, have engaged in art, science, complex communication, philosophy, the making of tools for making tools, and all the rest that separates our species as a species from all others. None of this is to say, however, that only human beings in the universe are capable of conceptual reasoning.

As for the challenges of the future, these will have to be met by those who encounter them. If and when artificial intelligence develops so far as to produce machines that think at will and abstractly, or some hybrid of human and machine or human and other species is produced, we may have to rearrange our taxonomy and refit ourselves within it. The possibilities that we presently imagine and that we may eventually actualize should not make us despair of our present understandings or of our ability to adjust our thinking so as to understand new and strange phenomena.

STABLE BUT NOT FIXED

In the meantime, we can confidently follow the ancients and consider answering the question of how we should act by reference to what we are, and what would make us good at being that. Having said this much, we must distinguish the present account of standards of right and wrong compared to the methods of the ancient philosophers.

The fundamental difference is that universals or definitions in ancient philosophy had been molded on geometrical concepts. These are purely formal and thus have a fixed status: When a circle is defined, it is as pure and timeless a definition as we can conceive. Defining justice or horses or human beings is quite different. We cannot travel to the end of time to tell whether we know human beings as they will have finally become. We can only know them to date, up to our time. Our definitions must not aspire to timelessness, even as they must attempt to be as stable and firmly grounded in reality as we can observe and assess it.

As to the content of the definition of human nature, we have already noted the major difference—in the ancient philosophy human nature tended to have a dualistic character, with the rational part accorded supreme importance. Thus it came to be that attending to the mind was of greater importance in human life than attending to the rest of oneself. But this seems not to be justified, unless the dualism is linked firmly to a metaphysics that is true and does justify it.

In fact, there is just one reality, not two or three, and this one is where human beings exist. So it is in this reality that we need to learn to do well at living. We need not show loyalty to some other realm, only to the complexity and diversity of what this, the only, reality contains. The standard by which human conduct is to be evaluated must let us know whether trade, commerce, business and, ultimately, free market capitalism have merit.

SOME CONSERVATIVE CRITICISMS

There are conservative critics of these efforts to defend standards. They tend to be skeptical of the view that we can reason ourselves from an understanding of human nature to a conclusion about how people ought to act. They believe that all we can have is a tradition of belief about what we ought to do. In their view, human beings are too fallible to reach conclusions based on reason concerning these matters, so the best approach is to trust the collective wisdom of culture, society, or race. As Edmund Burke put the point, "We are afraid to put men to live and trade each on his own private stock of reason, because we suspect that this stock in each man is small, and that the individuals would do better to avail themselves of the general bank of nations and of ages."[10]

It is not to our purpose here to muster all the challenges against this conservative approach to ethical and political matters. What can be said is that such an approach has its own serious problems. In particular, there are divergent, contradictory traditions that purport to direct our conduct so we will always be left with the

10. Edmund Burke, *Revolution in France* (Indianapolis, Ind.: Hackett, 1987), p. 76.

task of making rational judgments. There is also Burke's message of caution against a kind of absolutism or dogmatism that various rationalist views seemed to foist on us. The main target of conservatives is the belief that final answers are possible in ethics and politics. Reason can surely mediate between more or less good ideas.

Burke and Hume objected to a standard of right and wrong that requires *incorrigibly* superior answers to our problems. This seems to have concerned the best of the pragmatists as well. There is also the point that traditions themselves are built out of microdecisions made by individual human beings. These decisions are not always made self-consciously, so they do not exhibit explicit, deliberate reasoning. Rather, these decisions are the type we make from moment to moment as we navigate our lives, and for which we take ample personal responsibility, despite their inarticulate, nondeliberate nature.[11] If they didn't involve some measure of reflection or reasoning that individuals initiate and can carry out, there would be no point to much of the criminal law's doctrine that people are to be held responsible for their consequential errors and negligence. This institution, present in nearly every society, supports the view that reasoning carefully about matters of ethical and political conduct is vital for human life.

Defendants are often charged with negligence, omission, failure to attend to what is right and wrong, important and negligible. The reasoning demanded of them is not usually the kind carried out in mathematics, science, or scholarship, a self-monitoring or deliberative type of reasoning. Rather, it is often tacit, nearly habitual, yet still requiring the effort of initiative of individuals. Such reasoning, of course, may always be evaluated as

11. For a development of this point along lines of F. A. Hayek's discussions of the nature of human action, see Machan, *Capitalism and Individualism*, pp. 122ff.

being better or worse. Furthermore, Burke and other cautious thinkers would do well to realize that their own caution rests on assumption of some measure of their own successful thinking, otherwise, why should anyone take *their* advice?

Finally, although the kind of thinking involved in ethics and, especially, in politics may not make an immediate impact on actual conduct and institutions, that is no argument against it. Trends can be set, aborted, maintained, brought to fruition over time by means of careful thought and research. Custom, habit, and law are not simple to move toward reform, but they are not unbending either. Just as individuals take time to reorient habitual behavior, so large numbers of them, with relatively rigid institutions surrounding them, will also take time to respond to whatever ethical or political wisdom may be forthcoming in efforts along present lines.

For these and other reasons, conservative efforts fail to come to terms with our ethical and political problems. If we conclude, with good reason, even if not with finality, that commerce is decent and that the profession of business is honorable, this may eventually make a difference in concrete terms.

FROM HUMAN NATURE TO HUMAN VIRTUE

How are we to judge the matter, then? We should consider that human life is temporal and a part of the natural world, even if it does have aspects so distinctive as to introduce facts into the world that require new categories such as free will and moral standards. Despite that distinctiveness, the human species is a natural phenomenon. Accordingly, when human beings embark on a life that has on its agenda small comforts as well as grand tasks, all these elements deserve respect.

Surely, one can exaggerate the significance of the various items;

one can be immoderate about modest purposes and overbearing with high-minded projects. But prudence requires ample care for this life and all dimensions of it. This analysis requires a recasting of the concept of greed itself. As David Kelley and Jeff Scott have put it:

> The concept of greed can properly be applied only when the desire for money is divorced from any concern with achievement. Some people want money without having to earn it—a life of luxury without the effort of producing. Some people want the prestige and social status that comes with wealth. Some want power over others. In motive, greed is a desire for wealth without regard for achievement or creation. In action, greed is the unprincipled pursuit of wealth. This includes the use of force, fraud, and other illegal means. It also includes the violation of ethical norms, both the universal standards of honesty and fairness, and the specialized standards that apply to particular professions. . . .
>
> So there is such a thing as greed, and it is, as another common definition says, a reprehensible form of the desire for money. But what makes the desire reprehensible is not a matter of degree. If our standard is human life and happiness, we cannot set any arbitrary upper limit on permissible levels of material comfort— any more than there can be too much knowledge or beauty in our lives. It is not greed for a person with expensive tastes to work hard for the wherewithal to satisfy them. It is not greed for an entrepreneur to seek the capital he needs to make his vision real— even if the sums involved are huge.[12]

Thus, there is nothing inherently ignoble about trade, contrary to what Plato and even Aristotle are commonly understood to have thought, and in outright contradiction to much of what is taught by the world's great religions, as well as by most moralists. It has been traditionally held that economic concerns divert our

12. David Kelley and Jeff Scott, "Gekko Echo: A Closer Look at the Decade of Greed," *Reason*, March 1993, pp. 31–37.

attention from supposedly more important spiritual values. We are not here arguing against the tenets of religion or against spiritual values, however those may be defined. Indeed, it is no doubt possible to interpret the various sacred texts so as to be at least neutral, if not respectful, of material concerns and worldly desires. For example, even the famous passage of Jesus chasing the money changers out of the temple could be interpreted as righteous indignation for failure to respect a place of worship, rather than as an attack on money as such. Be that as it may, it is sufficient to have shown that business and commerce are not in themselves ignoble but are rather an integral part of what living a full human life requires. To think otherwise is a sad, even tragically misguided view, which could lead to serious neglect of one's proper goals.

GREAT MINDS GONE ASTRAY?

If one may be held responsible for promulgating ideas that one holds, it is arguable that many prominent minds, both past and present, are guilty of having misled many. This is especially serious when the thinkers condemn those who fail to strive for the pronounced ideals or, worse, who try but fail because the ideals themselves are inherently confusing and impossible to realize. Such seems to be the case with dualism and supernaturalism, ideas on the basis of which many have been guided to conduct their lives so as to deny the value of much that is naturally good. Again, our point here is not to take issue with religion as such or to deny the benefits that religious institutions have offered. Rather, we are trying to show the harmful effects of any view that devalues much of what makes for a full and flourishing human life, and we believe that the metaphysics of dualism and supernaturalism has led to such devaluing. Unless there is compelling reason to believe in such a metaphysics, it seems unwise to deny the value of what is present to all of us, in its name.

This can be put more reservedly: If there is no common method by which to ascertain the supernatural realm, then it is dubious, at best, to ask ordinary mortals to aspire toward or strive to gain admittance to such a realm. There is good reason to think that this is precisely how matters stand: No justification for the supernaturalist position exists, and all we have are unsubstantiated, at times incredible, reports requiring us to take matters not just on trust but on blind faith. But even if there were reason to believe in the supernatural, it does not follow from the existence of such a realm that the present world of our commonly shared experiences, the world of pleasures and pains, joys and sorrows, disappointments and achievements, discoveries and losses, is any less real or less valuable. On balance, it would seem that the wise view to take on these matters is to render to this world its proper due, not only because it may be the only world, the only life we have, but, more important, because it is a world and a life deserving in itself.

Even if a supernaturalist metaphysics poses no insurmountable obstacle to our embracing as worthy the economic dimension of life, there remains the fact that some secular ethics proclaims the superior life to amount to one that renounces pleasure, enjoyment, and delights. We need to address this.

SECULAR MISCONCEPTIONS ABOUT COMMERCE

Interestingly, many secular doctrines and ethics are reminiscent of aspects of the dualistic doctrine. Freud's division of the self into the id, ego, and superego comes to mind; as does Lawrence Kohlberg's theory of levels of moral development, in which the altruistic attitude is designated as the morally most advanced;

and John Stuart Mill's division of "higher" and "lower" pleasures, valuing the pleasures of the mind over those of the body.

Why should we dispute these? Simply because there is no sound reason for thanking that human nature is any less integrated than the nature of other living beings. Is there justification for viewing the lives of zebras or cats as fundamentally divided within themselves? Are these other living entities so different as to enjoy an unalienated form of life? There is no reason to think that nature is inherently contradictory. The fact of our distinctiveness as moral agents does not imply that our nature is necessarily, irreconcilably, divided. It means, rather, that keeping our integrity is a personal task and a uniquely human achievement when successfully attained. If we do not accept that nature exhibits inherent contradictions, why should we expect human nature to do so?

Karl Marx's philosophy is sympathetic to this doctrine of the fundamental alienation of human life, illustrated in his belief that humanity as a concrete universal entity—an "organic whole"—is still at an immature stage of development.[13] Clearly, babies, infants, children, and even adolescents are not fully developed and can thus experience basic instabilities in their lives, which parents and others in the community can help them overcome in the maturation process. But this model seems inapplicable to the whole human race, Marx and Hegel notwithstanding. Instead, since the emergence of Homo sapiens some 100,000 years or so ago,[14] human beings as individual biological entities of a certain kind have been able to reach adulthood and thereby live an una-

13. Marx, *Grundrisse*, p. 39.
14. Vitaly Shevoroshkin, "The Mother Tongue," *The Sciences*, May/June 1990, pp. 20–27.

lienated life.[15] In short, human beings need not find themselves innately torn within by their very nature. However, it is possible that, given that human beings live by their own wits, they may frequently fail to be fully integrated. But self-alienation is not the same type of inherent human alienation Hegel and Marx find as the necessary condition of human life prior to the attainment of some kind of collective emancipation.

The sort of ethics that a self-consistent human nature would imply itself exhibits a hierarchy of scale of moral principles. Not all such principles are equally binding in all circumstances; just as one may at times lie so as to protect the higher value of innocent human life, so courage may be less important than prudence. Accordingly, there is something to the claim that exclusive dedication to commerce, above all other possible endeavors, is misguided. Just as exaggerated devotion to feats of courage is misguided bravado, not the practice of a virtue, so too might one be rightly criticized for having too keen an interest in values that are on a lower scale, sacrificing values that are higher. Of course, to know which are higher and which are lower often requires knowledge of a person as an individual, for different people may have different value scales. Not all values are of equal weight for everyone. Opportunity, talent, temperament, and the like all play an important role in determining what is the morally proper life for someone in particular.[16]

Within the modified Aristotelian ethical theory that we have outlined in this book, the morally good life will have some common features for all persons in all times and places, including, among other things, a life exhibiting the virtues of courage, hon-

15. But see J. Roger Lee, "Morality and Markets," in Machan, *Commerce and Morality*. Lee's essay contains a brilliant account of the morality of financial and related speculation, one of the most frequent targets of moral criticism of the marketplace.

16. For a discussion of this in some detail, see Machan, *Individuals and Their Rights* (La Salle, Ill.: Open Court, 1989).

esty, generosity, prudence, and the like. But human lives can manifest themselves in great variety. The moral good, just as other aspects of nature or being, can be exhibited in a plurality of ways, not necessarily mutually exclusive. Just as the human potential for language can be actualized in indefinitely unique ways, with particular systems of communication, so too can the human potential for a morally good life be actualized in ways unique to each individual, yet recognizable to all.

In day-to-day terms, as we make assessments of our alternatives and of what our fellows make of their lives, this pluralism implies that different individuals may live morally exemplary lives doing very different things, following very different paths, from engineering to nursing to painting to philosophy to carpentry to taxi driving to parenting and on and on, including the various careers in business and commerce. Although some careers may be more significant for human life in general than others, it is not the career as such that determines the moral quality of those who have embarked on it or even whether anyone in particular ought to have done so.

Since we are not here advancing a fully developed and justified ethical theory, what we have said thus far will have to suffice for a reconsideration of the nature of commerce and business and its place on the moral hierarchy of human life. From what we have considered, it makes good sense to appreciate commercial activities as part of a prudently conducted human life. We ought to take care of ourselves as natural parts of the world; we should heed our wants, desires, needs, wishes, and the like, provided these have been ordered in a fashion consistent with human nature in general and in line with our individual personal attributes, opportunities, talents, and similar constraints and possibilities.[17]

In general terms there are constraints on commerce that have

17. For more detailed discussion of these notions, see Tibor R. Machan, *Generosity: Virtue in Civil Society* (Washington, D.C.: Cato Institute, 1998).

always been recognized and are still the most plausible standards by which to tell whether the activity is decent. There can be misconduct in commerce, as in any other human endeavor, but we would know of this only by reference to specific cases, based on a sensible moral standard. If commerce is conducted without deceit, fraud, force, or cruelty, there is clearly nothing in general wrong with it. It is one thing to profit from trade with others in normal circumstances but another to profit from the misery of a relative or a friend. It is one thing to realize great profits in times of peace, quite another to insist on them when one's country is at the brink of destruction. But this is just commonsense ethics, not a call for asceticism, self-renunciation, or self-abnegation.

If business is conducted honestly, forthrightly, prudently, wisely, productively, and with general awareness of life's other values, there is everything in general fitting about engaging in it. And, perhaps most important, the goal of commerce and business, the enhancement of one's well-being as a human being here on earth, is in no respect lowly or base, as suggested by Plato's philosophy, sometimes by that of Aristotle, and most of all by the dualistic doctrines throughout most of human history.

CHAPTER ELEVEN

Commerce
Morally Affirmed

*There is nothing so useful to man in general, nor so beneficial to
particular societies and individuals, as trade. This is that alma
mater, at whose plentiful breast all mankind are nourished.*
— Henry Fielding

STRUCK BY MENTALITY

It may be helpful now to summarize the basic thesis of this work.
A major reason business is bashed and commerce is maligned is
the widespread belief that institutions and endeavors that provide
joys here on earth are ultimately distractions and enemies of what
is truly important: the spiritual dimensions of human existence.
Underlying this belief are dualistic and idealistic philosophies,
the various permutations of which, in the innumerable layers of
culture, have conspired to make something that is undeniably
vital to human life also something that is demeaned.

In this book we have focused on those ideas that have influ-
enced commerce and business in many cultures, admittedly ignoring other factors that exert a cultural influence. Indeed, commerce might be placed in an unfavorable light for a variety of
factors. Of these, we have noted the special interest that intellectuals, artists, and the clergy may have in denigrating trade. As
those who trade in words and may seem themselves disadvantaged by a favorable view of commerce, intellectuals, such as
academicians, may engage in special pleading. Plato has been

accused of this for recommending, in his very prestigious Socratic dialogues, that the philosopher is most fit to rule the ideal society.

Historical accidents may also have contributed to the ill repute of commerce, as do certain emotions such as envy and resentment, although the latter, we have suggested, are likely not fundamental but rest on certain prior views about the lowly status of the role of commerce in human life. Also, other ideas, such as the view that greed motivates us all, indirectly tarnish the reputation of commerce, for if we cannot help desiring worldly goods, then there can be nothing commendable about seeking them. We found this to be implicit in Immanuel Kant, who grafted a moral theory on certain ideas developed by Thomas Hobbes, namely, that everyone is, by nature, greedy. For Kant, our greedy lower nature must be overcome by an act of will, itself apart from nature, in order for us to be moral. On Kant's analysis, prudence, the virtue of attending to one's own well-being, is stripped of its moral value.

Despite these interesting challenges to the reputation of commerce, the most serious is the prominence of the idea that human beings ought to eschew worldly satisfaction and embrace only or mainly the spiritual sides of their nature. Let's consider once again why there is such a widespread inclination for human beings to reach for some supernatural dimension, to give prominence to the idea of another reality, the realm of forms or spirits. Why are so many people inclined to anoint this realm with such an elevated status in reality as to require the denigration of the realm of earthly existence, which is our only verifiable, knowable habitat?

We should make clear the question being asked here, lest we confuse it with the earlier one concerning the content of this dualism. This is our question: What is it about the kind of life human beings live that could suggest to them that dualism is sound even if it is not? What is there about our commonly shared human experience that can give rise to a belief in dualism and the supernatural? Furthermore, why would someone embrace this view, despite its problems?

Since human beings are rational, our beliefs have origins, the discovery of which may shed light on the nature of the belief. For example, at one time, most people thought that the earth was flat and at the center of the universe. This was not an unfounded or *irrational* belief, though it turned out to be false. Part of the evidence offered for this belief was the nearly compelling testimony of the senses: In our common experience, the world does indeed look flat, the sun does appear to rise and set, and the heavenly bodies do seem to circle the earth, which certainly does seem to be motionless itself. It took some time and education to dislodge this belief from the body of widely held beliefs about the nature of things. Part of that education includes understanding how we came to have the belief in the first place and then offering the ultimately simpler view in its place, showing how it accounts for how things seem as we experience them, as well as for other phenomena that our former, false, belief could accommodate only with the increased complexity of additional beliefs. Since the new explanation honors, rather than contradicts, the testimony of the senses and offers simpler explanations of observed phenomena than the old view, the new explanation becomes more compelling, more rational. So too, we submit, is the case with the belief in dualism. Our question concerns the possible origins of this belief in our common experience, so that we can discover the truth behind a problematic, probably false, but seriously and widely held opinion. We are concerned to explore what is plausible about dualism.

UNDERSTANDING THE APPEAL
OF DUALISM

The explanation that we believe makes the best sense, and underscores the insight on which dualism is based, is this: Once human beings become aware of their uniqueness in nature as rational, thinking, reflecting, contemplating beings whose entire life is infused with this unique mentality, it is tempting to regard themselves as linked to some higher reality. We are, after all, by common observation, uniquely different from the rest of nature, as evidenced by our art, science, religion, technology, and other creative and self-consciously initiated expressions. It is human beings who have tamed nature, domesticated animals, built bridges, and sailed the seas, long before recorded history. Nothing else in nature comes even close to our achievements, which in themselves transcend nature. We are different because something about us is above nature, not just subject to it.

This metaphysicalization of the psychological experience of our uniqueness as conscious and valuing, and thus spirited— spiritual—beings, is most fully captured in the dualistic and idealistic views found in both East and West. Heraclitus contends that the soul has a *logos* that increases itself, indicating a nature quite different from that of the body, which may be increased by various causes but not by itself.[1] Consider, also, Augustine's observation, cited earlier, about human mental life being an infinite multiplicity: "This thing is the mind, and this thing is myself." Augustine is awestruck by the fact of human memory and awareness, something evidently not paralleled elsewhere in nature, indeed, not part of nature! Augustine's is a particularly eloquent expression of this experience, though certainly not the first or last of its kind.

We are suggesting this: When human beings begin to become aware of their unique mode of awareness, begin to notice how different they are from the rest of the living world by virtue of their capacity to think, to ask questions, find answers, to wonder, be amazed, and to give expression to such abstract reflections,

1. Heraclitus (DK22 B118).

they quite often and understandably imagine themselves to be not simply a unique part of nature but somehow a being that transcends it. They imagine themselves to be in part supernatural or to have some relationship to a supernatural realm. Such is the grand quality of the experience of discovering our unique faculties, capacities, unmatched by anything else in the natural world.

It would be futile to deny this experience—after all, this is how it *feels* to be utterly amazed, to be struck by the fact that we think, forge ideas, imagine stories, write books, compose operas, establish museums, propound scientific theories, attempt to make the various features of our world intelligible, and devote serious attention to considering what is good and bad, right and wrong, in every phase of our lives, in a world where nothing else does this. There are those, such as Daniel Dennett,[2] who argue that regarding ourselves as unique in this way is contrary to evolutionary science (since Darwin's idea also threatened to spread all the way up, dissolving the illusion of human authorship). But their argument tends to be self-refuting: They fail to see that every serious evolutionary theorist, particularly Darwin himself, clearly and unambiguously exemplifies authorship. The *Origin of Species* can hardly *itself* be considered a product of natural selection. Likewise, every normal human being's life exhibits a degree of authorship.

This plain fact of our distinctiveness is undeniable, but it is also susceptible of being misunderstood and leading us astray. Dualism is precisely the result of such a misunderstanding, which in turn has led to a suspicion of all activities, notably business and commerce, that serve earthly, natural, needs and desires, for

2. Daniel C. Dennett, "Darwin's Dangerous Idea," *The Sciences*, May/June 1995, p. 37. This is an excerpt from Dennett's book, *Darwin's Dangerous Idea: Evolution and the Meaning of Life* (London: Allen Lane, 1995). See, however, the list of works in note 5, chapter 7, in which the reductivist, determinist position is rejected.

such activities are seen as distractions and detours from the more laudable focus on spiritual concerns.

It might be argued that, by disputing the dualistic account, as we have, we are trivializing a sacred aspect of human existence, our link to the holy and the divine. Do we subvert human reverence and reroute it toward something lowly and base, the merely natural and mundane? Put another way, are we begging the very question we raise by providing a naturalistic account of our tendency to transform the "awesome" into the supernatural?

In a word, no. It is because we human beings are unique in seeking explanations that we ought first to attempt the naturalistic route. We ought first to proceed along such lines rather than give ourselves over at once to what nearly everyone admits to be at best a realm beyond human comprehension. Our wonderment, made possible by reflecting on the faculty of understanding, has, quite ironically, led in the opposite direction of the comprehendable!

Given our concern about why, despite its importance, commerce and business have such a poor reputation, it will not advance our understanding to invoke an explanation that is itself incapable of being grasped by us. To say that what puzzles us is something that belongs to the province of faith is to abandon the effort to understand and, instead, yield to what must remain fundamentally mysterious. It is primarily for this reason that Thomas Aquinas, in developing Roman Catholic theology toward an Aristotelian view of reality, rejected the more mystical path of Saint Augustine. Whatever its merits, faith alone is inadequate for helping us to understand our existence; it is, by definition, neither a faculty of the understanding nor an instrument of reason.

Were it not for its tragic implications for this life, including the demeaning of business and commerce, the dualistic, supernaturalistic view might be harmless enough, but such is not the case. Commerce and business are, after all, essential to a successful life, especially in modern society. Even the generally admired virtues of compassion, generosity, and charity, which rightly call on us to respond to the needs of others, would be nearly impossible to exercise had we not the means provided by economic industry and prudence. The prospects for a reasonably flourishing life are negligible without the fruits of commerce and business. Such flourishing is inhibited if we relegate these human endeavors to the lowly, the shameful, the constantly reprehensible and lamentable. To reject commerce is tantamount to rejecting our essential humanity, a failure to heed the injunction Know Thyself.

CHOOSING BETWEEN EXPLANATIONS

None of this proves that the explanation or account offered is sound but rather fends off the charge that such an explanation begs the question and embodies an intolerable irreverence. We have already noted that the popular explanation of envy will not suffice since envy cannot conquer without the aid of just resentment, righteous indignation. Envy is an ignoble condition, and its efficacy is assured only when combined with something that can vindicate it. It is the demeaning of commerce and business or, rather, of the aspirations of human beings engaging in business, that makes envying its achievements appear respectable. Nor is the power of commerce sufficient grounds for its debasement, for other sources of power do not suffer a similar fate: Science is powerful, as are education, medicine, literature, and public life. Each meets with its share of criticism but not the activities as such. Only commerce and business are subjected to such thoroughgoing devaluation that to be involved in them requires some excuse, some vindication. And so the private vice that is business requires a public benefit, such as philanthropy, to merit praise.

It seems, then, that a more fundamental explanation is required, one that is plausible in light of our understanding of human nature. It should also be consistent with the inventive capacity of human beings striving to find their place in the world and to make their presence acceptable to them. The invocation of the divine dimension as a way to comprehend our uniqueness as creative, speculative, contemplative, and knowing mental beings seems initially plausible enough to embrace and cling to, despite the scarcity of evidence for such a dimension.

A point to note about explanations of the kind advanced here is that they are not causal in the ordinary sense of that term. Scientism has extrapolated the mechanistic causal explanation to nearly all realms of human inquiry, including intellectual history. This view demands that, to explain anything, we must not do so by reference to what people have thought or to what people have done based on their thinking. Such explanations are deemed unscientific and are held in low esteem within much of the intellectual, especially social science, community. People are not accorded full causal powers or initiative since what a person does is itself always supposed to be in need of further explanation by reference, say, to upbringing, DNA, ethnic or cultural membership, economic class, the climate, and so on. Thus, we find that such fields of research and theorizing as sociobiology are always met with some measure of enthusiasm since they attempt to explain in ways derived from classical physics, even when some deference is shown toward the need for updating the language of causes, as, for example, with the language of variables.

But this preference for explanations in terms of efficient causes is itself often a prejudice based on metaphysics. Such is reductive materialism, which sees all causes as having to be of just one kind. It inclines many who are concerned to understand human behavior and institutions to await some future materialistic explanation even when none is in sight.

Were we to see that a pluralistic, rather than a reductionist, ontology is sound, so that nature manifests itself in irreducibly different types of beings, this kind of mechanistic bias would beg the question of what types of causes we may find in nature. In fact, of course, ordinary thinking, the kind that usually transports us through our days successfully, does embrace pluralism: We do not confuse the causal relations on a pool table with those that operate when Mozart produces a sonata, Rembrandt a painting, or Newton, a scientific theory. Nor do we take it that when we advance an explanation, this itself is something to be explained by, say, a childhood trauma or unconscious mechanism. In short, we see multiplicity in nature, various ways that the world works, not just the single model of mechanical causation. This common-sense stance has its metaphysical framework, developed early on by Aristotle and contributed to since, but it is not widely embraced by intellectuals, mainly because scientism prevails.

However, even in our day, the reductive materialist outlook faces serious challenges. All the concern with values in our culture, which fits ill with such a position, suggests the need for an alternative view. It is intellectually embarrassing, to say the least, to find major commentators embracing wholly incompatible modes of understanding human life, some including serious emphasis on morality, yet others discounting ethics completely and seeking only sociological or other social scientific explanations. Even our politicians exhibit the confusion when, on the one hand, they react with moral outrage to bombings, racism, sexism, and the like but on the other hand seek to remedy all this by vigorous social engineering.

In the present work we have invoked a pluralistic ontology that holds, in essence, that when we are concerned with human behavior, it is justified to believe that human beings can be first causes, initiators of action, mainly by reference to the original thinking they may choose to engage in or to evade.

EXPLANATIONS NEED HELP

The antinaturalist explanation or account cannot stand by itself.[3] Many other aids are required. For example, the accompanying debasement of the human individual in favor of the concrete universal of humanity helps the myth to survive. To give credit to nature is also to give credit to oneself in particular, not just as a humble manifestation of universal humanity. It is to accept that oneself is unique and dear, a valued being in and of itself, without having to make that value derivative of some higher being. So, by blocking the option of self-importance, the prospect of naturalizing human life itself is made to face an added obstacle. Combining all this with the dualistic and/or idealistic hypotheses, despite the evident ultimate mysteriousness of that option, helps make antinaturalism palatable. It conforms to the view that there is something greater than ourselves to which our self needs to be sacrificed, consistent with the perspective that our happiness on earth should be demeaned.

Ayn Rand has noted that religion has preempted naturalism by appropriating nearly all such terms as elation, rapture, ecstasy, exaltation, joy, glory, nobility, reverence, and worship.[4] Little remains by which the elevated possibilities of the natural world may be conceptually delineated and linguistically expressed.

Clearly, what we are suggesting is a secular or godless approach to human life but hardly a valueless or amoral one. It is

---

3. The term *explanation* in our time tends to suggest the mechanistic model of understanding action and behavior. *Account*, however, is broader. It suggests making sense of something, whatever the appropriate approach to that task may be. For example, in some cases understanding is achieved best by exploring what facts would make the best sense of some phenomena (e.g., would the fact of human free will make better sense of the enormous variety of what we know human beings to be doing than, say, determinism). (This is widely used in the criminal law!) For more, see Rose, *Lifeline*.

4. Ayn Rand, preface, *The Fountainhead* (New York: Signet Books, 1967).

an approach that any honest religious person should find some sympathy with, given that in nearly all the major religions there is a fundamental mystery, incomprehensibility, about the divine. The American founders, mostly deists, saw and attempted to adjust to this fact: They approached political life in secular terms, seeing that a religious approach would leave things inaccessible to common human understanding. The idea was that God had made the world essentially right, had given us the means to live our lives well, and had left us to proceed on our own, without further divine intervention. Believing that God intended, so to speak, to be left out of our political lives, the founders saw fit, and wisely, to honor that.

The accessible truth of religion, with which we agree, is that life is marvelous, amazing, immensely rich and varied and that human life in particular is rare and immeasurably valuable, given to free choice, and accountable thereby. Without in any way diminishing the wonder and the value and the moral worth of human life, we wish to provide a more humanly accessible account that, we believe, would be of enormous benefit to us all. We would then not have to declare ourselves estranged from nature in order to make room for our remarkableness.

PERSISTENTLY OFF

A major obstacle to widespread embrace of our thesis is that most people have believed otherwise for a long time. This certainly could be an obstacle to what we are arguing regarding the merits of commerce and the natural life that it serves. There is some sense to the traditionalist idea that a proposition held long and widely has merit by that alone. This is because beliefs are usually put to use and would not manage to help us with our lives unless they were reasonably close to the truth. We would eventually become disenchanted with unhelpful beliefs and replace them with others. This is clearly one way that science proceeds. This "democracy of the dead,"[5] or reliance on the trial-and-error process of sorting out our beliefs, would appear to support beliefs that persisted over time, such as dualism and, of course, the religious perspective on life that so many embrace, within which dualism finds its theoretical home. How are we to respond to the traditionalist view here?

First, as a matter of logic, the number of believers and the longevity of a belief are irrelevant to the truth of a belief. For example, as a matter of fact, countless generations of people falsely believed that the earth was the center of the universe, but they did so mainly because it *appeared* thus and for centuries no alternative theory was prominently propounded.

Second, many beliefs, though essentially false, survive over time because they serve some important value other than truth, such as social cohesion or moral education. It is undeniable that the various religions of the world have helped societies to cohere, as well as to be guided through life according to moral principles, many of which are universal in application and rationally supportable apart from particular theologies.

Third, one can be wrong without being wrong through and through. In the present case, it may be that many people are

---

5. Take the following comment from Edmund Burke, which supports this view in no uncertain terms: "Men have no right to risk the very existence of their nation and their civilization upon experiments in morals and politics; for each man's private capital of intelligence is petty; it is only when a man draws upon the bank and capital of the ages, the wisdom of our ancestors, that he can act wisely." (Quoted in Kenneth M. Dolbeare, *Directions of American Political Thought* [New York: John Wiley & Sons, 1969], p. 11.) Burke adds that "we are afraid to put men to live and trade each on his own private stock of reason, because we suspect that this stock in each man is small, and that the individuals would do better to avail themselves of the general bank of nations and of ages." *Reflections on the Revolution in France* (Indianapolis, Ind.: Hackett, 1987), p. 76.

wrong about the merits of commerce and business but not wrong about there being more important matters in their lives. Devotion to one's children, friends, political ideals, and such are more important than devotion to shopping, calculating risks of financial investments, or speculating on the futures market. Indeed, because of an inappropriate or disproportionate interest in financial success, many people have foolishly ignored more important values, such as nurturing intimate relationships. But here the fault lies in the person.

Fourth, there is not one body of a widely embraced doctrine called dualism. There are scores, with widely varied twists and turns, sharing a family resemblance but committed to widely divergent specifics. H. L. Mencken's *Treatise of the Gods* lists roughly 1,100 different monotheistic religions throughout recorded history, each different from the others.

Fifth, religiosity is not being dismissed as wholesale nonsense. Most beliefs that human beings entertain are far from being totally bizarre. There is much that is valuable and true in most systems of belief, and the dualist thesis contains elements that suggest important insights about reality (e.g., that there is some manner of hierarchical order of being). As Somerset Maugham put it:

> I have read much philosophy, and though I do not see how it is possible to refuse intellectual assent to certain theories of the Absolute, I can find nothing in them to induce me to depart from my instinctive disbelief in what is usually meant by the word religion. I have little patience with the writers who try to reconcile in one conception the Absolute of the metaphysician with the God of Christianity. But if I had any doubts, the [First World] war would have effectually silenced them.[6]

6. W. Somerset Maugham, *A Writer's Notebook* (London, England: Penguin Books, 1967), p. 145.

As we have already noted, a similar idea was expressed by G. W. F. Hegel, one of the modern era's greatest thinkers, when he proposed that Christianity is a symbolic rendition of the truths of metaphysics. Another modern philosopher, Ludwig Feuerbach, argued in his *The Essence of Christianity* that God is a formidable projection human beings make of what is essentially a collection of fully developed human qualities: Omniscience is the extension of our own fallible capacity to know, omnipotence of our limited power, eternity of our short lives guided by our awareness of much of history, and omnibenevolence of our finite goodness. Thus, God is the vision of ourselves fully developed, given cosmic proportion and significance, a powerful guiding principle for many of us.

One need not, by any means, dismiss the *source* of dualistic thinking. We are fully sympathetic with the profound awe and wonder that has tempted some toward dualism. Rather, it is our contention that dualistic thinking itself embodies psychological and ethical elements that have been distorted into metaphysical theses and moral misconceptions, as well as damaging prejudices.

Thus, in consequence, commerce and business may have been highly undervalued in Western and other societies, even while it is true that they ought not to be regarded as the highest values in our lives. But what such persistent and widespread undervaluing has done is to make commerce and business not just a low priority for people but an outright menace, a kind of necessary evil at best and an enemy of the people at worst.

We must also consider that perspectives other than the dualistic have given support to business bashing. Many fail to appreciate the spiritual dimension of the material stuff of which much of what is traded consists. Creativity, design, imagination, and beauty are found in many of the goods of commerce. Commerce also provides people with power over their lives, by providing goods and services that can reduce labor, increase available time, advance good health, and keep us informed and in touch. These benefits are overlooked and rarely praised by the business bashers. And, given the sheer overtness of commerce, when people in business go astray, the commercial malpractice gets writ large, energizing the prejudice against business with the inevitable calls for laws and regulations. Finally, working against business is the fact that "you can't take it with you," meaning that the temporal nature of the goods of commerce makes them less real and significant than spiritual goods. On this view, to show an interest in business and commerce and the goods that they provide is to demonstrate a commensurate degree of one's own spiritual poverty. In the words of Thoreau, "A man is rich in proportion to the number of things that he can let alone." The critics are famous and formidable.

What can be done in the face of such resistance? Essentially, an alternative perspective about all of this needs to be fully developed and vigorously advanced. We have only begun that project here by offering some naturalistic ideas as alternatives to the dualism that pervades our culture and underlies the maligning of commerce and business. We have offered a sketch of the rationale for such a view and why it makes better sense than dualism. Of course, deeply ingrained attitudes and prejudices are not easily changed. A good beginning is with serious reflection on this topic, which we hope this book may generate in readers.

Let us assume as true beyond a reasonable doubt that commerce and business are honorable human endeavors. Assume, again, that they ought to receive respect as such, that those involved in them ought to have all the benefits and rights accorded to members of other respected professions. Still, putting that idea into circulation and applying it to concrete human realities is a long and arduous process. Ideas are important, but they need to be put into practice. The idea that commerce is noble will meet with considerable resistance from the established institutions, laws, habits, practices, and attitudes that have been prejudicial in ways that we have discussed.

However, it seems that, based on what we have shown in this work, there is good reason to at least begin the process of rethinking the value of commerce and business in human societies and to continue the dialogue begun here. Those who have devoted much of their lives to careers in business and commerce deserve at least this much. We ourselves, in turn, deserve as much if, in good conscience, we are to be straight and just in the conduct of our lives and in the character of our communities.

BIBLIOGRAPHY

Adler, Mortimer. *The Difference of Man and the Difference It Makes.* New York: World Publishing Co., 1968.

Appleby, Joyce, Lynn Hunt, and Margaret Jacob. *Telling the Truth about History.* New York: W. W. Norton, 1994.

Aristotle. *The Athenian Constitution,* trans. P. J. Rhodes. Middlesex, England: Penguin Books, 1984.

Bacon, Francis. *The Advancement of Learning.* Oxford, England: W. A. Wright, 1868.

Bakewell, Charles M. *Source Book in Ancient Philosophy.* New York: Gordian Press, 1873.

Baldacchino, Joseph. "The New Public Order: Within and Above." Review of Charles Taylor's *Sources of the Self* in *Humanitas,* fall 1992/winter 1993.

Barry, Vincent. *Moral Issues in Business.* Belmont, Calif.: Wadsworth Publishing Company, 1983.

Beauchamp T. L., and N. E. Bowie, eds. *Ethical Theory and Business.* Englewood Cliffs, N.J.: Prentice-Hall, 1983.

Becker, Gary. *The Economic Approach to Human Behavior.* Chicago: University of Chicago Press, 1976.

Bellah, Robert, et al. *Habits of the Heart: Individualism and Commitment in American Life.* New York: Harper and Row, 1984.

Bloom, Allan. *Plato's Republic.* New York: Basic Books, 1972.

————. *Giants and Dwarfs*. New York: Simon and Schuster, 1990.

Borshi, Magen. "Children of Light." Correspondence in the *New Republic*, May 2, 1994.

Bowie, Norman E., and Ronald F. Duska. *Business Ethics*. Englewood Cliffs, N.J.: Prentice Hall, 1990.

Buchanan, Emerson. *Aristotle's Theory of Being*. Cambridge, Mass.: Greek, Roman, and Byzantine Monographs, 1962.

Buchanan, James M. "Boundaries of Social Contract," *Reason Papers*, no. 2 (1975).

Buono, Anthony F., and Lawrence T. Nichols. "Stockholder and Stakeholder Interpretations of Business Social Role," in [citation missing]

Burke, Edmund. *Revolution in France*. Indianapolis, Ind: Hackett Publishing Co., 1987.

————. *Reflections on the Revolution in France*. Indianapolis, Ind.: Hackett Publishing Co., 1987.

Coase, Ronald. "The Problem of Social Cost." *Journal of Law and Economics* 3 (1960).

Cunningham, Robert L. *Liberty and the Rule of Law: Essays in Honor of F. A. Hayek*. College Station: Texas A&M University Press, 1979.

Clark, Stephen R. L. *The Moral Status of Animals*. Oxford, England: Clarendon Press, 1977.

De George, Richard T. *Business Ethics*. New York: Macmillan, 1982.

Den Uyl, Douglas J. *The New Crusaders*. New Brunswick, N.J.: Transaction Books, 1984.

————. "Corporations at Stake." *The Freeman*, July 1992.

————, and Tibor R. Machan. "Recent Work in Business Ethics: A Survey and Critique." *American Philosophical Quarterly*, April 1987.

————. *The Virtue of Prudence*. New York: Peter Lang Publishers, 1991.

Dennett, Daniel C. *Darwin's Dangerous Idea: Evolution and the Meaning of Life*. London: Allen Lane, 1995.

————. "Darwin's Dangerous Idea." *The Sciences*, May/June 1995.

Derrett, J. D. M. "A Camel through the Eye of a Needle." *New Testament Studies* 32 (July 1986).

Donaldson, Thomas. *Corporations and Morality*. Englewood-Cliffs, N.J.: Prentice-Hall, 1982.

Eagleson, John, ed. *Christians and Socialism*. Maryknoll, N.Y.: Orbis Books, 1975.

Ehrenfeld, David W. *The Arrogance of Humanism* London: Oxford University Press, 1978.

Emerson, Ralph Waldo "Nominalist and Realist." In *The Complete Writings of Ralph Waldo Emerson*. New York: Wm. H. Wise & Co., 1929.

Estes, Ralph. *Tyranny of the Bottom Line*. San Francisco, Calif.: Berrett-Koehler Publ., Inc., 1996.

Etzioni, Amitai. *The Moral Dimension*. New York: Free Press, 1988.

———. "Money, Power & Fame." *Newsweek*, September 18, 1989.

Ezorsky, Gertrude, ed. *Moral Rights in the Workplace*. Albany: State University of New York Press, 1987.

Farr, Richard. "The Political Economy of Community." *Journal of Social Philosophy* 23 (winter 1992).

Feyerabend, Paul. *Against Method*. London, England: Verso Press, 1987.

Friedman, Milton. *Capitalism and Freedom*. Chicago: University of Chicago Press, 1961.

———. "The Line We Dare Not Cross." *Encounter*, November 1976.

———. "The Social Responsibility of Business Is to Increase Its Profits," *New York Times Magazine*, September 13, 1970.

Garrett, Garret. "Business." In Harold E. Stearns, ed., *Civilization in the United States: An Inquiry by Thirty Americans*. New York: Harcourt, Brace, 1922.

Goldwater, Barry. *The Conscience of a Conservative*. Chicago: Regnery, 1962.

Green, Peter. "The Care of the Soul." *New Republic*, September 5, 1994.

Hamburger, H. *Money, Coins: The Interpreters Dictionary of the Bible*, vol. 3. Nashville, Tenn.: Abindon, 1962.

Hardin, Garrett. "The Tragedy of the Commons." *Science*, no. 162 (December 13, 1968).

Hasnas, John. "Social Responsibility of Corporations and How to Make It Work for You." *Freeman*, July 1994.

Hastings, James. *Dictionary of the Bible*. New York: Charles Scribners Sons, 1963.

Hessen, Robert. *In Defense of the Corporation*. Stanford: Hoover Institution Press, 1979

Hetherington, John A. C. "Corporate Social Responsibility, Stockholders, and the Law." *Journal of Contemporary Business*, winter 1993.

Hinman, Lawrence M., ed. *Contemporary Moral Issues*. Upper Saddle River, N.J.: Prentice Hall, 1996.

Hoffman, W. Michael, and Jennifer Mills Moore, eds. *Business Ethics*. New York: McGraw-Hill, 1990.

Hospers, John, ed. *Readings in Introductory Philosophical Analysis*. Englewood Cliffs, N.J.: Prentice Hall, 1968.

Hugo, Victor. *La preface de Cromwell*, Maurice A. Souriau, ed. Geneve: Slatkine Reprints, 1973.

Hume, David. *The History of England*, vol. 2. Indianapolis, Ind.: Liberty Fund, 1983.

Hunt, Lester H. "An Argument against a Legal Duty to Rescue." *Journal of Social Philosophy* 36 (1994).

Johnson, M. Bruce, and T. R. Machan, eds. *Rights and Regulation*. Cambridge, Mass.: Ballinger Books, 1983.

Jones, Donald G., and Patricia Bennet, eds. *A Bibliography of Business Ethics 1981–1985*. Lewiston, N.Y.: Edwin Mellen Press, 1986.

Kelley, David, and Jeff Scott. "Gekko Echo: A Closer Look at the Decade of Greed." *Reason*, March 1993.

Kenney, Anthony. *What is Faith?* London, England: Oxford University Press, 1992.

Ketcham, Ralph L., ed. *The Political Thought of Benjamin Franklin*. Indianapolis, Ind.: Bobbs-Merrill, 1965.

Kirk, Russell. *The Conservative Mind*. Chicago: Regnery Publ. Co., 1953.

Kirzner, Israel. *Competition and Entrepreneurship.* Chicago: University of Chicago Press, 1973.

———. "Producer, Entrepreneur, and the Right to Property." *Reason Papers*, no. 1 (fall 1974).

Langer, Susanne K. *Mind: An Essay on Human Feeling*, vols. 1 and 2. Baltimore, Md.: John Hopkins University Press, 1967/1972.

Letwin, Shirley Robin. *The Autonomy of Thatcherism.* London: Fontana Books, 1992.

Lucey Kenneth J., and Tibor R. Machan, eds. *Recent Work in Philosophy.* Totowa, N.J.: Rowman and Allenheld, 1982.

Machan, Tibor. *Liberty and Culture: Essays on the Idea of a Free Society.* Buffalo, N.Y.: Prometheus Books, 1989.

———. *Individuals and Their Rights.* La Salle, Ill.: Open Court Publishing Co., Inc., 1989.

———. *Capitalism and Individualism.* New York: St. Martins Press, 1990.

———. "Pollution, Collectivism and Capitalism." *Journal des Economists et des Estudes Humaines* 2 (March 1991).

———. "Do Animals Have Rights?" *Public Affairs Quarterly* 5 (April 1991).

———. "How to Understand Eastern European Developments." *Public Affairs Quarterly* 6 (1992).

———. "The Right to Private Property." *Critical Review* 6 (1992).

———. "Between Parents and Children." *Journal of Social Philosophy* 23 (winter 1992).

———. "Evidence of Necessary Existence." *Objectivity* 1 (1992).

———. "Applied Ethics and Free Will." *Journal of Applied Philosophy* 10 (1993).

———. "Environmentalism Humanized." *Public Affairs Quarterly* 7 (April 1993).

———. *The Virtue of Liberty.* Irvington-on-Hudson, N.Y.: Foundation for Economic Education, 1994.

———. "Professional Responsibilities of Corporate Managers." *Business and Professional Ethics Journal* 13 (fall 1994).

———. *Private Rights and Public Illusions*. New Brunswick, N.J.: Transactions Books, 1995

———. "Reason in Economics versus Ethics." *International Journal of Social Economics* 22 (1995).

———. *A Primer on Ethics*. Norman: University of Oklahoma Press, 1996.

———. *Generosity; Virtue in Civil Society*. Washington, D.C.: Cato Institute, 1998.

———. *Classical Individualism, The Supreme Importance of Each Human Being*. London: Routledge, 1998.

———. "Prima Facie v. Natural Human Rights." *Journal of Value Inquiry* 10, no. 1, 1976.

Machan, Tibor R., ed. *Commerce and Morality*. Lanham, Md.: Rowman & Littlefield, 1988.

———, ed. *The Libertarian Alternative*. Chicago: Nelson-Hall Co., 1974.

Mack, Eric. "Bad Samaritarianism and the Causation of Harm." *Philosophy and Public Affairs* 9 (summer 1980).

MacKinnon, Catherine. *Only Words*. Cambridge, Mass.: Harvard University Press, 1994.

Macpherson, C. B. *The Political Theory of Possessive Individualism: Hobbes and Locke*. Oxford, England: Clarendon Press, 1962.

Marx, Karl. *Grundrisse*, trans. D. McLellan. New York: Harper Torchbooks, 1971.

Matson, Wallace I. *A New History of Philosophy*. San Diego, Calif.: Harcourt Brace Jovanovich, 1987.

Maugham, W. Somerset. *A Writer's Notebook*. London, England: Penguin Books, 1967.

Mavrodes, George. "Property." In Samuel I. Blumenfeld, ed. *Property in a Humane Economy*. LaSalle, Ill.: Open Court Publishing Co., 1974.

McGee, Robert, ed. *Business Ethics & Common Sense*. Westport, Conn.: Quorum Books, 1992.

McKenzie, Richard. *The Limits of Economic Science*. Boston: Kluwer-Nijhoff Pub., 1983.

Midgley, Mary. *The Ethical Primate*. London: Routledge, 1994.

Miller, Fred D., Jr. *Nature, Justice and Rights in Aristotle's Politics*. Oxford, England: Clarendon Press, 1995.

Mitchell, Roy. *The Exile of the Soul*. Buffalo, N.Y.: Prometheus Books, 1983.

Moorehouse, John C. "The Mechanistic Foundations of Economic Analysis." *Reason Papers*, no. 4 (1978).

Muller, Herbert J. *Freedom in the Ancient World*. New York: Bantam Books, 1964.

Murchland, Bernard. *Humanism and Capitalism: A Survey of Thought and Morality*. Washington, D.C.: American Enterprise Institute for Public Policy Research, 1984.

Nederman, Cary J. "Political Theory and Subjective Rights in Fourteenth-Century England." *Review of Politics* 58 (spring 1996).

Neuman, Harry. "Nihilism: Objections and Answers." *Claremont Review of Books*, fall 1985.

Norton, David L. *Personal Destinies: A Philosophy of Ethical Individualism*. Princeton, N.J.: Princeton University Press, 1976.

Novak, Michael. *The Spirit of Democratic Capitalism*. New York: Simon & Schuster, 1982.

Nozick, Robert. *Anarchy, State, and Utopia*. New York: Basic Books, 1974.

Olson, Mancur. *The Logic of Collective Action, Public Goods and the Theory of Groups*. New York: Schocken Books, 1971.

ONeill, John. "Altruism, Egoism, and the Market." *Philosophical Forum* 23 (summer 1992).

Palmer, Thomas. "The Case for Human Beings." *Atlantic* 269 (January 1992).

Peikoff, Leonard. *The Ominous Parallels*. New York: New American Library, 1982.

Pols, Edward. *Mind Regained*. Ithaca, N.Y.: Cornell University Press, 1998.

Popper, Karl. *Unending Quest*. Glasgow, Scotland: Fontana/Collins, 1974.

Rand, Ayn. *The Virtue of Selfishness: A New Concept of Egoism*. New York: New American Library, 1964.

———. *Introduction to Objectivist Epistemology*, 2d ed. New York: New American Library, 1989.

———. *Philosophy, Who Needs It?* New York: New American Library, 1982.

Rawls, John. *A Theory of Justice*. Cambridge, Mass.: Harvard University Press, 1971.

Regan, Tom, ed. *Just Business, New Introductory Essays in Business Ethics*. New York: Random House, 1983.

———. *The Case for Animal Rights*. Berkeley, Calif.: University of California Press, 1984.

"Rethinking Foundationalism: Metaphilosophical Essays." *Reason Papers*, no. 16 (fall 1991).

Roberts, Edward B., and Ian C. Yates. "Large Company Efforts to Invest Successfully in Small Firms." *Journal of Private Enterprise* 10, no. 2 (spring 1995).

Rollin, Bernard. *Animal Rights and Human Morality*. Buffalo, N.Y.: Prometheus Books, 1981.

Rorty, Richard. *Objectivity, Relativism, and Truth*. Cambridge, England: Cambridge University Press, 1991.

———. "The Seer of Prague." *New Republic*, July 1, 1991.

Rose, Steven. *Lifelines: Biology beyond Determinism*. London: Oxford University Press, 1998.

Saint Bernardino of Siena. "Decontractibus et usuris." New Haven, Conn.: Research Publications, 1974. Microfilm.

Schmookler, Andrew Bard. *The Illusion of Choice*. Albany: State University of New York Press, 1993.

Searle, John R. *The Rediscovery of the Mind*. Cambridge, Mass.: MIT Press, 1992.

Shaw, William H. *Business Ethics*. Belmont, Calif.: Wadsworth Publishing Co., 1991.

Shevoroshkin, Vitaly. "The Mother Tongue," *The Sciences*, May/June 1990.

Shorris, Earl. *A Nation of Salesmen: The Tyranny of the Market and the Subversion of Culture.* New York: W. W. Norton, 1994.

Smith, Adam. *Inquiry Into the Nature and Causes of the Wealth of Nations.* New York: Modern Library Edition, 1927.

Sorell, Tom. *Scientism.* London, England: Routledge, 1991.

Sowell, Thomas. "Middleman Minorities, Why the Resentment?" *American Enterprise,* May/June 1993.

Steiner, Hillel. *An Essay on Rights.* Oxford, England: Blackwell Publishers, Ltd., 1994.

Stigler, George. *The Economist as Preacher and Other Essays.* Chicago: University of Chicago Press, 1982.

Stone, Christopher. "Should Trees Have Standing?" Palo Alto, Calif.: William Kaufmann, 1975.

Tierney, Brian. "Origins of Natural Rights Language: Texts and Contexts, 1150–1250." *History of Political Thought* 10 (winter 1989).

Trucker, Robert C., ed. *The Marx-Engels Reader.* New York: W. W. Norton, 1978.

Von Mises, Ludwig. *Human Action.* New Haven, Conn.: Yale University Press, 1949.

Watts, Fraser. "You're Nothing but a Pack of Neurons." *Journal of Consciousness Studies* 1 (1994).

Werhane, Patricia, and H. Persons. *Rights and Corporations.* Englewood Cliffs, N.J.: Prentice-Hall, 1985.

Zeller, Eduard. *Aristotle and the Earlier Peripatetics,* trans. B. F. C. Costelloe and J. Muirhead. London: Oxford University Press, 1897.

INDEX